"The problem of priorities and managing our time is especially important for Christians, who want their hours and days to count in the service of their Lord. How can we be confident, amid a list of unfinished tasks, that we are making the most of our time? Smith's book tackles this problem head-on. He offers solutions based on his own experience, lessons learned from his failures as well as successes. A readable style and practical suggestions keep the pages turning."

—Charles Hummel, author of *Tyranny of the Urgent*

"*It's About Time* is an excellent tool for those who would like to better organize their lives, and an essential tool for those who know they need to. Ken Smith has done an excellent job of integrating God's Word into a meaningful application of everyday techniques that can be used again and again."

—From the Foreword by Larry Burkett

"It gives me great pleasure to recommend *It's About Time*, written by one of God's faithful and choice servants. Ken Smith has been dedicated to helping others manage two of their scarce resources, money and time, over the past several years. I have known Ken for at least eight years and have been impressed with his faithfulness to the Biblical principles of money and time management. The principles presented in this book are consistent with God's Word, point you to the Savior, and will result in a more effective life for anyone who practices them. Heartily recommended."

—Ron Blue, author of *The Debt Squeeze* and *Managing Your Money*

"Ken Smith's new book *It's About Time* deals with time management in a superb way—and never makes a statement that cannot be backed up with the Word of God. Read it!"

—Ted DeMoss, past President, CBMC of USA

"Today's society is super time-conscious. And yet no one, including Christians, seems to have time to do what is necessary. This book will be a great help to all who want to learn how to manage their time. Here are the answers—all in one place!"

—Herbert E. Ellingwood, former Special Counsel to President Ronald Reagan

"Having had dynamic life-changing experiences through Ken Smith's seminars, it is indeed reassuring to know his principles of life management are now available through his equally powerful book, *It's About Time*. Thousands have benefited from his one-on-one teachings in the seminars; with this new book, millions will now have the opportunity to dramatically change their lifestyles."

—The Honorable Mark D. Siljander,
    former member of the U.S. House of Representatives

"Ken Smith has written a very practical and useful book for guiding Christians in faithful stewardship of God's most precious gift to us, the gift of time."

—Alden M. Hathaway, Bishop, Episcopal Diocese of Pittsburgh

"I highly recommend *It's About Time* for every Christian. It will be especially helpful to those experiencing the frustration of disorganization and overcommitment, which may be robbing them of the peace and joy of the Lord. Ken Smith has provided a blueprint which, if followed, will lead to a very productive and fulfilled life that brings honor and glory to our Heavenly Father."

—Wilmer "Vinegar Bend" Mizell, baseball legend and
former member of the U.S. House of Representatives

"In the 31st Psalm David cried out, 'My times are in Your hands,' and indeed, it is through the ordering of our daily actions that we uncover His plan for our lives. In *It's About Time* we are given a rich reference to guide us through the process of getting our lives in order. This book will be the starting place for many of an exciting journey toward a life of peace, order, and entrusting the Lord with the time He Himself has given us."

—Beverly LaHaye, President, Concerned Women for America

"For people who want to be more organized, I recommend you keep this book handy with bookmarks in the sections on how to say no, punctuality, setting goals, making the crucial 'to do' list, and how to organize both your disgustingly cluttered desk and your hopelessly messed-up file cabinet. The section on procrastination is worth the price of the book alone. I know six people who need this desperately!"

—Leonard E. LeSourd, Associate Publisher, Chosen Books

"As one who has been intrigued by all aspects of personal time management, I am delighted with this helpful, meaningful, Biblical treatise on using our time in a redemptive, pro-active mode. Ken Smith is a recognized expert in this discipline, and his book's practical, Scriptural suggestions and principles will be of great help to all—whether business person, professional, laborer, homemaker, or student. Here is a book filled with eminently practical suggestions for everyone who wants to honor Christ in every aspect of life."

—Ted W. Engstrom, author and President Emeritus, World Vision

"Ken Smith begins this book with a gripping account of how the Lord rescued him from alcoholism and brought him into a new life of committed obedience to Christ. Over the years Ken has developed a splendid self-discipline of the stewardship of *time*. This book is a strategy and tactics manual beginning with basic principles, then moving to nitty-gritty suggestions about how to put an effective time-management program into practice. Abundant stories and case studies illustrate his points. I recommend this book for people serious about improving their time-effectiveness."

—John W. Alexander, President Emeritus, Inter-Varsity Christian Fellowship

"Ken Smith rightly urges us to see success in terms of obedience to Jesus Christ. He offers many practical ideas on how we can be obedient to the Lord with our time, whether we are a homemaker or an executive."

—Doug Sherman, coauthor of *Your Work Matters to God*

IT'S ABOUT TIME

Ken Smith

CROSSWAY BOOKS

A DIVISION OF GOOD NEWS PUBLISHERS

WHEATON, ILLINOIS • CAMBRIDGE, ENGLAND

It's About Time.

Copyright © 1992 by Christian Stewardship Ministries (CSM).

Published by Crossway Books, a division of
Good News Publishers, 1300 Crescent Street, Wheaton, Illinois 60187.

Cover design: Dennis Hill

First printing, 1992

ISBN: 0-89107-666-2

Printed in the United States of America

Unless otherwise noted, all Bible quotations are taken from *Holy Bible:
New International Version*, copyright © 1978 by the New York International
Bible Society. Used by permission of Zondervan Bible Publishers.

00	99	98	97	96	95	94				
15	14	13	12	11	10	9	8	7	6	5	4

First British Edition 1992

ISBN 1 85684 044 1

Production and Printing in the United States of America for
CROSSWAY BOOKS
Kingfisher House, 7 High Green, Great Shelford, Cambridge CB2 18G

To my mother Katherine, my wife Pat, my sons Ken Jr. and Robbie, and my cousin Jim. Mother prayed me into the Kingdom, Pat encouraged me to enter (and remain in) full-time ministry, Kennie and Robbie were my guinea pigs for many years, and Jim provided the impetus and the means without which this book would not have been written

TABLE OF CONTENTS

LIST OF CHARTS

ACKNOWLEDGMENTS

My heartfelt thanks goes out to the following men and women, without whose encouragement, loyalty, and wisdom this book would have never become a reality. When you try to thank everyone, the absence of some names is painfully obvious to whoever is omitted. If your name should have been included here and it wasn't, please forgive me and please let me know. I'll find a way to make it up somehow.

First, I would like to thank the present and past members of the Christian Stewardship Ministries Board of Directors. Not only have these friends been responsible for the policy and direction of CSM, but they have been a source of tremendous strength and encouragement to me personally throughout the years this book has been on the drawing board.

Present Board members are Mark Brehm, Chris Call, Steve Craven, Bart Fleming, Steve Gaskins, John Keith, Bill Peterman and Edie Rittinger.

Past Board members are Ed Prichard, Frank Deierhoi, David Jones, Jerry Tiahrt, Carl Meyer, David Barnett, and Jim McIlvaine.

The distinguished, dedicated, and godly men who have served on the CSM Board of Reference also deserve a very special thank you. They are John Alexander, Bill Bright, Larry Burkett, (who not only offered to write the Foreword but has been a friend and encourager from the beginning), Reid Carpenter, Herb Ellingwood, Ted Engstrom, Dick Halverson, Alden Hathaway, Charlie Hummel, and Mark Siljander.

The following friends of mine serve on the ministry's Advisory Council and have provided valuable insight into the overall direction of the ministry. To them, too, goes my deepest thanks and appreciation: Chuck Annis, Ron Boehme, Sandy Bowen, Dave Boyd, Ed Britton, Vince Buchinsky, Andy Buist, Frank Cerutti, Tom Clark, Margy Cleaver, Mary Ann Cochran, Armand Dauplaise, Dan Derrick, Amos Dodge, Jim Eckhardt, Jon Elliott, Bill Findler, Beth Fleming, Frank Foley, Dick Franklin, Joe Grieco, Bud Harper, Larry Hoffman, Ron Jenkins, Ed and Libby Koepenick, Len Larson, Frank Lewark, Glenn and Arlene McGee, Tony McGraw, Gene McGuire, Gerry

Moore, Bob Mulligan, John Mumford, Roger Penn, Burton Pierce, Mike Riley, Dick Schwaab, Bruce Scott, John Sellers, Jay Schabacker, Mark Siljander, Katherine Smith, Pat Smith, Steve Skancke, Linda Spruill, Steve Templeton, Jerry Tiahrt, John Viccellio, John Vogt, Tom Wartha, Brenda Wilberger, Charlotte Wiles, Mike Woodruff, David Yeakel and Ray Zook.

I would also like to thank the following men and women who have waged war in the heavenlies for the ministry and for the completion of this book. They are the members of the CSM Intercessors Ministry. Their faithful prayer support has meant more than any of them could know, and my love and thanks go to each of them: Georgenne Assur, Eric Assur, Roy Benson, Sharon Boots, Marjorie Bottorff, Margaret Cleaver, Pat Dalzell, Dan Derrick, Ted Farmer, Debbie Farmer, Susan Gladwin, Helen Hamilton, Bud Hancock, Phil Herrell, Rob Huey, Josey Ingley, Marilyn Kirk, Gordon Klooster (my friend and confidant), Roberta Klooster, Lydia Lopez, John McKendree, Nancy McKendree, Vickie McNamara, Edward Mullins, Laurie Porter, Marilyn Schwankoff, Gig Settle, Annette Settle, Becky Shamess, Bob Shamess, Pat Smith, Katherine Smith, Tamy Smith, Scott Smith, Bill Spengler, Malachy Vance and Lester York.

I would also like to thank the following friends who contributed their time and expertise to help improve the manuscript in all of its many shapes and sizes: John Alexander, Chuck Annis, David Barnett, Ivy Barnett, Ron Boehme, Chris Call (whose wife Callie proved to be a wonderful model), Dan Derrick, Amos Dodge, Ted Engstrom, Lou Enoff, Ted Farmer, Bart Fleming (who provided especially helpful suggestions on content), Steve and Jan Gaskins, John Guernsey, Tom Hall, Veletta Hall, David Harper, Charlie Hummel (whose booklet *Tyranny of the Urgent* was very meaningful to me as a young Christian), Ron Jenkins, John Keith (whose good judgment has made the difference numerous times), Joe Kitts, J. C. Lasmanis, Sandy Lesourd, Len Lesourd (who served as an encourager and an expert advisor throughout each stage of the manuscript), Sheila MacPherson, Jim McIlvaine, Mike Mintor, Kathie Nee (who devoted many long hours to editorial work), Bruce Newell (who has been my friend and confidant for many years), Dick O'Driscoll, Bill Peterman, Suzanne Peyser, Edie Rittinger, Katherine Smith, Pat Smith, Linda Spruill, Jerry Tiahrt (who also contributed greatly to the seminars that preceded this work), John Viccellio, Sally Vogt and John Yates.

The following men and women provided financial assistance which has made this book a reality: Vince Buchinsky, Chris and Callie Call, Steve and

Gaye Craven, Armand and Linda Dauplaise, Bart and Beth Fleming, Bud and Jill Harper, Earnie and Jan Heatwole, Bob and April Kelly, Joe Kitts, Don McIlvaine, Jim and Mary McIlvaine, Carl and Kay Meyer, Bruce Newell, Milt Peterson, Bruce and Barbara Reyle, Gary and Robin Rockwell, Jay Schabacher, Dick and Lynn Schwaab, Mark and Nancy Siljander, Steve and Nancy Skancke, Steve Templeton, and Bob and Mary Landon Walton. In addition, my home congregation, Truro Episcopal Church, has provided significant mission and outreach support for both the book and the ministry behind the book.

A special nod of appreciation must go to the following men who have provided computer support for the ministry and have enabled me to move from a yellow pad and pencil to becoming an accomplished word processor — even though I am still baffled by bytes, rom, ram and DOS: my stepson Brett Ames, Chuck Annis, Ken Harshbarger, Les Kent, Ivan Penkoff, Rick Rump and Doug Stites.

My thanks also to the following ladies, who slaved to convert hand-written radio scripts into typewritten texts, which in turn formed the basis for much of this book: Consuelo Moreno, Jan Jennings, Linda Rump, Clarissa Teves and Ellen Tyson.

Also, thank you to Bobbi Johnson, Jean Moore, Kelly Peren, and Suzanne Billman, who kept the ministry's mailing list and contributions flowing while Linda and I struggled to keep the rest of the ship afloat.

Thanks also to two individuals who contributed to this manuscript in significant ways. Sybil Harp was the first writer to begin to articulate the things God was showing me in a way to which others could relate. She wrote the workbook that we still use as a time management seminar text. David Hazard broke ground by getting me started on this project and introducing me to someone who could help me see it through to completion.

This third person in the furnace has become one of my closest brothers in the Lord and is a writer's writer. David Wimbish produced not one, but two full book manuscripts in the course of this project. Not once did he complain or become defensive as his work was criticized, critiqued, rejected and finally praised. Thank you, David, for a job well done in the midst of great personal trauma and challenge. My prayers continue to be with you and Diane.

I must say thank you too to a very special person, Linda Spruill. In the dark days of 1988, when it looked as if Christian Stewardship Ministries would close its doors, one person stood in the gap — and that was Linda.

She offered to be a staff of one to handle seminars, counseling coordination, the newsletter, donor development, material sales, and administration. She persisted, God provided, and CSM survived. This book is a product of that survival. Thank you, Linda.

I also want to express my gratitude and affection for Ted Engstrom, whose copyright philosophy is "copy it right." His book with Ed Dayton, *Strategy for Living*, formed much of the basis for my first time management seminar. Much of the material in this book grew out of that process, and I am grateful to Ted for his mentoring.

My deepest thanks and appreciation also go out to the man who has carried me the many miles that represent my written contribution to this book. That man is John Vogt, the president and general manager of WCTN radio in Potomac, Maryland. John and his staff (especially Ivan Penkoff and Jimmy Peck) have produced for me, free of charge except that of love, almost two hundred daily radio broadcasts since October 3, 1988. John and his wife Sally are extraordinary people in their commitment to Christ, to each other, and to God's work through them. Without John's encouragement and commitment there would have been nothing upon which to base this book.

FOREWORD

by Larry Burkett

I have known Ken Smith for nearly ten years now. One of the first impressions I had of Ken when he volunteered to organize and host one of our seminars on Biblical finances in the Washington, D.C., area was that of a highly organized person. I have learned over the years of teaching conferences that often the success of a conference is directly related to the organizer's personal habits. Too often people volunteer out of a sincere but misguided emotional attraction to a particular topic that benefited them in their spiritual walk. But the rigor of organizing other workers, making myriads of telephone calls, and countless hours of committee work usually burns them out. As a result most never attempt the task twice. In Ken's case what impressed me was that he immediately volunteered to organize a second, even larger conference. His organization plan was adopted by other volunteers around the country and greatly aided the ministry of Christian Financial Concepts in the early growth period.

It is with this introduction that I heartily endorse Ken as an expert in the area of organization and time management. Perhaps nothing in our "drive-through" society is more lacking than effective organization. I am reminded of what I heard one of my college professors say once: "We all have the same number of hours per day, whether we are the President of the United States or an inmate in a penitentiary. It is not the amount of time that is the issue. It is the way you use it."

I have tried to remember that when I feel frazzled and hurried by my schedule. Ken's book *It's About Time* is an excellent tool for those who would like to better organize their lives, and an essential tool for those who know they need to. Ken has done an excellent job of integrating God's Word into a meaningful application of everyday techniques that can be used again and again.

The one caution that I would give any reader is the tendency to procrastinate, even when reading a book on organizing. The Apostle James told us that we should be effectual doers of the Word, not merely hearers. I trust that you will apply the principles taught by Ken Smith in this excellent book.

PREFACE

When I began to seriously address the question of whether another book would add anything to the billions of words already written on every conceivable subject under the sun, I must confess that I felt very inadequate. On the one hand, I felt that God wanted me to write this book. I procrastinated and rationalized for years because I neither felt equipped to write a book, nor could I imagine that I had anything to add to a subject as familiar to all of us as that of time management and personal organization. Not that lots of people didn't have plenty to learn on the subject — but how could I contribute anything that had not already been developed in the past?

But the longer I put it off, the more convicted I became that it really wasn't a question of whether I had anything to add or whether anyone would learn from what I had to say. The question was: Is God telling me to write this book? If He was, then I had to get on with the job or else be willing to suffer the consequences.

I can tell you without fear of any skeptical response that God told me to write this book. Whether it is for your benefit, only you can judge. For me, it was and is an exercise in obedience. And when all else is said and done, that's exactly what this book is all about: obedience. For whatever reason, God took a lawyer and decided to make him a writer. Or maybe he took a writer and let him practice law for a while.

The things you will read and the examples I will share with you are all real, either from my own life or from the lives of others. Many of the things I have learned have come through great pain. My life has not been easy, but it certainly has been blessed. I don't think for a minute that I have suffered unduly or that the pain I have experienced has been greater than the pain any one of you has experienced. And the final result of the pain in my life has certainly been great joy and fulfillment.

You see, the thing that motivates me even more than my love for God is my fear of Him. Not that I see God as a great big meanie in the sky, looking

xv

for ways to make me suffer. On the contrary, I see Him as a loving God cheering for me to succeed in everything I attempt. But I have learned the hard way that God has a plan for my life, and when I act in a fashion that is inconsistent with that plan, it can become very painful.

The bottom line is obedience.

Now, God's plan for my life is too big for me to comprehend. If I try, I am quickly overwhelmed. But what I can do is learn the principles that dictate how He wants me to walk each day. Once I know those principles, then it's simply a matter of applying them. When I do apply them, I'm being obedient and will receive the rewards God gives to those who obey Him. When I do not live by God's plan, I am being disobedient and will suffer the consequences.

The ultimate reward for obedience on this side of eternity is what the Bible calls "the peace . . . which transcends all understanding" (Philippians 4:7). I call it "freedom from anxiety." I'm not going to tell you that I will face everything in the future without anxiety, but I can tell you that since I began to identify and practice the things this book is all about, I have been totally free from anxiety — and that has been more than fifteen years. This comes from a person who once thought he had an obligation to worry, and if I had nothing else to worry about, I'd worry that there was nothing to worry about.

The reason for the change is that I have developed an attitude of obedience. That's not to say I am always obedient, but rather that I have within me a deep desire to be obedient. When I am consciously disobedient, or discover after the fact that I have been disobedient, I act as quickly as I can to overcome that area of disobedience. And it is that desire, that attitude, that has protected me from the pain of anxiety.

Will you join me today? Will you purpose to develop an attitude of obedience to God as you read this book? Decide that you will uncover areas of your life which have not been submitted to God, and ask Him to show you how to become obedient in those areas. If you ask God to give you the desire to become an obedient person, you can be sure that He will do it. The Scripture that God gave me as a new Christian to motivate me to major in obedience was Matthew 13:1-23, the Parable of the Sower. I determined that I would strive to multiply a hundredfold, and I realized that the only way to do that was to become committed to becoming obedient.

As you and I learn the things that will produce in us a lifestyle of obedience to God, we can begin to make an impact on those around us. In my experience, there are not many people today who have the attitude that will produce a lifestyle of obedience. And until the Body of Christ recognizes this need as paramount to everything else, the mission of the Church will not be fulfilled. We cannot effectively go to Judea and to Samaria and to the uttermost parts of the earth to spread the gospel of Jesus Christ until we, the Church, have acquired the ability to be obedient. And we will not acquire that ability without a commitment to do so.

Before we move on, let me say that it is extremely important that you put into practice the things we are going to talk about in this book. Knowledge without application breeds frustration. For that reason, I have included exercises where appropriate to help you follow through on the things you learn. It is my hope that you will not only read this book, but that you will continue to use it as a tool.

You can only apply so much knowledge at any one time. So if you will take one or two of my suggestions the first time around and master them, you are much more likely to return for additional suggestions. If you permit yourself to be overwhelmed by the magnitude of the task the first time around, you are likely to become discouraged and fail to apply anything.

But begin the process now with the realization that you can add more and more until your life is a model of order, peace and, most importantly, obedience.

INTRODUCTION

From Chaos to Order

You are about to embark on an exciting journey — a journey toward success and fulfillment in life. I know because it's a journey that I have taken myself.

Every once in a while I counsel someone who seems to think I couldn't possibly understand a disorganized life. "It's easy for you," he'll say. "You've always had your act together! But my life is such a mess — well, it's a completely different story!"

Despite that opinion, the truth is, my life hasn't always been one of order and control.

Quite the contrary.

In fact, when it comes to disorder and chaos, if I hadn't once been there myself, I doubt that I would try to suggest to anyone else how to overcome it.

I suspect that if those counselees had known me "back then," their attitude might be, "If he could get his life together, so can I." That's why I think it's important for you to know something of my background and how Christian Stewardship Ministries came into existence.

It all goes back to Washington, D.C. — a heady place for a fifteen-year-old boy entering Capitol Page School. I was excited to be one of the elite few who run errands for United States Congressmen. I was meeting famous people — the movers and the shakers that others only read about in newspapers.

Delivering messages through those polished halls gave me a sense of self-worth I'd never felt at home. I was accepted here. They considered me worthy of attention and respect. It was so different from my home, where things seemed to go wrong much of the time. Everyone seemed on edge there, snapping and sniping at each other. The normal noise my little brothers made only added to the tension and confusion I felt. But it was different here, and I felt as if I had escaped from an invisible prison of uncertainty.

But even though home was, for me, an increasingly unpleasant place, I was still shocked and depressed when my parents separated. Looking back, I know I should have seen it coming. But as much as they fought and argued, they were still my mother and father — and with the breakup of their marriage, the only roots I'd ever known were gone. All I had left was my position as a Page.

Feeling like a lost soul, I moved into a rooming house, not realizing that I would never live at home again.

NOT-SO-INNOCENT BEGINNINGS

One night I went out with some other Pages and got drunk. It was a wonderful experience. When the alcohol began to take effect, I felt giddy and laughed as I hadn't laughed for years. Drinking also made me feel grown-up and in charge. I knew right away that drinking was something I was going to be doing often.

And I did.

At first it didn't take much to knock me for a loop, but gradually it took more and more. I didn't mind, though. Things were going well for me. I achieved the highest possible position, serving as the Speaker's Page under Sam Rayburn. I reasoned that the drinking hadn't interfered with my Page duties; it just helped me shut out the gnawing sense of loneliness that welled up in me at night.

There was one area where my drinking did hurt me, however, and that was in the area of my grades. By the end of my junior year they were so low I knew that if I didn't do something fast I might never get into college.

So I enrolled in the Bolles School, a military prep school in Jacksonville, Florida. The disciplined atmosphere there left me no opportunity to drink, and it did wonders for my grades, which shot up high enough to get me scholarship offers from a number of colleges. I chose the college that offered the highest scholarship — which also happened to be my mother's and my uncle's alma mater, Tulane University in New Orleans.

By now my mother was trying to provide for my two brothers essentially by herself, and I knew that the least I could do to help her was to keep my expenses to a minimum. I didn't know how she always managed to pay her bills, but somehow she did. What made that fact even more astounding to me was the knowledge that she insisted on giving 10 percent of her income to the Lord.

That didn't make much sense to me — since I didn't have much use for anything religious in my life at the time — but my mother simply would not have it any other way. One tenth of her income belonged to the Lord, and it was always the first tenth.

As for me, I enjoyed the college life — particularly the parties. Yet gradually I came to see that many of the other guys didn't drink as much as I did. Nor did they drink in the same way I drank. I drank before a party to "loosen up." Most of them didn't. I had to have some alcohol in me in order to have a good time. Most of them seemed to be able to have fun even when there wasn't anything to drink. I began to wonder if perhaps there was something different about me, something wrong.

When those kinds of thoughts came to me, I did my best to push them out of my head. I didn't want to worry. I just wanted to drift through my classes, doing the minimum amount required to maintain my scholarship.

During my last year of college, I got married. Alba was a nice Catholic girl who loved me very much. The priest said I'd have to agree to raise our children as Catholics. I quickly agreed because it didn't matter much to me one way or another.

At the time of my marriage I was a midshipman in the Naval Reserve Officers Training Corps — and one of the conditions of that program was that I would remain single until after receiving my commission, which would not occur for another nine months. But I was young and in love, and I rationalized that what the ROTC brass didn't know wasn't going to hurt them — or me either, for that matter.

Besides, no one had to find out.

Unfortunately, however, one day, about six months after my wedding, I was called into a meeting by the executive officer. It seems that someone had written a letter, alleging that several of the midshipmen were married.

I stood there listening to him, trying to appear as nonchalant as possible, as if what he was talking about didn't apply to me.

But it didn't work, and he finally asked me point blank, "Is it true? Are you married?"

"No, sir, I'm not," I lied.

He said he was relieved to hear it and told me I was free to go.

As I walked out into the sunlight, I was relieved that he had believed me. But by the time I got home I knew it was never going to work. I had to go back and admit the truth, even though I knew it would mean the end of my naval career — something I had dreamed about for years.

I retraced my steps and admitted to the executive officer that I had lied to him. The truth was that, yes, I was married.

I never returned to the Navy building.

I was absolutely crushed. Since the age of thirteen I had always assumed I would have a career in the Navy. I had even appeared on a Navy recruiting poster when I was in high school and had autographed photographs from admirals and commanding officers wishing me well.

All of my aspirations were tied up with the Navy, and now that option was no longer available to me. I would have to do something else with my life.

I decided to enroll in law school. Even though I was hurt by my dismissal from Navy ROTC, I had to admit that I enjoyed married life. It was nice to have someone to come home to, and Alba didn't even complain about my drinking. We had two children while I was in school, and by the time my second son was born I didn't spend much time at home. I had to work and study. And if I wasn't doing one of those things, I was usually drinking.

Somehow I managed to make it through law school and graduate in the middle of my class. I then returned to northern Virginia to begin my legal career. Only one more obstacle loomed ahead of me. I had to pass the Virginia Bar Exam. In those days bar exams weren't standardized, and the percentage of those who passed the first time around was very low — less than 50 percent.

I studied harder than I had ever studied in my life. I was running scared because I didn't have the time or the money to afford not to pass the first time. Alba had confidence that I would pass, but the more I studied, the more discouraged I became. There was just so much to learn and so much information to digest — and if I failed the exam, I had no idea what I would do to take care of my family.

Finally I decided I would call on God. That was an unusual step for me to take because at that point in my life I wasn't even sure there was a God. Or if there was, I wasn't convinced that He cared about me at all. But somehow my Christian upbringing had developed within me the attitude that God is the best person to turn to in times of trouble. My mother had always taken her sons to church, and I had been baptized and confirmed in a mainline denomination. Up until my entry into Page School, I had believed in God, read the Bible on occasion, and was active as an acolyte. After my parents separated and I began life on my own, I quickly forgot that training and had even come to the point in college where I had debated the existence of God.

Nonetheless, I did turn to God and in an attempt to bargain with Him said that if He would help me pass the bar exam I would go back to church and attend regularly for the rest of my life.

I'll never forget Alba's shriek the day we got the postcard telling us that I had passed the exam. God had come through for me. Now it was my turn to uphold my end of the bargain.

Alba was not very interested in church, but I took the boys with me and attended her church, faithful to my vow that the boys would be raised as Catholics.

A SUCCESSFUL FAILURE

Soon my life was full of "important" matters. I was an up-and-coming attorney with valuable political experience. I became president of the local Lion's Club and held the same office with the Young Democrats. I managed political campaigns, served as a substitute judge, and began working as an Assistant County Attorney for Fairfax County in Northern Virginia.

To anyone looking in from the outside, I had it made. I was on the way to becoming a "success" by all the world's standards.

Yet something was missing. I didn't spend as much time at home; that same atmosphere of tension was there — just as I'd remembered as a boy. My children represented responsibility I wasn't willing to assume. I wasn't really focused on my boys or my wife. It was like we were all strangers. Finally Alba decided she had had enough of Mr. Success. She packed up the kids and headed for Atlanta. My marriage, like my earlier naval career, was over.

In a way it seemed like a relief. I could finally be a young, successful single attorney and live the way I wanted to live. Best of all, I still had my faithful friend — the bottle. Life seemed good — at first. I went wherever I wanted with whomever I wanted and did whatever I wanted. I also drank whatever I wanted. I had plenty of time for Mr. Budweiser and Jack Daniels, as well as for various social and civic organizations, but one thing I gradually had less time for was church.

By 1974, nine years after I had made that vow to attend church for the rest of my life, I stopped attending. It wasn't that I intended to stop. I was just having so much fun that I forgot to go. It wasn't until I looked back later that I even realized I had stopped going. I had long since lost sight of my vow. I had come to view my church attendance as more of a habit than as the fulfilling of a promise to God, and when I broke the habit I didn't realize I was also breaking a vow.

LIFE AT THE BOTTOM

It wasn't long before things began to really fall apart, as I began to drink more and more. I became less and less responsible, and, as a result my life became almost meaningless. A deep depression settled over me. There was no joy in anything I tried to do. It was as if all the sadness in the world lay just beneath the surface of my life. The depression caused me to have difficulty breathing, and it was to be more than fourteen months before I was actually able to take a deep breath. I literally gasped my way through those months, feeling that at any moment I could run out of air and suffocate.

Soon those clubs and organizations that had once seemed so important to me began to lose their appeal. Gradually I lost interest in them as I found myself spending more and more time drinking. When I wasn't drinking, I was either anticipating my next drink or getting over the effects of the last one.

My life consisted of going to work, coming home, drinking until I went to bed, and then getting up to go to work again. I even stopped eating regularly. By the end of that fourteen-month period of depression, my weight had dropped to 119 pounds (I now weigh in at 160). I knew I was headed for destruction, but there was nothing at all I could do to stop the downward spiral. The alcohol fueled the depression, the depression led me to seek oblivion in drinking, and so it went.

Part of me knew that the alcohol didn't really help and that what I thought of as a friend was in reality a deadly enemy. Gradually it began to dawn on me that I was an alcoholic, but at least I prided myself on the idea that I was a "functional" alcoholic. My drinking hadn't seemed to hurt my career.

Several times I tried to go without drinking for a few days, but the drive inside me wouldn't let me stop — and eventually my law practice did begin to suffer.

I argued with myself constantly, attempting to rationalize my behavior and making excuses for my excesses. But before too long I was forced to admit that things were worse than I'd let myself believe.

For one thing, I simply could not keep a secretary. Because of my lack of organization in my practice, I went through a long succession of them. I began attracting fewer new clients, too. The worst thing was, the fewer clients I had, the more time I had on my hands, and that meant more time to spend drinking.

Finally I came to the conclusion that the only way out was death. I seriously began considering various ways of taking my life. The only thing that kept me from carrying that out was that I couldn't decide on a socially acceptable way of killing myself.

Yet, as I was going through this alcohol- and depression-induced hell, something else was happening to me.

Through the fog of despair, a tiny light was shining. Maybe it was God. Maybe He had an answer for me.

So in search of His answer I went to some Christian businessmen's fellowships and even attended a couple of prayer groups. The men I met seemed friendly enough, but I was worried that they could see through my smiling disguise and knew that I didn't really "belong" with such spiritual people. Perhaps they could see how totally dark my life had become.

Maybe they *could* see through me. But if they did, they didn't let me know. They accepted me as their friend and brother. But even though I was appreciative, the pain deep down in my soul didn't lessen.

Maybe I should try to discover who God is, I thought. *Maybe that'll do it.*

So I prayed to accept Jesus as my Lord and Savior, hoping for a brilliant flash of light that would lift this terrible darkness and fill me with the joy and peace these new Christian friends of mine were always talking about.

But nothing of the sort happened. I didn't feel a thing, and I knew I was the same old person. I really did want Jesus to rescue me, but I knew I was still a slave to alcohol. I wanted Him to be my Savior, but I knew that whenever I felt down and depressed I turned to alcohol, not to Jesus.

The despair seemed deeper than ever, so I asked my Christian friends what I should do, and they all said the same thing: "Read the Bible and pray."

The only problem with that was that every time I tried to read the Bible I found it boring and hard to understand. As a lawyer I was used to reading contracts containing the most complex and obtuse language. But for me the *King James Version* of the Bible was much harder to comprehend.

THE TURNING POINT

Then, just before Lent, I wandered into a mainline denominational church and sat in the back pew. The young priest was preaching about giving up something for Lent. The thing he chose to give up did not say much for his spiritual condition, but it hit too close to home — it was scotch and water at cocktail parties. I could almost taste the smoky coldness of the scotch. Unconsciously I licked my lips — and then looked around quickly to see if anyone had noticed.

No one had, apparently, but I still felt a deep uncomfortableness — like a loving sadness. I knew God was dealing with me about my drinking.

"Will you give it up for Lent?" He seemed to ask. But I knew I couldn't, despite all the times I'd tried.

But then I remembered one other time in my life when I had asked God for a favor — made a bargain with Him even — and He had come through for me. I knew it had been His help that had enabled me to pass the Virginia Bar Exam on my first try. Perhaps He would help me this time too.

"If You'll help me stop drinking during Lent," I prayed silently, "I'll do all I can to help You help me."

The result was immediate and overwhelming. A great sense of relief flooded through me. Tears welled up in my eyes and poured down my face. I couldn't stop them. I knew beyond any doubt that God had heard my prayer, and I felt sure that He was going to help me. For the first time in a very long time I had some hope. Despite the new strength I felt, I was quite embarrassed by my unexpected and uncharacteristic show of emotion. I sneaked out of the church as soon as the service was over, still not sure exactly what was going to happen.

The first week after that dramatic experience I frequently thought about popping open a can of beer. But when I really thought about it, I realized that I didn't need to do that anymore. I thought about drinking only because it was a long-time habit of mine. But the deep-down need for a drink, the over-whelming desire, had been taken away from me. Just like that.

By the middle of the second week, I was no longer even thinking about drinking anything stronger than coffee or black cherry sodas.

After that, many other doors opened. No longer was the Bible so con-fusing. It actually became "a lamp to my feet and a light for my path" (Psalm 119:105). A hunger and thirst for righteousness began to grow in me. I started using the Word of God to fill the long hours I had once spent drink-ing. I'd rise early in the morning to spend time reading the Bible, come home from work and lunchtime to read it, and stay up late at night reading.

I am no expert on the subject of supernatural healing, but I do know that without God's miraculous intervention I would be lying in a gutter somewhere right now — or perhaps be dead from an alcohol-related accident, disease, or suicide.

I have come to believe that the things we consider to be supernatural or miraculous are really quite consistent with God's Laws. It's just that we have not and never will discover or understand all of the Laws under which the universe operates. We all see certain things happen that we can't explain. Some of us can easily attribute them to God without feeling the need to understand the explanation, whereas others are reluctant to attribute things to God at all. Unsaved doctors are known to acknowledge that things happen which they cannot explain, but refuse to acknowledge God as the source of such occurrences.

What adds to the magnitude of what God did for me is that alcoholism is deeply imbedded in my family tree, on both the paternal and maternal branches. I knew before I ever took my first drink that I was playing with fire. Drinking was a temptation and a sin into which Satan was able to easily lure me — and I believe that there was no escape for me except through the blood and the power of Jesus Christ.

I also believe that even though God delivered me from the desire to drink, it would be possible for me to become tangled in the same trap all over again. I am still an alcoholic, but I am an alcoholic who does not drink, one who sees no reason to tempt myself, or the Lord, by consuming alcohol. The Lord's Prayer says, "lead us not into temptation," and even though I do not have a compulsion to drink, I plan to stay as far away from that potential temptation as possible.

LIGHT IN OTHER CORNERS

Once God had dealt with my drinking problem, He began to deal with me in other areas of my life too. One day as I sat in my office wondering what I could do to reestablish my interest in life, I began to realize that the Lord wanted me to make some changes in my way of doing things. Eventually, thanks to His leading, bit by bit, my chaotic and disorganized life became orderly.

I learned how to use my time in ways that reflected God's well-ordered universe. Each new discovery I made about God's ways of doing things left me hungry to learn more.

Then I heard about a way to apply God's principles to the management of my finances. At my mother's urging I attended a Christian money management seminar, and the Bible-based principles I heard there captured my attention and my imagination.

I began budgeting my money and arranging my finances to eliminate all of my personal debt.

I had already begun tithing, so I reduced my expenditures to allow for increasing my offerings to the Lord.

I began to share what I'd learned with others, and soon Christian friends and acquaintances were asking me to share with them the principles of Christian money management. Finally there were so many interested people that I arranged to teach a seminar where I could tell all of them about it at the same time.

The response was tremendous, and several of those who attended the seminar shared with me how much they had benefited. Word of mouth spread, and I received numerous requests to conduct additional seminars.

Two years later Christian Money Management began. And shortly after that, I began teaching time management seminars and changed the name of the ministry to Christian Stewardship Ministries.

CSM conducts both time and money management seminars, counsels people who are in need of special help with regard to the management of their time or money, and assists Christian-owned businesses and other Christian organizations with the task of bringing Biblical principles into the conduct and management of those organizations. I also teach a daily radio program and distribute a newsletter (*Glad Tithings*) on time and money management.

So that's the story of how Christian Stewardship Ministries came into being — an organization that God created out of the chaos that once was my life. Whenever I read the first chapter of Genesis, which says that when God began creation "the earth was formless and empty" (v. 2), I feel a special sense of recognition. For just as God created our beautiful planet from that "formless and empty" blob, so He has transformed my "formless and empty" life to the point where I can now teach people the benefits of godly order within their lives.

This book will draw upon my personal and professional experience in time and money management, presenting the principles I've learned from this experience and from the continuous study and application of God's Word. These principles have helped many people discover a new life of order and peace. I know that these same principles can help you manage the greatest resource you have.

Before we begin this adventure, I have to ask you an important question: Have you accepted Jesus Christ as your Savior? That's where the adventure begins. All you have to do is acknowledge that you are a sinner and that the penalty for your sins is death and eternal separation from God. Next, accept the fact that Jesus Christ paid the penalty for your sins when He died upon the cross and that His resurrection from the grave symbolized the new life you are now able to begin with God.

Once you've made Christ your Savior, you still need to make Him the Lord of your life. That's a position He deserves and requires. But whereas making Christ your Savior is a one-time decision, making Him Lord is a life-long process. It's something you do over and over again in many situations. Unless you acknowledge Jesus Christ as Savior and Lord, your life will never be all it could and should be. Without Him this book may help you, but it will not be as beneficial as it can otherwise be.

So if you haven't surrendered your life to Christ, do it right now. All it takes is a simple prayer — like this one:

> Lord Jesus, I acknowledge that I am a sinner, and I understand that the penalty for sin is death and eternal separation from God. I know, Lord, that You paid the penalty for my sin — that You were crucified in my place, and that only through the shedding of Your blood is it possible for my sins to be forgiven. I ask, Lord, for forgiveness and cleansing through Your blood, and I acknowledge You as Lord and Savior of my life. Help me, Lord, to live close to you every day of my life. Amen.

Now let's get on with the adventure!

PART ONE

THERE'S NOTHING YOU AND GOD TOGETHER CAN'T DO

1

Obedience: The Key to Fulfillment

It's been more than twenty years now since Frank Sinatra had a hit record with the song called "My Way." You may recall that song and its message of a man looking back over his life and declaring proudly that he was a success because he had always done things in his own way — that he had never allowed anyone else to tell him what to do. That record was a very big hit, so it's obvious that millions of people identified with its message.

The problem, though, is that doing everything "my way" isn't really going to lead to true success. Instead, it usually brings disappointment and failure, or at least doesn't produce inner peace and fulfillment. Truthfully there is only one way to be truly successful in life, and that is to learn to do things *God's* way. Obedience to God will undergird everything we talk about in this book. It is the foundation on which all else is built. Without an attitude of obedience and a desire to follow God's leading, you will never achieve true success. On the other hand, if you strive to be obedient, your horizons are limitless.

Obedience isn't always easy, but it's always beneficial.

I remember one of the first lessons I learned about obedience. When I became a Christian, I was smoking two to three packs of cigarettes a day. I had gotten to the point where I was embarrassed to smoke in front of other Christians, and yet I couldn't seem to shake the addiction. I knew that God wanted me to stop smoking, but I couldn't do it. I had begun to limit the number of cigarettes I smoked by allowing myself no more than one every half hour — and then every hour. But it had taken me several months to reach that point, and giving cigarettes up totally seemed like an impossible thing to do.

As I studied the Biblical concept of the authority of the believer, I realized that He who is in me is greater than he who is in the world. I suddenly believed that God gave me that and other Scriptures for the purpose of conquering my smoking habit. It was one of those times when the living Word of God had specific application to a very tangible point in my life.

To limit my smoking, I played a little game with myself. I would wait until just a minute or so before the hour was up to have my cigarette for that hour. That way, I knew that I could have one for the next hour a couple of minutes later if I wanted to. I never smoked the next one until that hour was almost up, but I knew that I could if I wanted to.

It was Labor Day weekend of 1976, and the time was 11:55 A.M. on a Saturday. It had been almost an hour since I lit up last, and I had looked forward to the only cigarette I could have for that entire hour. I really struggled. I knew God was giving me a chance to break my smoking habit. I also knew that if I didn't have that cigarette in the next five minutes I could *never* have it. Never! Well, God won that battle. I got up and threw my cigarettes in the trash. I was at my mother's apartment at the time, and I told her to forget the lunch she was fixing for me because I had some serious business to attend to. I drove the twenty minutes to my house and got ready for what turned out to be the most dramatic experience I've ever had in the realm of spiritual warfare.

I spent that day and the next two days acting like a crazy man. I prayed to God. I yelled and screamed at the devil. I would head for the store to get cigarettes, then stop myself and pray some more. I spent that weekend in as close proximity to Satan as I ever want to.

Finally it was Tuesday morning. I went to my law office as usual, and I called my mother early to see how she was doing after the long weekend. While I was talking to her, I realized that I was still reaching for cigarettes that were no longer in my shirt pocket. But the *urge* to smoke was gone. I still had the habit, but I no longer had the urge. It was then that I realized for the first time in over twenty years of heavy smoking that there was a difference between the habit and the urge. It was the urge that had always defeated me in times past when I had tried to stop, and now that urge was gone. I quickly lost the habit and haven't been tempted to have a cigarette ever since.

It was a difficult thing to do, but I knew that God wanted me to quit smoking, and I needed to obey Him. As you can imagine, the benefits of that decision have been many: improved health, improved personal hygiene, a cleaner environment, and so on. And one of the biggest benefits was that I learned for myself the importance of obedience and the availability of the power of God to aid those who are determined to obey.

OBEDIENCE IS THE FOUNDATION OF SUCCESS

God's Word tells us that "To obey is better than sacrifice" (1 Samuel 15:22) and that God will give His Holy Spirit only to those who obey Him (Acts 5:32). Obedience underlies our entire relationship with God. As Christians, we have accepted what God did for us at Calvary. But how many of us have taken the steps to make Him our Lord. Accepting Christ as Savior is reflective of what He did for us. Making Him our Lord is reflective of what He wants us to do for Him. Accepting Him as Savior is something we did. Making Him Lord is recognizing who He is.

To make Christ the Lord of our lives is to engage in a process — a never-ending process — of becoming the person He wants each of us to become. God has a plan for each day of our lives — a plan He designed before the beginning of time. David says in Psalm 139, "All the days ordained for me were written in your book before *one* of them came to be" (v. 16). Our job is to discover that plan on a daily basis. Obedience consists of 1) discovering the plan, and 2) doing our part to implement that plan.

In order to do that, we must spend time with God. We must get to know Him well enough so that we understand what He wants us to do and when He wants us to do it. Conversely, we need to understand what He does *not* want us to do and have the discipline to *not* do it.

Obedience is an attitude, a state of the spirit. We are either obedient or we are not obedient. It's not so much what we *do* as it is who we *are*. Yes, we all have little areas of disobedience — of doing what we know is not God's best for us. But if we have an *attitude* of obedience — a spirit-deep commitment to being the person God wants us to be — we can conquer those little pockets of disobedience.

If obedience can be defined as making God the Lord of your life, then disobedience can be viewed as *not permitting* Him to be Lord of your life. Perhaps you remember this old joke: "Question: How do you eat an elephant? Answer: One bite at a time." Now *all* of life is like a very big elephant. In order to take a closer look at disobedience, we need to carve that elephant into some bite-size pieces so we don't choke.

First, can you think of some things you presently do that you should not be doing, or that you're not doing that you should be doing? It could be poor use of time, poor use of money, or a poor relationship you haven't sought to mend. Perhaps there are some things you should or should not be doing in your relationship with God or within your family.

Once you've done that, the next step is to determine what it is about this area that is actually disobedient. Is it bad in and of itself, or is it only bad for *you* to do it? Is it an area that you have rationalized to the point that you've convinced yourself it's all right although you know deep down that it's really not?

For example, I have a problem when it comes to movies. Now, there is certainly nothing wrong with going to movies. I doubt that an occasional movie represents a poor use of time if it provides recreation and relaxation.

But the problem with my going to the movies is that God doesn't *want* me to go, and He has gently let me know that in any number of ways. He objects to what I hear and what I see at my local theater. That's primarily because my tastes run to action films, and unfortunately Hollywood doesn't produce action films that do not include language or scenes that offend God. For years I have rationalized, and for years I have been disobedient. It is an area of disobedience that I am presently trying to overcome.

WHY IS OBEDIENCE SO IMPORTANT?

Perhaps you have similar areas in your life. Again, it is extremely important that you identify those areas of disobedience and then try to determine what it is about those areas that displeases God. The next step is to find the answer to the question, "Why should I worry so much about whether I'm living in obedience?"

There are at least two ways to answer this question. From the positive side, obedience pleases God and brings His blessings. If you want to see how much God desires to bless people who are obedient to Him, read the twenty-eighth chapter of Deuteronomy. When we are disobedient, we preclude God from providing us with many of the things He wants us to have. He is constantly having to rework the wonderful plan He has designed for our lives in order to compensate for our disobedience. Disobedience forces us to miss out on some things entirely and brings a delay in our enjoyment of other things.

The negative answer to the question about obedience is that if we are disobedient, we reap the consequences and pain of disobedience. Not only do we miss the blessings, but we incur the pain. Why should we be so stupid as to disobey an all-knowing, all-loving God?

Now it is true that there may be some pain associated with obedience. But it will often be short-lived, and the obedience will produce a joy and an ultimate result that will make the pain that was felt seem insignificant in comparison. It is as Paul said in Romans 8:18: "I consider that our present sufferings are not worth comparing with the glory that will be revealed in us."

Now it's certainly not necessary to be physically tortured to suffer for being a Christian. When I was very young in the faith, a very close friend of mine was killed while driving drunk. He lingered for six long months without recovering consciousness before he died. At the funeral his wife, who was a Christian, had the pastor announce that my friend had been an alcoholic and that his drinking had been the reason for his accident. The pastor explained that his wife hoped the publicity would deter others from driving and drinking. Up to that moment the fact of his intoxication had been carefully covered up. He was a prominent lawyer, and the police had not reported it as an alcohol-related accident.

The pastor then invited those in attendance to share their memories of the deceased. A number of people did. But not me. As the testimonies drew to a close, I began to tremble. I knew God wanted me to speak. Now there were hundreds of people present, including everyone in the community whose respect I ever wanted to have. If I spoke, I knew I would instantly be discredited by many of these most-important people. I asked God not to make me speak, but His persistent urging continued, and I knew that to remain seated would constitute gross disobedience. If I wanted to please God I had no choice. Suddenly I found myself standing and saying that I, too, was an alcoholic. I testified that God had healed me of alcoholism a few months before and that He had the power to heal others in that auditorium of the same addiction.

Talk about suffering! That was fifteen years ago, and I remember it as if it were yesterday. Ever since then I have been labeled as a Christian in the legal community, and some people whom I considered to be my friends began crossing the street when they saw me coming. I didn't like that at all, but I knew I had been obedient to God, and I was at peace within myself because of that.

And then the benefits began to occur. People I hadn't known before but whose respect I would have liked to have started coming *across* the street when they saw me coming, so they could shake my hand and congratulate me on my courage. What's more, because of my outspoken and very public statement about God's healing power, I have had a platform from which to boldly proclaim Christ ever since. In fact, it's been expected of me, and I've been able to do it without worrying what anyone else might think about me.

You see, there was suffering in obedience, but it was temporary, and the obedience brought tremendous benefits my way.

On the other hand, the pain that comes from disobedience is the kind that will not let go of you and sometimes lasts for years.

My own experience in this area might provide another helpful illustration. When I accepted Jesus as Savior and pledged to make Him the Lord of my life, I did so in response to *very great* pain. As I have already told you, I was severely depressed and had been for fourteen long months. I was so depressed that I had not been able to take a deep breath for all that time. I constantly gasped for air and always felt as though I was about to suffocate. I contemplated suicide on a continuing basis, and one of the miracles of my life is that I survived that period.

But I did survive, because I found Christ — or He found me. I then began the *process* of learning to live in obedience to God. And the more I brought my life into line with His wishes, the less I hurt. Whenever I am tempted to be disobedient, or when I realize that I am being disobedient, the primary motivating factor to be obedient is my very personal knowledge of the pain produced by disobedience.

HOW CAN I BECOME OBEDIENT?

1) Recognize Disobedience

The first step in becoming obedient in an area is to acknowledge that you are being disobedient. Take a pencil and pad of paper and list five to ten areas of disobedience in your life. If you can't think of that many, list as many as you can think of. Just to get you started, think of the relationships you need to work on, the things you need to do that are health-related, and the things you should improve on in your relationship with God.

2) Reflect on the Significance of Disobedience

After you've made your list, carve out time to seriously think about it. Give yourself the opportunity to think through the significance of each of these areas. Reflect on not only your disobedience, but on the consequences of that disobedience, in *your* life *and* in the lives of others.

3) Confess and Request Forgiveness

Once you've identified an area as conscious disobedience — and therefore as sin — you can begin to deal with it. The next step is to acknowledge to God that it is sin. That's called confession — "God, I acknowledge my sin to You, and I ask You to forgive me for it." By the way, when you ask God for forgiveness, keep in mind that He isn't going to grant it unless you have forgiven those who have sinned against you (Matthew 6:14, 15; Mark 11:25). Even if another person is treating you shabbily, you have to forgive him before God will forgive you. That's not always easy to do, but it should motivate you to be obedient in an area that is often difficult to master.

4) Repent

Along with confessing areas of disobedience and asking God's forgiveness, we need to be sorry for our sin. That's called *repentance*. Very often the reason we've never really changed our ways in an area of disobedience is because we really aren't sorry. On the contrary, we're enjoying them, or at least think we are. Now if you're sleeping with someone who is not your spouse, you most likely have figured that one out. You may not be sorry, but at least you know it is a sin. However, if it's the movies you go to that are the problem, you may never have focused on going to them as something to be sorry for. Once you're at the point of knowing that you *should* be sorry, then ask God to give you a repentant heart. Ask Him to make you feel sorry — sorry to the point that you're willing to become obedient.

5) Change

Once you're sorry, or at least *willing* to be sorry, start working on what you need to stop doing or start doing. If you need to lose weight, don't focus on skipping the next meal. Focus instead on forming new eating habits. If you need to get better grades, don't focus on asking your teacher for another chance; focus on spending more time on your class work and homework. If you need to stop going to certain movies, don't concentrate on not going, but focus on what you should do instead.

If your problem has to do with someone else, look inward, not outward. God may have plenty of changes for the other person to make, but until you've succeeded in becoming the person He wants *you* to be in that relationship, the other person isn't likely to change at all. In fact, as you're obedient and make the necessary changes in yourself, you free God to work on the other person.

6) Relinquish Areas of Disobedience

As you go through this process of identifying areas of disobedience, confessing them, repenting, changing your behavior, and becoming a different person, look for the areas in which you're trying to hold onto something or someone. It may be that you're refusing to surrender something that God wants you to be willing to surrender. This process is called *relinquishment*.

There is freedom ahead for you as you are able to let go. In fact, there is bondage in trying to hold on when God wants you to turn loose. You may even find that you don't have to lose whatever it is you're afraid of losing, but until you're *willing* to lose it, you'll never know whether it's yours to keep.

DEVELOPING GOD-DIRECTED DISCIPLINE

It takes self-discipline to be obedient to God. Or actually it takes God-directed discipline, because it is through His empowering that you can continually bring more and more of your life under His control.

The first step in acquiring God-directed discipline is to want to have it — to be motivated to want to do the things He wants you to do. Often that will happen without any sort of struggle. For some people it just comes with the territory of being a Christian. But for others it takes a great deal of effort to develop that motivation. If that is the way it is with you, you'll need to ask God to give you the desire to be obedient to Him.

The next step is to position yourself with God so He can provide you with ongoing direction. The only way you can know consistently what God wants you to do is to spend sufficient time with Him on a regular basis. (More about that in the next chapter.) The reason for this is twofold. Not only do you need to be available to hear Him when He has something to say to you, but you also need to have the assurance that if you haven't heard from Him, He hasn't had anything to say on the subject. If you know you have done what you need to do to receive His direction and still haven't gotten any, you can keep moving without fear that you are contradicting His will in a particular area.

If you develop the discipline of spending time with God on a regular basis, all other God-directed discipline will follow. Until you form the habits that enable you to be God-directed, much of what you do, accomplish, and achieve will be dead works.

What are some of the areas where you need to discover God-directed discipline? What about your physical well-being? Do you exercise and eat properly? What about your relationships, your responsibilities within the church, etc.?

If you're still at a loss for direction on where you might start bringing your life into line with God's will, ask your spouse or your children. If you're not married, you might ask your close friends or your coworkers. It might also be beneficial to ask your pastor.

Usually the problem isn't so much where you need self-discipline as it is a matter of getting started in one of any number of areas. If that's your situation, I suggest that you make a list of several areas in which you have not exercised the discipline you know you need. Then pick the one that will relieve you from the most stress or frustration. Set aside some time to decide just what the best approach might be. For example, if it's in the area of physical exercise, you might enroll in a weight lifting course (and attend the sessions!). It's not necessarily that you want to increase your strength, but that you want to establish a routine of getting regular exercise. The idea is to begin somewhere — anywhere — but begin!

OBEDIENCE IN FASTING

One of the greatest lessons I learned in this area of discipline had to do with fasting.

Now whether God expects you to fast is a question that only you can answer. In my case, as a brand-new Christian God supernaturally led me into and through a three-day fast that dramatically changed the course of my life. I can still relate things that happen in my life to that particular fast. For several years following that experience, I continued to believe that I *should* fast, but as disciplined as I was becoming in other areas, I could not bring myself to engage in even a one-day fast.

As time passed, I became more and more convinced that God did want me to fast again. Finally, seven years after my first three-day fast, I knew that if I did not readdress the matter of fasting, I would be guilty of conscious disobedience to God. So I sat down and developed a plan for fasting. I was still not *committed* to following the plan, but at least I had gone through the mental process of making one.

I decided that if I was going to go to all this trouble, I may as well make it worthwhile, so I set a goal of working toward a forty-day fast. Now that was something I could get excited about. I knew that if I ever did achieve that goal, I might one day be in the big leagues in my relationship with God, and I really did desire to become a spiritual giant.

I determined that I would fast one day the coming month, two days the month after that, and so on. I figured that I'd try to increase each fast by one day per month, and if that worked, I'd reach a forty-day fast in forty months. While it didn't work out exactly that way, I did begin my one-day fast in November 1983, and with God's help I completed my first forty-day fast in April 1987, a total elapsed time of forty-two months.

A year later I completed another forty-day fast. Now I just fast from time to time. I no longer aspire to forty-day fasts, but I feel that what I did in the past was for a reason. When and if God asks me to go on another extended fast, I trust I'll be willing to repeat the effort.

By the second or third month of working up to a forty-day fast, I realized it would be very helpful to keep a journal. I had not decided to fast in order to make things happen in the heavenlies. I was not asking God for anything during the process. In fact, it almost seemed in the beginning that there was no spiritual dimension to my fasting. I was doing it because I knew God wanted me to do it, and it was simply an exercise in discipline and obedience.

Nevertheless, there were some times of great spiritual insight. My journal entry for February 28, 1984 shows that I was up at 3:15 A.M. and spent from 4:30 to 7:30 in Bible reading and prayer. I recorded on that date "tremendous enthusiasm for fasting. Most rewarding time with God I can remember; prayers shouting through the roof. . . . I can't begin to do justice to the feeling I have regarding my relationship to the Lord." On May 5, 1984 I entitled the entry "Spiritual Breakthrough" and went on to record an insight that would have great significance in the future.

Perhaps the greatest benefit I received from fasting was in the form of increasing intimacy with God. I've just become more comfortable with Him. He seems much less a stranger and much more a friend. As Jesus said so encouragingly in John 15:13-15,

> "Greater love has no one than this, that one lay down his life for his friends. You are my friends if you do what I command. I no longer call you servants, because a servant does not know his master's business. Instead, I have called you friends, for everything that I learned from my Father I have made known to you."

OBEDIENCE IN TITHING

Another area in which obedience to God produces great freedom is in our finances — specifically, tithing — returning a minimum of 10 percent of what He has entrusted to us to His work. The third chapter of the book of Malachi has some things to say about the importance of tithing:

> "Return to me and I will return to you," says the Lord Almighty.
> "But you ask, 'How are we to return?'
> "Will a man rob God? Yet you rob me.
> "But you ask, 'How do we rob you?'
> "In tithes and offerings. You are under a curse — the whole nation of you — because you are robbing me. Bring the whole tithe into the storehouse, that there may be food in my house. Test me in this," says the Lord Almighty, "and see if I will not throw open the floodgates of heaven and pour out so much blessing that you will not have room enough for it." (vv. 7–10)

If you want to have maximum freedom in your financial affairs, you need to be obedient in managing your money His way.

I began tithing even before I was a Christian. I opened my own law practice in 1972. I had been with a small firm, had served as Senior Assistant County Attorney in Fairfax County, Virginia, and had even formed a very short-lived partnership with a former chairman of the County Board of Supervisors. But now I was on my own, and I needed help. I knew nothing about operating a solo practice, and for the second time in my legal career I decided that I needed God to be involved. In 1965 He had helped me pass the bar exam, and as my part of that deal I had agreed to attend church regularly for the rest of my life. I was seven years into that vow when I opened my own practice in September 1972.

The means by which I chose to ask Him to be part of my new practice was a commitment to tithing. I knew nothing about tithing from a Biblical perspective, but I did know that my mother had tithed for many years and that God had not only rescued her from potential financial disaster, but she had reached her middle sixties with financial security for the future. So I asked God to be part of my practice, and in return I agreed to tithe.

All I knew about tithing was that it was 10 percent, so I decided to set aside one-tenth of my net income for God. I had no idea what He wanted me to do with the money, so I just accumulated it in a savings account for three years. The only withdrawal during that time was $100, which I contributed to a youth club football team to purchase trophies.

It wasn't until 1976, after I became a Christian, that I began to understand how God wanted me to use that money. And it wasn't until I attended a money management seminar in 1978 that I began to understand the principles underlying the concept of tithing.

And yet God honored my heart attitude back in 1972. He was involved in the financial end of my practice. I didn't make a great deal of money, but I didn't come close to starving either. And by 1976 I had accumulated enough money that I was able to make a difference in the lives of people He brought my way. I was able to help a neighbor avoid having to sell his home because of debt; I helped a woman pay off her legal fees, knowing that her lawyer also had serious financial problems; I was able to help churches, pastors and laypeople, all because of God's blessing in my life.

Most importantly, God began to give me a desire to give. I began to get excited about achieving higher and higher levels of giving.

How much should you give to God's work? It's really up to you. But if you're not at least tithing, you run the risk of not being obedient. I've had people tell me they can't afford to tithe, but my response is that perhaps they cannot afford *not* to tithe. The less you have, or the more in debt you are, the more important it is that you have the confidence you are being obedient, and I believe that in the area of money management, obedience begins with giving.

In the next chapter I'll tell you how to improve your life by getting to know God in a very personal way.

PRACTICE OBEDIENCE

1) List five areas of your life where you know you could do a better job of living in obedience to God's will.

2) How has your disobedience in these areas impacted upon your life?

3) How has your disobedience in these areas impacted upon the lives of others?

4) Why are these five areas particularly difficult for you?

5) Are there specific steps you can take to begin living obediently in each of these areas? If so, list the steps you intend to take.

2

The Importance of
Daily Time with God

When God reached out to me in 1976, He supernaturally healed me of alcoholism. It was not something that happened gradually, over a long period of time, but was an instantaneous event that took place in a particular place and at a particular moment. It was a very dramatic experience, and those who knew me then knew that God had done it. My old drinking buddies instinctively shunned me, and I withdrew from them.

During the ensuing six months, I spent many hours daily with God. I would go to bed late at night and rise early in the morning. I would come home at lunchtime and as early in the evening as possible in order to spend time with Him. I knew instinctively that the answers to my problems lay with knowing God better, and the only way I could think of to get to know Him better was to spend time with Him. The only way I knew to spend time with Him at that stage of my Christian walk was to read the Bible, pray, and meditate.

It's a shame more of us don't spend a regular daily "quiet time" with God. Just think of it — we have the privilege of spending time with the One who created the entire universe. He is willing to listen to our concerns, fears and desires — and not only to listen but to intervene in our behalf. He is willing to give of Himself and in fact *desires* to do that. And all it takes on our part is a little bit of discipline, just long enough to make it a habit, a routine.

There are a number of very practical reasons why it's important to meet with God on a daily basis. Here are just a few:

1) Because He Expects It
Scripture is clear, both in words and through example. God expects us to spend quality time with Him on a daily basis, and there is no way to become

or remain spiritually strong without doing so. The first Psalm, for example, tells us that the man who meditates upon God's laws day and night is blessed. In other words, his heart is never far from the Lord because he spends time with Him daily.

2) Because You Will Get to Know Him Better

When my wife Pat calls me on the telephone, I don't have to ask, "Who is this?" Why? Because I know her voice. And how do I know her voice? Because I spend time with her.

When you spend time with God regularly, you learn to recognize His voice. You become more familiar with how He communicates with you, and you also gain insight into how He operates the universe, especially your part of the universe.

3) You Will Get to Know What He Wants You to Do

In spending daily time with God you will come to see that He has a perfect plan for your life. That plan existed before you were born and anticipates every mistake you will ever make. This morning when you woke up, God had a perfect plan for the remainder of your life. It took into consideration all the faults and imperfections that make you who you are. When you go to bed tonight, He'll still have a perfect plan for the rest of your life that takes into consideration the mistakes you made today. It is absolutely essential to understand this concept. When problems and challenges that would produce discouragement come your way, you need to understand that the answer does not lie in your solving that problem, but rather in your discovering what God's perfect plan is for you in that situation. You cannot discover that plan if you do not spend time with Him, letting Him reveal it to you.

If you believe that God not only has *an* answer, but He has the *best* answer, then your job is to discover what God's answer is. And the only way you'll ever do that consistently is to spend regular time with Him.

Once you have established that regular, consistent quiet time and have learned how to use it effectively, you can know in advance that whatever problem comes your way will be resolved with God being part of the solution. It is this foreknowledge that will provide you freedom from anxiety, or "the peace . . . that transcends all understanding" (Philippians 4:7).

4) You Will Have Confidence in Making Decisions

One of the most uncomfortable times for a Christian is when you know after the fact that you missed God. You can look back and see that if you had only done something differently, things would have turned out better. Is there really a way to avoid those uncomfortable times? I think there is, and it involves spending enough time with God on a regular basis so that in most instances we can know what He wants us to do ahead of time instead of just running to Him for a quick answer in a time of crisis.

Look at it His way. If you are trying to tell a child something that will help him, but he's just too busy to listen, chances are good that you'll wait until he slows down long enough to hear you. In fact, you might even slow him down yourself. He might have to stand in the corner for a while until he's willing to listen to you. Similarly, the only way to effectively hear God in advance on a regular basis is to spend time *listening* to Him regularly. It's one thing to ask for direction and then hope that everything turns out okay. It's quite another thing to know that you've gotten that direction or that you've made yourself available and He hasn't had anything to say.

How do you know what to do when you have heard absolutely nothing from Him — when you've spent time with Him, you've sought direction, and you haven't heard Him say a thing in reply?

Let me share how I handle not knowing what God wants. First, I know that I've been available to hear, and I know that God hasn't spoken. That assurance grows out of the habit I've formed of spending at least an hour a day in Bible reading and prayer. Part of that prayer time is devoted to listening. After I've told God that I need direction for a particular decision, I spend enough time waiting for an answer so that if I don't get one, I can rest in the knowledge that He didn't give me one.

If I don't receive God's direction, I won't make a decision unless it is imperative. Until then I permit the status quo to be maintained. Very often it turns out that I don't have to make any decision at all. Time and circumstances take care of the matter without my having to decide or do anything.

I also take the position that God will direct my steps. If I've been available and heard nothing, and if the situation has developed to the point that I must take the initiative, I make the best decision I can. I don't decide more than I need to decide to take care of the situation; but rather than let my indecision become my decision, I take the initiative.

Following that, I await the results. It may be that one decision leads to another. But each time I repeat the process. Over the years I've learned to wait and to exercise patience. That combination of listening and being patient has produced within me the freedom from anxiety that escaped me for so long.

WHERE SHOULD I SPEND MY QUIET TIME?

I am often asked if there is a best place for spending a daily quiet time with God. Though there is no single answer to that question, there are some important considerations to be made when choosing the place where you will meet with God.

The first requirement is that it be a quiet place where you are unlikely to be disturbed or interrupted. That would eliminate your automobile or the bus or subway. It would also preclude restaurants and busy offices. On the other hand, a public library might be quite satisfactory for most of the things you would do during your quiet time.

Secondly, look for a location that is convenient to you every weekday at the same time so that you can establish the routine of being there consistently. If you work in your home, the den or the basement might be ideal. If you have a home office, that's a most logical place. A corner of the living room, the dining room table, or a spare bedroom can do just fine. Unless you are fairly well disciplined, your own bedroom is not a particularly good place unless it's large enough for the use of a desk and chair. Sitting in bed is generally not the best idea.

If you work outside the home, it may be that you can find a place that's even more suitable than somewhere in your home. For example, I began my relationship with the Lord by spending time with Him at my desk at home. But I discovered that very often during the day at work I wanted access to the materials I had at home. Gradually I began to take resource materials to my office, and finally I realized it was much more logical to just shift my quiet time to the office. Now I have my Bible and certain other things at the office, as well as a more extensive library at home.

WHEN SHOULD I HAVE MY QUIET TIME?

Very often during the question and answer sessions in my time management seminar, people will ask me when I think they should have their daily time with God. My answer is another question: "When do you think God wants you to?"

There is certainly much Scriptural support for the proposition that early morning is to be preferred, but many of the great men of the Bible had several quiet times each day. For example, Jesus clearly rose early to pray, but He didn't limit Himself to mornings. Evenings were also a popular time for prayer.

The real answer for each of us lies in knowing when *God* wants us to spend quality time with Him. But there is a big difference between spending *quality* time with God and spending *ordinary* time with Him. All too often someone will say to me, "I spend all day with God" or "I pray all the time." Both of those statements might be true, although I wonder how someone can pray while he's sleeping or trying to concentrate on doing all the things God has already told him to do. The point is, however, that we need to carve out time to spend with no one but God, and unless you're in a cloistered monastery or the middle of a desert, there's no way to do *that* all day long.

Certainly God wants you to spend time with Him when you're most mentally alert. Decide when that is, and propose to spend your quality time with God then. How can you give Him *less* than your *best* mental time and really believe you're doing what He wants you to?

When I became a Christian and began to examine the use of my time as God's steward, I came to realize that reading the morning paper really wasn't necessary. I had rationalized that as a practicing attorney I had to stay abreast of current affairs just to maintain my credibility. Now there are lawyers whose practice is such that that may be true. It wasn't for me. It's just that in Washington, D.C., there is a mind-set that everyone needs to know everything there is to know just as soon as possible. I was spending time reading the newspaper which I should have been spending with God. I finally decided that instead of reading the paper every morning I would rely on a weekly news magazine for my knowledge of current events.

I still listen to the news on the radio and read a local daily newspaper, but I no longer do either in the early morning. I realized that my morning was my highest quality time and that I should spend it doing the things that were most important to me — and that meant spending time with God.

The Bible says that those who "wait upon the Lord" will soar with wings of eagles (Isaiah 40:31, KJV), and I came to realize that I couldn't "wait" on the Lord unless I spent time with Him. It's really very simple: If you want to soar with the eagles, you must spend time with God.

HOW MUCH TIME SHOULD I SPEND WITH GOD?

Have you ever taken the time to think about how much time there is and how you spend it? There are 168 hours in each week. Subtract the time you spend sleeping and you will have about 110 hours left.

Do you believe it's appropriate to spend as much as one-tenth of that time with the Lord? That's eleven hours. That may sound like quite a bit of time, but after allowing time for church on Sunday, that leaves eight or nine hours for everything else: Bible studies, prayer and praise, and quiet time. For a committed Christian, the fact is that it's very difficult to cover the basics in just eleven hours a week.

Assuming you can get to the point of spending one hour a day five days a week in quiet time, that leaves you five hours for everything else. You may ultimately decide you need to carve out more than that.

WHAT SHOULD I DO DURING MY QUIET TIME?

There are at least five ways you should spend your private, quiet time with God, and these are:

1) Prayer

2) Bible reading

3) Listening to God (meditation)

4) Bible study

5) Memorizing Scripture

Let's take a closer look at each of these areas.

First, prayer. There are any number of ways you can approach God in prayer, but it is helpful to have a method for communicating. If you met daily with the President of the United States, would you just show up in his office and begin to talk, or would you have an agenda? Of course you'd have an agenda.

A helpful acronym that can help you prepare that agenda is: A-C-T-S (adoration, confession, thanksgiving, supplication).

The first thing you might want to do as you prepare to converse with God in prayer is to acknowledge Him for who He is. You need to worship and praise Him, remembering that He inhabits the praises of His people (see Psalm 22:3).

The second step is perhaps to be willing to acknowledge all areas of disobedience as sin and to ask for forgiveness. I've found that if I skip over this second step, the quality of my remaining time with God is not nearly so good. That's because I'm not fully reconciled with Him until I've confessed areas of conscious disobedience. I also need to let Him show me what I need to do to be reconciled with those around me whom I've offended. Until I've been reconciled with them too, I can't be truly reconciled to Him.

The third part of the acronym is to thank God for the things He has done and for His answers to past requests. I haven't always spent much time on this, for two reasons: I didn't keep track of what God had done for me, and I was in a hurry to get on with the things He hadn't yet done. Then I got a little pocket computer that had the capacity to store 32,000 bits of information. I decided to put my prayer list on the computer. Then, as God answered prayer, I began to keep track of all the answered prayers. When I began to realize just how many of my prayers were being answered I really got excited. I began to list those things that God had done for me without my even having asked, and I finally began to have a grateful heart. I got to the point where I was having more fun thanking Him and appreciating what He had already done for me than I was asking Him for more.

The final part of prayer consists of making your requests known to Him — and He is concerned about every aspect of your life, on down to the minutest of details.

You may not have a computer to keep track of your prayer requests and answers to prayer, but I've found that a stack of 3 x 5" index cards can work just as well when it comes to keeping your prayer life organized.

You might begin by captioning four of them with the four priorities of life: God, family, job, and service to others/ministry. (We will discuss these in more detail in Chapters 9 through 11.) As you list your own priorities under each of these captions, you may see other logical relationships emerge. Be sure to have a large supply of cards, and experiment with them. You'll find combinations that fit together very nicely.

As God answers specific prayers, they can be removed from the card, and new ones can be added. If you wish, you can keep track of the answered prayers on another card.

Another very helpful tool for organizing your prayers is a prayer diary. I use mine in conjunction with the 3 x 5" cards so I can remember to pray for people and situations in my diary that may not be on my regular prayer cards.

From time to time I also maintain a prayer journal which lists those prayer requests I've made which have not yet been answered, together with the date the prayer request was first made. I continue to pray for each of those items on a regular basis, until they are answered. If the answer is yes, it's time for rejoicing. If the answer appears to be no, I list the date it's removed from the list.

One thing I found in my prayer life was that after I learned to look beyond myself and pray for the needs of others, God began to expand my horizons. I moved from praying for those I knew to those I didn't know. I even began to translate my irritations with other people into prayer, and as I did I began to develop a compassion I had not had before.

Then I discovered the excitement of praying as God is supernaturally directing. A friend gave me a Youth With A Mission prayer diary that had all kinds of information on every country in the world. I began to pray regularly for a different country every day. I got a geographical atlas and began to bone up on my geography and world history. Then I really got excited. God gave me the insight to pray for an individual in each of the countries for which I was praying. Every morning I would identify the country and then I would let my mind visualize a person in that country. Day after day and week after week I was able to bring to mind a picture of someone in the country I had selected. As a result I've prayed for tribesmen in Africa and women and children in Europe. I've prayed for sick people, dying people, unsaved people. I've prayed for missionaries and doctors. Although I've never met any of these people, I know beyond any doubt that they really do exist. They are people God gave me in prayer.

Another practice I have found helpful is to set aside specific days to pray for specific requests. For example, on Tuesday I might pray for all of the missionaries in a certain country, and Wednesday might be the specific day to pray for my next-door neighbors, and so on. This is another way of keeping track of prayer requests and of being faithful with regard to my promises to pray for particular people and situations regularly, though not necessarily every day.

The second thing you'll want to do in your quiet time is read the Bible.

You need to spend time reading the Word of God, letting it speak to your heart. As you read, allow yourself to bask in God's promises to His people, see how the Scriptures apply to you personally, and understand that you are reading a message from a friend — a friend who is the Creator of the entire universe.

How much you should read each day is entirely up to you. There are several Bible reading and devotional guides that can direct you in your reading and that can help you read through the entire Bible in a certain amount of time. For example, if you read just one chapter a day, you will be able to read through the entire New Testament in less than a year. Four pages a day will get you through the entire Bible in one year.

The third thing you need to do in your quiet time is to meditate, or listen to God. No matter how much time you spend in talking to God, unless you establish the habit of listening to what He may have to say, either on His own initiative or in response to what you have said to Him, you're not going to get much out of the conversation or the relationship. Unlike people, God does not impose Himself on us. Not that He can't make Himself heard when He wishes, but He usually speaks with a still, small voice, and you may hear Him only if you are listening intently.

During your time of listening to God, you may wish to record your thoughts so that you have a list for future reference.

The fourth thing you need to do is move on to deeper study of the Bible. To do that, first gather together the tools you need: your Bible, pencil and paper, a highlighter, 3 x 5" cards, a timer, and any prepared Bible guides and Bible studies you wish to use. There are a number of excellent guides available to help you ferret out the deeper truths and meanings of the Word of God.

You can develop your own system of study or you can purchase prepared studies arranged by topic or book. I find it helpful to vary my approach to studying the Bible. I both develop my own studies and use those developed by others.

How much time should you spend in Bible study as opposed to praying and the other activities of your quiet time? That is really up to you, as God directs you. But it is important to have enough time for each of these areas, so decide in advance how you'll spend your time or it's likely to get away from you.

The fifth part of your quiet time could well be spent in Scripture memorization. A few years ago my wife Pat and I attended the Christian Business Men's Committee National Convention in Orlando, Florida, and one of the highlights of our time there was getting to know Dan Hayden, a pastor and the director of Christolized Ministries. Dan has developed a system of Bible memory which works extremely well for me. If you'd like to know more about his system, write to him at 500 N. Bumby Avenue, Orlando, Florida 32803.

Why should you memorize Scripture? There are several reasons:

1) The first and foremost benefit to memorizing God's Word is that it will enhance your devotion and prayer times. In fact, you will be able to com-

municate with Him according to His Word at any time of the day or night, even if you don't have a Bible with you.

2) Bible study will become more meaningful to you if you have the ability to recall passages of God's Word from memory. Your mind will be like a computer scanning its program to correlate areas of related information to gain a more complete knowledge of Bible truth. Your overall familiarity with the Bible will increase.

3) Another important benefit of Scripture memorization is that it will arm you for occasions of temptation and spiritual struggle. The ability to immediately recall the Word of God at a time in which you are in need of His instruction and encouragement is extremely helpful. This is how Jesus was able to defeat Satan during a period of intense temptation (Matthew 4:1-11).

4) Knowing Scripture by memory will increase your effectiveness and confidence in sharing the gospel with others. The ability to bring the right verse to bear upon a particular situation can make you a better soul-winner or counselor.

5) Your mind will be occupied with good things from God (Philippians 4:8), which will in turn have a purifying effect upon your life (Ephesians 5:26).

Before moving on, let me just remind you how important it is that you get enough sleep so that your mind is alert and receptive to God's input. If you find yourself tending to drop off to sleep in the middle of prayer and Bible study, you're not going to get much out of your quiet time, nor are you likely to hear God when He speaks to you. There are many reasons why you need to be sure you are getting enough sleep, but one of the most important is so you can be refreshed and alert for your time with God.

We will discuss this in more detail in Chapter 9, but coming up next, I'm going to give you some keys for discovering God's plan for your life.

PRACTICE THE PRESENCE OF GOD

1) How much time daily do you believe God would like you to spend with Him?

2) Make a list of things you need to bring before God.

3) Develop a tentative plan for reading the Bible (two pages a day? one chapter a day? a book a week?).

4) Of your total quiet time, how much should be devoted to quietly *listening* for His input (ideas, thoughts, flashes of insight)?

5) Ask God whether He wants you to sign the following pledge:

I will, with God's help, spend at least _____ minutes per day, five days per week, with God in prayer, Bible reading, and meditation. I will begin this discipline on _____.

     Your Signature:_____

                            Date_____

3

God Has a Plan
for Your Life

*All the days ordained for me were written in your book before one
of them came to be.*

(PSALM 139:16)

We began this book by talking about success, and I told you that the only way you can truly be a success is by doing things God's way. Why is that? It's because He has developed a perfect plan for your life. A plan which, if followed, will lead you to a fulfilled and meaningful life, a life in which you will have contentment and joy in everything you do. Some people have fame and fortune, but if they don't have contentment or joy, there is no way they could be judged successful by God's standards.

What exactly is success? One of the best definitions I have ever run across is that "success is the continuing realization of a worthwhile goal." If the objectives and goals we set for ourselves are reflective of the things God wants us to do, they are by definition "worthwhile." That being the case, each day that we take another step, however small, toward the realization of one of those objectives or goals, we are a success for that day. With this as our definition of success, each of us can be successful every single day for the rest of our lives.

You see, God knows what is best for you — and His plan for you is more than you could ever do for yourself. In Matthew 6:33 Jesus said: "Seek first [God's] kingdom and his righteousness, and all these things will be given to you as well." That is part of what I'm talking about, but it goes beyond that, too. Seek the general advancement of God's Kingdom, certainly — and you will find His blessing upon your life. Make sure you are living within that Kingdom, absolutely — so you will be blessed by His presence. But move beyond that and seek to understand and uncover God's specific plan for you as an individual. We've already talked about the importance of spending a regular, daily quiet time with God, during which you will get to know Him better and thus receive His direction for your life.

But there are other specific steps you can take to facilitate your understanding of His plan for your life, to move you off square one and into the process of actually living out this plan.

In this chapter I'm going to tell you about some of those steps.

OVERCOMING PROCRASTINATION AND INERTIA

There are two things that must be overcome before anyone can discover and live by God's plan. They are: procrastination and inertia. Procrastination is where it all begins. Put off doing one thing and another thing gets piled on top of it, on and on until you have a mountain of things to do. That's when inertia sets in. You don't know *where* to begin and so you simply *don't begin* anywhere! And before long anxiety becomes a factor.

I know this very well because there was a time when I was behind on virtually everything of importance in my life. When God supernaturally rescued me from the pain that procrastination represented, I began what has become Christian Stewardship Ministries.

When I was in college I had a terrible problem with both of these areas. Instead of seeking early morning classes and getting a jump on the day, I sought late morning and afternoon classes. I bragged about never studying and always cramming for exams. I looked for shortcuts and ways to put off things until the last minute and still survive.

God surely had His hand on me during college and law school. He had things to accomplish through me that surpassed my ability to be self-destructive.

After I began practicing law, I found that I was a member of a profession that majors in procrastination. The entire system of statutory deadlines reflects the commitment to procrastination that our legal system represents. I'm sure there are many good lawyers who do not procrastinate, but I was not one of them.

Eventually, through God's involvement in my life, I became aware that procrastination and inertia were leading to stagnation and defeat, so I took steps to overcome them. You can too.

FIRST, MAKE A LIST

The first step in the battle to overcome procrastination is to identify those areas in your life where you have been procrastinating.

I suggest that you devote a notebook or yellow pad to the process. Begin by making a list of the various areas of your life. For instance, you might begin with God, Family, and Job as areas in which to look for procrastination. Other possible areas might include Relationships, Finances, and Future Ambitions. Don't be too concerned about identifying all possible areas. You'll soon find them. Next, make a list of all of the things you've left undone in these key areas of your life. For example, in the God-related area, have you carved out the things He wants you to do to develop your relationship with Him? Do you read the Bible regularly and spend time daily in prayer and meditation?

In the family and self area, what have you left undone around the house? Have you developed a personal or family budget? Do you have a plan for keeping things maintained, such as your automobile, the exterior of your home, and your yard?

In the area of your job, what projects have been left unfinished? What are your boss's high priorities that you've not found time for? If you're a student, do you have a schedule for doing everything that needs to be done during the semester or quarter? Do you know what hours you should be devoting to study, to term papers and projects, to reading? If you're a homemaker, are your closets organized? Is your kitchen orderly?

What about personal correspondence? What about all the bills, receipts, and other paperwork in your life?

Once you've identified all those areas of procrastination, you've made a good start toward getting things in order. For many of us, the pain of acknowledging some of those areas is so intense that we can't even put them on a list. If that is the case with you, ask God to help you begin to be honest with yourself. Just because you don't know how to do something, or don't feel you have the time, is no reason not to list it.

Figure 1 illustrates how to do this. Form 1 in the back of this book is designed for duplication or use as a model for your own list.

PROCRASTINATION WORKSHEET

Here are twenty examples of areas of procrastination to prioritize. Using the A-C-B, 1-3-2 system of prioritizing, the person who made this list used the first column to identify all the areas of procrastination which would relieve the most pressure, giving them an A. He then used that same column to identify all the areas of procrastination that would relieve the least pressure, giving them a C. Everything else was automatically given a B. Then, moving to column 2, he reviewed all his A priority areas of procrastination. The highest priority A's were given a 1, the lowest priority A's were given a 3, and all other A's were automatically given a 2. He then followed the same process for each of his B and C areas of procrastination, giving them a rating of 1, 3, or 2. The end result was that he determined the order in which each of his areas of procrastination should be dealt with.

THE ACB TECHNIQUE
A — What is most important (Must do — high value)
C — What is least important (Can do — low value)
B — Everything that is not A or C (Should do — medium value)

AREAS OF PROCRASTINATION	PRIORITY	
	A-C-B	1-3-2
1. Answer Elena's letter	A	3
2. Clean the garage	C	3
3. Wax the car	B	1
4. Catch up on filing	A	2
5. Make a budget	A	1
6. Take a course in word processing	B	3
7. Establish a date night with Pat	C	2
8. Take Kennie fishing	B	2
9. Repair my relationship with Sally	A	3
10. Set some deadlines on the Cerutti case	C	1
11. Clean out the filing cabinet	B	3
12. Clean out the attic	C	2
13. Read Ken Smith's latest book on time management	A	2
14. Repair the roof	A	1
15. Schedule bridge with the Flemings	C	3
16. Register for CSM's next money management seminar	B	1
17. Plan how to celebrate our anniversary	A	2
18. Have the cable channels disconnected	C	1
19. Get an answering machine	B	3
20. Plan a regular quiet time	A	1

Figure 1—also see Form 1 in back of book

NOW MOVE INTO ACTION

The next step is to sit down with your list and decide what to do and when to do it.

There are several ways to approach this. You might do the hardest thing first on the theory that you'll find it easier to do everything else. You might do the easiest thing first on the theory that you just need to get started somewhere. I believe it makes more sense to do the thing that will relieve the most pressure, so I can be assured of continued freedom from anxiety and have greater freedom to do everything else.

However you choose to approach it, after you've made your procrastination list, code it so that you know all of the top priorities. It might help to give your most important areas an A and the least important areas a C. Then make everything else a B. After that, go back over your A's and give the most important A's a 1, the least important A's a 3, and all the others a 2. If you want, you can do the same things with your B and C priorities.

Now look at all your A-1 areas of procrastination. Depending on how many there are, you can develop a plan for doing all of them. Some of the items you've listed can be taken care of relatively quickly, and it will be a source of encouragement to get them done and out of the way. Other items on the list will require you to make goals and subgoals, which we will discuss in a minute. But the key with each one is to take the first step and then decide what the next step is and when you will take it.

As you move through your list, you will gain more and more confidence and encouragement. You'll discover that many of those mountains are really just molehills. Others, you'll discover, really aren't as high a priority as you thought. And you'll probably decide that some things on your list don't need to be done at all.

Not long ago I had lunch with a lawyer friend of mine who told me he had been trying to overcome procrastination. He had made a list of the things on which he was procrastinating and came up with twenty-seven items. He was overwhelmed by the prospect of having to deal with them and asked if I had any suggestions. I told him he had already taken the most significant step, which was to create the list. My suggestion was that he choose the one item on that list which, when completed, would produce the greatest freedom from anxiety. He told me what it was without hesitation. I asked how long it would take him to complete that matter, and he said, "Oh, about fifteen minutes." I asked how long he had procrastinated on it and he said, "Six months." He had suffered for six months over something that would take fifteen minutes to do! I asked if he would do it before the close of business that same day, or call me if he didn't. He said he would do it, and he did. In similar fashion he set deadlines for all the other items on his list, and by the end of the month he had taken care of them all.

What was the key to his success? It was to set aside the time, in advance, to deal with the areas of procrastination. He agreed to dedicate an hour each day, at the same time, to nibble away at these twenty-seven items. At the end of each hour he would decide where he would begin the next day at the same time. He gained a sense of momentum and then maintained it. The entire list took him a total elapsed time of seven hours, one hour at a time. He could have accomplished all these things months earlier if he had only established a routine for dealing with areas of procrastination.

In my own life, whenever I discuss the topic of procrastination, my mind always goes back to a horrible metallic monster that used to give me nightmares. It was a filing cabinet — the most disorganized filing cabinet I've ever seen. I knew that eventually I would have to get it in order, but I hated the thought of tackling it.

But then one morning during my quiet time in my law office, I looked across the room and saw that cabinet standing there, its disarray mocking my desire to live an organized life. I didn't do anything just then, but over the next few days I gradually realized that God actually intended that I *do* something about this file cabinet. So I got up from my desk, walked over to it, and opened the top drawer. It was just as bad as I had thought. I emptied that top drawer onto the floor, and then did the same with each of the other four drawers. I then spent most of the day sorting, organizing, throwing things away, and filing things in other areas of my office.

When I had finished, the file cabinet had been transformed from a cram-packed, overloaded, disorganized pile of paper to a model of efficiency. There was now plenty of space for future filing, and the drawers were no longer bending under the weight.

I returned to my desk so fulfilled! I was ready to bask in the delight of having defeated procrastination as represented by that filing cabinet when what to my eyes should appear but the top of my desk. It was just as bad on the outside as that file cabinet had been on the inside.

Slowly, painfully, I began to realize that God wanted me to organize my desk too. So I eventually did the same thing with my desk that I had done with that filing cabinet. I put everything on and in that desk on the floor. Then I threw things away, put things elsewhere, and put back in my desk only those things that really belonged there.

There was a stack of legal files that had been on that desk for as long as five years. In fact, the desk itself had been taken apart and moved from one office to another, and that stack of files had survived the move. Those files had been the source of great pain because of my years of procrastination, but when I opened them I found there was nothing left to be done with them except close them out.

Once my desk was organized, I became so excited about conquering other areas of procrastination that I began making a list and catching up in other areas of my life.

You, too, can know the relief and pleasure that come from overcoming procrastination, and by overcoming it you can free yourself to move forward in obedience to the plan God has prepared for you.

Putting things off beyond the time they should be done is never helpful. The Bible contains many references to people who suffered because they procrastinated.

For example, in the Gospel of Matthew there is the account of a man who wanted to follow Jesus, but who said, "Lord, first let me go and bury my father" (8:21). In other words, he was saying, "As soon as my family obligations are taken care of, I'll come follow You, Lord. Right now I'm so busy I just don't have the time to follow You — but I'll be sure to follow You later." You see, this man's father wasn't dead. He just wanted to put off following Jesus until he had closed another chapter in his life. Because he procrastinated, he missed out on the opportunity to spend time with Christ.

In Acts 24:25 we find the words of Governor Felix, who was presiding over the trial of the Apostle Paul. When the apostle tried to persuade Felix to become a Christian, the governor responded by saying, "That's enough for now! You may leave. When I find it convenient, I will send for you." He put off making a decision on what he had heard and, as far as we know, wound up losing his soul.

Procrastination is always dangerous — in the realm of the spirit and everywhere else.

SETTING GOALS: SIGNPOSTS TO THE FUTURE

Once you've dealt with procrastination, the next step is to move forward through the setting of goals which you believe to be consistent with God's plan for you. In a moment we're going to talk about *how* to set goals for your life. But first, I want to talk about *what* goals are.

We can begin by defining a goal as "a very specific objective, measurable in time and quantity." The more measurable it is, the more effective it will prove to be as a device to move you in your intended direction.

Next, let's discuss the difference between a purpose or objective and a goal. I've found that what works best for me is to first reflect on my general direction (my purpose), and then narrow it down to what I must do first and second that will eventually get me where I think I need to go.

It works this way: When you have a general idea of what you want to do, that is your purpose. As you put hands and feet on that general idea, as you focus more and more on the details of what is involved to accomplish it, you will identify various general objectives or things to be achieved. Finally, you will define some very specific objectives which are measurable in time and quantity. These are your specific goals, which will lead you to the fulfillment of your purpose.

For example, as God directed me I formed the "purpose" or "objective" of writing this book. I then broke that purpose down into specific goals: I will develop an overall outline of the book by a specific date. I will complete the first draft by a certain date. In order to do that I will write a certain number of pages per day. And so on. All of the goals I came up with were aimed at the same purpose or objective; namely, to write a book. But until I established and achieved each goal, my purpose or objective would continue to be something that I intended to do, not something that I was doing or had done.

Now again, it's important to note that just because I set particular goals did not necessarily mean I had to achieve them. I might find that some were not realistic, some were not advisable, and some were just not necessary. But until I went through the process of determining what should be my goals, I wasn't going to discover what would and wouldn't work.

Another way of saying this is that goals are *motivators of life*. By this, I mean that a goal is something that keeps you moving forward. It is the setting and pursuing of goals which moves you from *knowing* God's will to *doing* His will — which produces progress from point to point along the pathway. Remember, again, that it's not so much the achieving of the goals you set that's important. It's the forward motion that counts. You don't have to wait twenty or thirty years before you can consider yourself a success in life. All you have to do is discover God's will for you each day and then work toward it. You can be a success today, tomorrow, and the day after as you progress toward reaching your goals.

I'm often asked why we need to set goals. It's because the way God works is that He gives you little parts of the puzzle of life. Then, as you begin to work on one part, He gives you another. You never have the really big picture, although you are likely to have increasingly large glimpses as the pieces of the puzzle come together.

Let's move on now to discuss some of the specific elements or requirements of a goal:

The first requirement is that it be in writing. Technically, it is possible to have a goal that is not in writing, but chances are, if it isn't in writing, you haven't put enough effort into its development so that it will have the other essential elements. You will want to write what I call a "goal statement" in which you commit your goal to paper as accurately and succinctly as possible. Spell it out so you know exactly what it is you hope to achieve.

The second requirement is that it have only one objective. Why is that? Why couldn't you have a goal that includes more than one objective? The answer is that by our definition, if you have more than one objective contained in your statement you have more than one goal.

The next requirement of a goal is that it needs to be specific and measurable so you know when it has been achieved. If you cannot easily determine how much or how many of something you need to do or have, you have not made your objective specific enough to qualify as a goal.

The fourth essential element of a goal is that it must have a deadline attached. You can always modify your goal by changing the timetable, so don't be too concerned over whether the deadline you've set is 100 percent perfect. The purpose of the deadline is to assist you in knowing when you've *planned* to act or accomplish or achieve something, not necessarily when you *must* act, accomplish or achieve. Deadlines don't limit your flexibility — they just increase your ability to identify and work toward achieving God's plan at the correct pace.

The whole purpose of goal-setting is to establish a plan with sufficient precision so that when it is accomplished, an objective observer with all the facts will be able to recognize its achievement or completion. A goal requires focus, measurability and deadlines.

The fifth and final requirement of a goal is that it be realistic. In order for a goal to be a constructive tool, the objective and the deadline must bear some semblance of reality to the ability of the person to achieve the goal. It is one thing to decide not to achieve a goal, and it's quite another to be unable to achieve it. Not all goals will be achieved, because circumstances do change. But all goals should be *achievable*.

If you have no experience in formal goal-setting, I would advise you to start small and assure yourself of moving from success to success rather than running the risk of too early a failure. If your goal is realistic, you can be a success. In fact, the only practical difference between success and failure may be the matter of being realistic.

HOW TO SET GOALS FOR YOUR LIFE

I believe that the most important goals we can set are the ones having to do with building a relationship with God. As a person matures in his relationship with God, the goals that are reflective of the Lord's will will emerge as those things we decide to do and achieve and become. What goals should you set for your life? In order to know the answer you must first discover what Scripture calls "the desires of the heart" that God has placed within you. These are things we want to do or be or become that *God* wants us to do or be or become. They are tied to God's long-range plans for our lives, and as we identify them and set goals to move toward them, we'll be moving toward reaching our God-given potential. Now, not all of our desires are God-given. Some are desires of the flesh, and others are from Satan. But in your regular quiet time with God, begin to seek His guidance about the desires of your heart — both as you listen for His voice and as you consult the Scriptures — and you will come to know for certain which are the desires He has placed within you.

What are some desires of the heart? Perhaps you think you'd like to be married, or be a ministry leader in your church, or become a manager where you work. All of these may be legitimate desires of the heart that God has given you. The next step is to take them before God to determine if they are from Him.

Ask God about each desire in prayer, and then check it against God's Word to make certain it is not inconsistent with Scripture. After you've determined that your idea, thought or desire is not inconsistent with Scripture, you need to determine whether you have "the peace . . . which transcends all understanding" (Philippians 4:7) with respect to it. An easy rule of thumb to apply to this form of guidance is, "If in doubt, don't." You will avoid many pitfalls if you'll just exercise patience until God makes the way clear to you.

If your desire is consistent with Scripture and you have peace with respect to it, then you may safely proceed to plan and achieve the goal associated with the idea. But if at any time you find that you no longer have the desire, or you begin to lose your peace with respect to it, then it's time to reconsider the situation. You may discover that circumstances are not supporting your efforts to achieve a particular goal. You may have to decide whether God wants you to persevere in order to overcome obstacles, or whether He wants you to reevaluate your direction.

Suffice it to say that if you continue to have the desire and the peace, and if you do not become aware of an inconsistency with Scripture, you may continue to assume that you are hearing God's voice and proceed on that basis unless and until He tells you to the contrary.

What if you know God wants you to do something, but you don't have the desire to do it? In that case, ask Him to give you that desire. For example, let's assume for a moment that you want to be obedient to God in a particular area, but you don't have the desire to be. You realize that to not do it will be an impediment to your obtaining things that already are desires of your heart, but you just haven't been able to achieve a desire to obey God in that area. What should you do?

The first thing would be to focus on the objective that you *are* motivated to achieve and which you believe is reflective of God's will for you. Let's say you're single and one of the desires of your heart is to be married, or that you're unhappily married and want to be happy in your marriage. You want this objective with all your heart, and you know beyond question that God wants it for you.

Next, focus on your objective of obtaining an attitude of obedience in the area of disobedience. Let's say it's an unhealthy relationship. You begin to see that terminating that relationship is a necessary step in your achieving the marriage you believe God has for you. Now set some goals. Let's say the first one you choose is to spend that amount of time with God that He wants you to spend daily. Your goal statement might read like this: "In order to achieve my objective of an obedient attitude with regard to this relationship,

I will spend thirty minutes with the Lord five days a week. During that time I will specifically ask Him to give me a desire to be obedient. During that time, I will also study the subject of obedience to God in the Bible. I will begin this time tomorrow at 6 A.M., and I will continue it Monday through Friday for one month." Once you have identified a worthwhile objective, which by definition is something God wants you to do, then decide what steps you need to move through to achieve your objective. It may be something simple, like saving enough money to buy a new sofa, which would simply require saving a certain amount of money each month until you have what you need. Or it may be something complex that will take much time and effort to achieve.

Suppose your objective is to achieve a better relationship with God. Let's assume that you presently spend about ten minutes a day reading the Bible and praying and that you manage to do that two to three times a week. You don't have a regular time or place, but you know it works best when you do it in the morning. You might draft a goal statement which says: "Beginning tomorrow morning I will spend from 7:00 to 7:15 in my basement in prayer and Bible reading. I will commit myself to this schedule five days a week for the next four weeks." How does this goal statement stack up against the requirements for a well-stated goal? It is in writing. It has only one objective — to improve the amount of time you spend with God. It is specific and measurable. It has a deadline — tomorrow for four weeks. Finally, it is reasonable.

At the end of four weeks you'll either be motivated to continue or even increase your commitment or you know you can quit if you want to. That is much different from an open-ended or long-range commitment. You've included an element of flexibility which will encourage you to stay with your goal for the short haul and reserve until later the question of whether it will last beyond the twenty-eight-day trial period. Obviously you hope to continue and increase the time spent with the Lord or you wouldn't have chosen this goal to begin with. But you don't have to labor beyond what you consider a realistic timeframe to discover whether this particular goal is for you.

Once you've achieved the goal, you'll be much more motivated to establish another one. After a while, you'll wonder how you ever managed without a lifestyle of setting and pursuing goals.

In the past few chapters, we've discussed the necessity of obedience, the importance of having a regular daily time with God, overcoming procrastination, and beginning to set goals that are consistent with God's plan for your life. Coming up next, we're going to move on to talk about a very important subject on the road to success. It's called planning.

PRACTICE MOVING FORWARD

1) Make a list of all the areas of procrastination in your life that you can think of.

2) Pick one or two areas from this list to begin working on. Usually the ones which will relieve the most pressure are the best ones to begin with. Set some goals that will enable you to conquer these areas of procrastination.

3) Choose an area of your life in which you would most like to make progress.

4) Write down several goals (as we have described them in this chapter) that will lead you toward achieving that progress.

PART TWO

PLAN AHEAD: BECOME ORGANIZED

4

Planning: An Essential Ingredient of Success

Have you ever known anyone who experienced one disaster after another? Someone whose life was a continuous round of confusion?

Well, while I admit that some things happen over which no one has control, experience has also taught me that many "unavoidable" problems could have been avoided — if the person involved had simply taken enough control of his life to plan ahead. To live without planning is to drift along with the tide, and that tide may carry you into some places you need not have visited. If you fail to plan, you plan to fail. It is true that those who plan will still face problems and challenges, but as they face and resolve those challenges, they will be ever closer to the objectives they pursue.

To some extent we all plan. The person who goes to the office plans whether he's going to drive or take the bus; the homemaker plans ahead regarding what she's going to fix for supper; the couple plans far enough ahead to know they will be in church this coming Sunday. But the truth is, most of us don't spend nearly enough time in planning, and the scope of our planning is not nearly broad enough. In the examples we just gave, probably circumstances were really driving the planning process.

Whatever plans you make certainly need to be consistent with what you believe God is saying to you. Actually the planning you do should be aimed at enhancing your obedience to God.

I believe *every person ought to spend some time every day in personal planning and organization*, which is the process one goes through to decide what to do and when to do it. It can be long-range planning, short-range planning, or somewhere in between the two. In Chapter 15, we're going to talk about long-range planning, which involves looking down the road another five years or more. But for now we need to concern ourselves with planning for today and tomorrow — remembering that *now* is the substance from which the rest of our lives will be built.

The most important thing to recognize about personal planning and organization is that it must be done on a regular, consistent basis. For a person who does not have an established routine which includes time for daily planning and organizing, it is next to impossible to understand its value. But until daily planning and organizing is a way of life, life is not going to run as smoothly as it otherwise would.

We have already discussed the fact that God has prepared a plan for each one of us and that He generally chooses to reveal His plan to us one piece at a time. I'll take that a step further to say that He expects us to expend time and energy to discover and develop that plan, and if we refuse to do so, we are being disobedient. Since conscious disobedience is sin and sin produces its own consequences, can any thinking person afford to consciously decide to not plan? Can we afford to refuse to discover His plan for each of our lives? Proverbs 14:15 tells us that "a prudent man gives thought to his steps," and Jeremiah 10:23 adds that "a man's life is not his own; it is not for man to direct his steps." In other words, a wise man will seek to discover the steps he needs to take — the steps that the Lord has ordained for Him — the plan the Lord wants him to follow.

Since we can't always know exactly what God wants us to do, one of the ways He has provided for us to learn is to develop a plan He can use as a base from which to lead us. If you haven't thought about where you're going, any old path will get you there. But if you have thought it through, then when you get to an unexpected fork in the road, you stand a much better chance of knowing which way to take.

In the sixth chapter of Matthew, Jesus tells us not to worry about what we should eat or drink or what we should wear. Instead, He says, we should seek first God's Kingdom and His righteousness and all these other things will then be given to us as well (v. 33). Verse 34 of that chapter says, "Therefore do not worry about tomorrow, for tomorrow will worry about itself. Each day has enough trouble of its own."

I believe that what God is saying here is that we don't have to worry about having our needs met because He has a plan for providing all of them. But in order for us to discover that plan, we must seek first His Kingdom and His righteousness. As we project ourselves into His Kingdom through prayer and through the process of spending time listening to Him, we will understand more and more of His plan. As a result, as we understand more of His plan, we can more accurately decide on a daily, even hourly and minute-to-minute basis what our own plan should be and what steps we should take. As we plan today and spend our time in accordance with that planning, tomorrow will take care of itself. Prayer plus planning equals obedience, which in turn equals freedom from anxiety about tomorrow. Let's discuss some of the benefits of planning ahead.

PLANNING AHEAD PRODUCES PUNCTUALITY

There are many important benefits that come from planning, including the fact that you can improve on your ability to be on time. Lack of punctuality can damage relationships. In his book *You Can Be Financially Free*, George Fooshee reflected on his own lack of punctuality, estimating that his usual arrival time at appointments averaged five minutes past the starting time. He computed what that five minutes had meant to him over the past sixteen years and was astounded to find that he was a full two months late! Two months of imposition on other people. A chronic lack of punctuality reflects a lack of respect for other people. It tells the other person that you think your time is more important than his is, which may damage the relationship. But if you are punctual, you demonstrate your respect for others, and that will impact relationships in a positive way.

I once had a good friend who was active in politics. I managed several of his campaigns, and he was elected first to a local and then to a state office. His political future was bright, and he could easily have been elected to national office. But from the very beginning of our relationship, he was not punctual. As time went on, he became less punctual, and then predictably late. Finally he became unpredictably late and sometimes didn't show up at all, even for important events. I finally became discouraged and lost my desire to support him because of his habitual tardiness. I lost a friend, and he lost a valuable resource.

Another reason to be punctual is that tardiness creates anxiety. Have you ever heard anyone say, "Boy, am I glad I'm late"? Of course not.

The most important reason to be punctual, however, is that it reflects obedience to God. Scripture requires that your yes be yes and your no be no — in other words, that you mean what you say (Matthew 5:37). If you agree to be at certain places at certain times and you are habitually late, you are exhibiting an attitude with which God is not pleased.

How can you become punctual? The cornerstone of consistent punctuality is planning to be early. The reason most of us are late is that either we don't plan at all or we plan to be on time. A few people actually plan to be late, and fewer still plan to be early.

The most common argument against planning to be early is that if you're early you've wasted time, that you could have put the time to much better use if you had spent it on whatever you were working on before you left. The fact is, you were probably late beginning to work on that too.

Even if you do actually arrive early, all you need to do is plan on how to use that time in advance. Depending upon the circumstances, you might even have extra quality time with the Lord or catch up on some reading. Very often, though, if you plan to be early you will actually wind up arriving on time.

If you have already gotten to the point of being punctual most of the time, there are still some things you can do to show respect for the other person when you are unavoidably late. If you're late leaving, try to have someone phone ahead and announce your delay. If you're the only one who can call, do it yourself.

If you're caught in traffic, your options are more limited unless you have a mobile communications unit. If you can reach a phone, you have to weigh that against the delay involved in getting out of and back into traffic.

Finally, when you've done everything you can, relax. Do some planning or other constructive activity. Or just commit the time to prayer, including prayer for the people who will be adversely affected by your tardiness. And learn the lesson to be learned so that you will be early in the future.

PLANNING WILL HELP YOU FIND OUT WHAT WORKS

If we could always know, without thinking too much about it, what was going to work, there would be less need to plan. After his ten-thousandth failed effort to invent the electric light bulb, Thomas Edison reportedly said that he was not at all discouraged. He had discovered ten thousand ways not to invent it, he said, and that meant he was that much closer to his objective. He would continue to follow his plan, even though that plan had to be refined and restructured at various points along the way.

The more planning you invest in a project, the less work you will have to do when it's time to execute your plan. When you have developed your plan in full, then you will have to spend much less time making it work.

PLANNERS CAN MEET DEADLINES

While serving as a consultant to a small Christian-owned computer engineering firm out west, I was asked to take a look at how the engineers used their time. There was one man in particular who was brilliant, but who never seemed able to meet deadlines — even though he had a part in setting those deadlines himself. Management was considering dismissing him because there wasn't enough money available to just put him in a corner and let him work until he got things the way he wanted them.

I spent some time with this man, Van, who told me he understood that deadlines were important, but that the deadlines being set just weren't realistic. Circumstances beyond everyone's control seemed to sabotage most efforts to meet those deadlines.

As we talked about gaining the ability to meet deadlines, I asked him what he was working on right then and what all had to be done before he could complete the project. He went on for quite a long time about all of the things that still had to be done, so I asked him if he could write down each thing that needed to be accomplished to achieve closure to that stage of the project.

Following his preparation of the list, I asked him if he knew when each thing needed to be done in relation to the completion of the entire project. I brought in Gordon, the project manager, to help with this. He knew precisely what the time lines were. The two of them talked about what could be done to make the list of things that needed to be done workable within the necessary timeframe.

Over a period of time we got to the point where Van was actually interested in focusing on the deadline as part of his ongoing effort to produce a good product. Then I began to teach him the value of taking a little time each day to go over his list and to try to decide in advance where he should be at the end of the workday. I said that even if he didn't get it all done, he should at least try. He agreed and began to have a regular time first thing each morning to organize his list.

Before I completed my work for the company I suggested to Gordon and Van that they meet weekly to go over Van's list. About three months later Gordon called me to thank me for what *he* had learned as a manager while

I was there. He also said that the company had decided to publicly recognize Van for the progress he had made and because of the example he was setting for the other engineers.

THE KEYS TO DEVELOPING A SUCCESSFUL PLAN

There are five keys to developing a successful plan for your life on a daily, weekly, monthly and long-range basis.

Those keys are·

1) Understand the past.
2) Be realistic.
3) Set aside time for planning every day.
4) Use a daily "to do" list.
5) Maintain a schedule.

Let's start with *understanding the past.*

It is impossible to produce a good plan in the vacuum of the present. It's next to impossible to develop a workable plan without knowing the background and history of what you are planning. In fact, one way of seeing the planning process is to view it as a link between the past and the future. The past has a direct bearing on where you are right now; you need to know where you have been in order to understand how to get to where you want to be.

It's easy to fantasize about the future, and it's easy to think you know where you are in the present. But unless you have an accurate picture of the past, it's virtually impossible to triangulate your position.

Of course, the past is very relative. What you don't know about doesn't exist as far as your plan is concerned. In my opinion, this is the biggest single limitation on our ability to know God's plan for our lives. Most of us don't know or don't invest the time in finding out enough about the past to make the best decisions for the future.

So begin your plan. Focus on where you want to be. That provides your motivation. But then study where you've been so you can understand where you are. Then you can navigate most accurately into the future.

Next, your plans must *be realistic.* I'm not suggesting that you shouldn't dream and fantasize. But if I tried to invent the next generation computer, it would be totally unrealistic because I don't have any aptitude in this area. Thomas Edison, on the other hand, was perfectly capable of inventing the light bulb and many other wonderful devices. He had great plans, and he had the aptitude to bring them to reality.

To achieve a successful attitude toward planning, the thing being planned must appear to be achievable.

The third thing we said is that if you would develop a successful plan, you need to *set aside time for planning every day*. We talked about this earlier, but it is impossible to overstress the importance of a regular planning time.

My suggestion is that you plan to spend at least fifteen minutes the first thing every morning planning and getting organized for the day. If you have your regular quiet time first thing in the morning, then I suggest you do your planning immediately after your time with the Lord. That is a particularly good time because you will be focused on what you have learned in your time with God, the things you believe He has told you to do.

During your planning time, focus on what you are going to do today and tomorrow. Perhaps you have several meetings scheduled during the day. If so, go over these, thinking about what is to be discussed and what you still need to do to prepare for each one. Focus on everything you need to do today, and think through just how you are going to approach each item. Thinking about how and when you're going to do what during the day leads me to point number four, which is the importance of a *daily "to do" list*.

If you learn how to efficiently use a "to do" list you can master the task of organizing your life. Here's how to go about it. During your planning time, write down everything you can think of that needs to be done. Then decide what should be done today and what can wait until another day. Then list the things you should do today in the order in which you plan to do them. After your planning time is over, you can start doing the things on your list. Take as much time as you need to develop this list. It's your key to success for the whole day and for your whole life.

And — this is a very important and — don't stop there. As you go through the day, write down all the things you think of during the day that need to be done in the future. Do *not* stop and do them when you think of them, but do write them down for tomorrow's list. Over the long haul it will be the rare exception that you really have to do something at the same time it first occurs to you.

Why not stop and do them? Because they will get in the way of the other things you have already planned to do. That's the way most people go through life. They are always doing what comes along rather than following a predetermined plan and doing what should be done. This approach pre-

THINGS TO DO TODAY

Referring to your Personal Procrastination Worksheet, as well as to your calendar and whatever else you use to remind you of what you have to do today, list those things that you would like to plan to do today. Prioritize the list as you have already learned to do, and then do the things in the order that your prioritizing dictates. Whatever you do not complete today will go on tomorrow's Things to Do Today list.

THINGS TO DO TODAY	PRIORITY	
	A-C-B	1-3-2
1. Rake leaves	A	2
2. Complete page proofs	C	3
3. Call Mother	A	1
4. Errands (see errand list)	A	2
5. ~~with Howard and Jill~~		2
. Call Chris and Callie	B	1
16. Vacuum	B	2
17. Write thank you note to Jan and Steve	B	3
18. Complete time sheets	C	3
19. Update day timer	C	2
20. Mow	C	1

Figure 2—See Form 2 in back of book

vents a sense of real accomplishment at day's end and produces the nagging concern that something important may have slipped through the cracks.

It is important to learn to stick to your "to do" list and to resist the urge to do things that are not on it. If something else comes along that seems important, put it on today's list and see how it compares with everything else you've already decided to do that day. Unless it is really important, use tomorrow's planning time to decide when to do it.

The fifth thing we said was that a key to successful planning was to *maintain a schedule*. Scheduling will be discussed in greater detail in Chapters 5 and 6, but I do want to introduce the concept now, since it is an important component of planning.

Suppose your daily "to do" list has ten things on it that you really want to get done today and another five things you'll do if you have time. As you review the list you will discover a logical order of sequence.

For example, consider the list I draw up for Thursday, which is my

THINGS TO DO THIS WEEK

Referring to the same sources as for the Things to Do Today list, list those things that you do not need to do today, but that should be done sometime this week. As you complete your Things to Do Today list, you can refer to this list for the next highest priority items. This list will soon become the source for the things that go on a future Things to Do Today list.

THINGS TO DO THIS WEEK	PRIORITY	
	A-C-B	1-3-2
1. Visit Mother	A	1
2. Get tires for Pat's car	A	1
3. Send radio tapes to Chuck	B	1
4. Complete materials inventory	C	2
5. ⁓ promotional letters		1
⁓. Get new software package	C	2
16. Review seminar video	C	3
17. Update rolodex	C	1
18. Send Kennie a birthday card	A	2
19. Learn how to do macros	B	3
20. Call Charles for registration figures	B	2

Figure 3—See Form 3 in back of book

errand day. I have my quiet time planned for 5:30-7:00 A.M., to be followed by a breakfast meeting. I have lunch with a friend at noon, and I have a Bible study with some Christian business owners from 4:00 to 5:30 P.M. I want to be home by 6:00 for dinner and to spend some time with my wife, Pat. That leaves from 8:00 A.M. until noon to be scheduled and from 1:30 to 4:00 P.M. to schedule — a total of six and a half hours. My first decision is to schedule my planning and organizing time at 8 A.M., right after breakfast. That is when I will develop the rest of the schedule.

Since I am committed to spending time with my mother, I call her to confirm that she can ride around with me while I take care of errands. We agree to meet at 1:30, right after lunch. Once that is squared away, I make a list of all the places I need to go. Because I have been making notes and building my Thursday errand list all week, I have everything there that I need. I will need to stop at several places around town, and I decide the order in which I will make those stops. If I don't get everything done that I had planned to do before lunch, then I can decide after lunch whether I can catch up or whether I need to plan to leave some things until next Thursday.

As the day wears on, I go from task to task, and because I keep my eye on the plan all day, I make sure that I do what is most important. I may not get to everything on my list, but what is left undone can simply be added to next Thursday's schedule.

After you have successfully established the habit of setting aside time on a regular daily basis for planning and organizing and have learned to use a "to do" list and a daily schedule, you are well on the way to living an organized and fruitful life. You will find, however, that whatever plan and schedule you begin with will need to be revised each week. This is true for several reasons. First, your priorities will change. What is a very high priority this month may not be so high next month. Also, circumstances may change. Or you may need to modify your schedule as the seasons change. Only after years of experience will you be able to maintain the same schedule month in and month out. Until then you will need to reevaluate your schedule on a weekly basis — or perhaps even more frequently.

Be sensitive to those areas where your schedule is not working. If you are missing appointments, not getting enough sleep, not spending enough time with the Lord, etc., then you know it's time to rethink and revise your schedule.

AIDS TO ORGANIZATION AND PLANNING

Over the years I have learned that several tools can help you stay organized and on top of the things you need to do:

Calendar: The most practical thing I can tell you about calendars is that unless you are extremely experienced or have a secretary who can coordinate them, you should never try to maintain more than one calendar.

Pocket organizers: A first cousin to the calendar is the desk or pocket organizer. In addition to a calendar, the typical organizer has space for a daily or weekly "to do" list and room for tracking the spending of money and use of time. One of the best I've found was developed by Time Systems, Inc. Interested? Contact Time Systems, Inc., 400 Interstate North Parkway, Suite 750, Atlanta, GA 30339, or 5353 North 16th Street, Suite 400, Phoenix, AZ 85016.

I have also found the Daytimer system to be excellent.

Index cards: 3 x 5" index cards, kept in a small file, can be a terrific help with regard to organization. For example, suppose I know that next week I'm going to meet with my friend Byron to discuss a particular matter. During the course of the week I might have various ideas I'd like to discuss with Byron. All I have to do is place his name at the top of an index card, and then every time I have an idea relating to that meeting I just jot it down on his card. On the morning of the meeting I can organize those thoughts and ideas in very quick fashion and be prepared immediately to discuss what's important to me. There's really no limit to the types of things that can be organized and tracked in this way.

Telephone message pads: To tell you how I use these, let's go back to my friend Byron. We may not have a particular time set up for a meeting, but I think of something I want to discuss with him. So I write his name on the appropriate line of the message pad together with a short one-line note that will remind me of that particular thought. Since it's not urgent, I don't place a call to him at that time. Later in the day I have another thought, and two days later I have yet another. They all go on Byron's message pad. Finally the opportunity presents itself to talk to him — either because he calls me or because I've got enough things to talk to him about to justify making the call. In this way I have kept track of the things we need to talk about, and I can be sure I haven't forgotten any of them.

Pocket recorder: For those who are interested in refining the organization and memory process, I have found that a pocket recorder enables me to do several times as much each day than I was able to do before I had one. Its use requires discipline, but if you're willing to pay the price, the results can border on the miraculous. My pocket recorder is small enough to be carried in my shirt pocket, although I actually carry it in a small leather "portable pocket." Whenever anything occurs to me that I want to remember, I just make a quick note on the recorder. The kinds of things I record are various ideas I have, commitments I make, and money I spend. If it's not practical to make a note on the recorder at the precise moment that an idea occurs to me, I may jot it down until I can comfortably convey it to the recorder and then throw the written note away. Regardless of when I put a note on the recorder I know that at 8 A.M. the following morning I am going to clear the tape and list the things I've recorded in my organizing and planning time. Then I transfer those notes to appropriate files, throw the list away, and begin again.

There are numerous other organizational and planning helps available, but the important thing is for you to experiment and determine the ones that work for you.

Once you begin to be an effective planner, you'll find that planning will aid you in a number of different areas of your life. For example, you can plan a project from start to finish, plan a vacation, and even plan the use of your leisure time.

Remember, having a plan actually increases your flexibility because it gives back to you time which would otherwise be lost because you didn't know what ought to be done next. Have you ever decided to spend a leisurely day with your family — or perhaps even by yourself — and "things" wound up getting in the way? If you habitually planned in advance what you were going to do on that leisurely day *and* planned when to do everything else, you probably would have had the sort of day you wanted to have. And if every day is well planned, your days off will unquestionably be far freer of interruption than if your "normal" days are out of control. Far from being restrictive or stifling, planning should and can set you free.

PRACTICE PLANNING

1) Decide on the best time to spend fifteen to thirty minutes per day planning and organizing your day over the next week, and make a commitment to give it your highest priority, second only to your quiet time.

2) Each day during your planning time, review what you did the day before and what you plan to do today.

3) Determine whether there is something undone from yesterday that still needs to be done today.

4) Determine what needs to be done today that you did not plan to do yesterday.

5) Decide what you will plan to do today and the order in which you will plan to do everything. Whatever *must* be done today is to be at the top of your list, and what can be done another day should be toward the bottom.

6) Decide *when* you will do what you plan to to during the day. If you cannot accurately estimate the time required, plan more time than can possibly be needed. Run the risk of ending up with extra time rather than not enough time.

7) In the case of any appointments, plan to leave early in order to arrive

early. If someone is coming to meet with you, plan to stop what you are working on at least five minutes before the meeting is scheduled to begin.

8) If you need a pocket organizer, will you order one today? Suggestions were given earlier in this chapter, or you can call Christian Stewardship Ministries at 703-591-5000, or write to us at 10523 Main Street, Suite 200, Fairfax, VA 22030.

5

A Schedule: The Key to Making the Day Flow Smoothly

In this chapter we're going to get down to the business of designing a daily schedule. First, we're going to talk about some key activities around which a schedule should be built, next we'll discuss some of the other components that go into designing a successful schedule, and then we'll begin the process of committing a schedule to writing. Now, when I mention schedules some people react negatively. They think I'm trying to take away their freedom to be flexible. But they're wrong.

Most of my teaching time is devoted to helping Christians get better organized in various aspects of their lives. Since the underlying assumption for most of what I have to say is that there needs to be more discipline in a particular area, many people assume I leave no room for flexibility. Nothing could be further from the truth.

The fact of the matter is, unless there is a proper balance between discipline and flexibility, the one can defeat the other. Too much flexibility can render the attempt to be more disciplined ineffective, and too much rigidity in the exercise of discipline can destroy the motivation to be sufficiently disciplined. The problem really isn't too much discipline, it's too much rigidity — or too little flexibility in the midst of the discipline.

Since most of us find it easier to err on the flexibility side of the spectrum than on the discipline side, most of what you hear from a person like me is designed to help you move from too much flexibility toward the other extreme. But it is important to realize that the objective is not to become more and more rigid, but to discover more and more of God's plan for your life. A great deal of that plan includes much greater flexibility, but very often we need to master the art of discipline in order to experience that freedom of greater flexibility.

I encourage every Christian who is committed to achieving a greater degree of personal organization in his or her life to see a momentary lack of flexibility as a short-term investment in a long-term process. Your return on that investment will be a trillionfold. For every minute you decide to be less flexible in order to become better organized, you will enjoy hours, days, weeks, months, and even years of greater flexibility in the long term. The joy and freedom produced by achieving greater personal discipline and organization far outweighs the cost.

The essence of establishing self-discipline for a Christian is to discover what God wants you to do and then to be willing to do it. The hard way to do that is to try to decide each day and each hour and each minute what God wants you to do and then try to figure out how to do it. The easy way is to determine in advance as much as you can what God wants you to do and then to establish a plan for how to do it.

THE PAIN OF OVERCOMMITMENT

Over the years I have counseled a great many Christians who didn't understand the importance of routines, who had no idea how to pace themselves, and whose lives had become unmanageable as a result. They were overcommitted — that much they knew — but they didn't know what to do about it. We'll talk more about overcommitment and how to overcome it in Chapter 7, but for now I simply want to say that the underlying problem here is disobedience. We have *not* done what God *wanted* us to do, and we *have* done what God did *not* want us to do. So the first step in shedding our overload is to begin to understand what God is saying *now*. What does He want you to do and what does He not want you to do? Certainly God doesn't want you to be like a whirlwind, always going in circles and never getting anywhere. He wants you to live a life of peace and order, and if you understand His will for you and plan your life accordingly, that's how it will be. You will be able to say good-bye to the vise of overcommitment and hello to more freedom and flexibility.

To avoid overcommitment, a good technique to apply is the axiom, "if in doubt, don't." Don't agree to something until it's clear to you that God wants you to do it. You may miss a blessing once in a while, but you'll save yourself tons of grief. I find it's much better to run the risk of lagging behind God than to bear the pain of getting ahead of Him.

UNDERSTANDING MAJOR ACTIVITIES

One of the keys to getting your day organized is to develop an understanding of what I will call major activities. These are certain activities that are common to all of mankind, regardless of generational or cultural differences or even spiritual awareness. When those activities are identified and made a matter of conscious deliberation, a proper balance can be struck between them that will provide the individual with the ability to move through the path of life with relative ease.

As you identify these major activities and strike the proper balance between them, God will certainly make more and more of His plan known to you in a tangible way.

There are at least five of these major activities, and they are:

1) Sleep.
2) Time with God.
3) Time for self (including personal planning and organization).
4) Time for family.
5) Physical exercise.

Let's take a look at these, one at a time, beginning with:

Sleep

I am sometimes asked why I give such a high priority to sleep. That's because I believe sleep is at the very foundation of a person's ability to perform at an optimum level. The human body is very adaptable and can be incredibly abused and still maintain its basic integrity, but at what cost? Science has produced relatively little insight on the human brain and the phenomenon we refer to as sleep. We know some of the results of sleep, and there is an increasing body of research on the subject — but as with other aspects of neurological science, we know relatively little about it.

There are those who can not only survive but prosper without much sleep, but they are rare. Ed Sullivan, the television personality of the fifties and sixties, was said to need no more than two to four hours of sleep per night.

Then there those who require much more than the accepted adult norm of eight hours per night.

But apparently most people need somewhere between seven and nine hours of sleep on a regular basis to maintain optimum performance. Understand that my focus is on achieving peacefulness, which includes optimum performance. I have discovered that most of the people I have counseled simply do not get enough sleep. I also realize that a person can obtain too much sleep, and that is also undesirable. But in an increasingly fast-moving world, getting too much sleep is less and less of a risk. So our first major activity that will contribute to a peaceful life is getting a sufficient amount of sleep.

How much sleep do you need? Only you can say for certain. Your body will certainly tell you if you're not getting enough or are getting too much, and your daily routine must be adjusted accordingly.

God knows sleep is important, and His Word promises those that love Him, "when you lie down, your sleep will be sweet" (Proverbs 3:24). A good night's sleep is a treasured gift from God. But you may need to make some changes in your daily routine in order to receive that gift!

Later on in this chapter I'll be telling you how to go about establishing a daily bedtime that works best for you.

Getting enough sleep can actually be the first step in revolutionizing your life.

For example, I remember Mark. When I first met him he was a relatively new Christian, a man who had been disorganized in many areas of his life prior to surrendering control to Christ. By the time we met, he had developed a system of listening to the Lord that worked so well it was obvious to anyone who met him that here was a truly different kind of person.

Mark rose early almost every weekday morning, had his quiet time, and was out of the house before anyone else was out of bed. After running, he returned to have breakfast with his family and then was off to work. He arrived at his office before anyone else, where he planned his day before being subject to the interruptions that were a part of any normal day. He tried to use his mornings for tasks that required quality mental effort because that was when he was at his best.

His plan was to clean and straighten his desk and leave the office every day at exactly the same time. He was home in time for dinner every evening and had the rest of the day to devote to family or personal commitments. When he had to put in extra time at the office, he would schedule that for

Saturdays. Because he was so well organized, his weekends were usually free for family. I asked Mark how he was able to make it look so easy. What was he doing that others could model? His answer was that the time he spent with the Lord each morning and the time he set aside for planning and organization before work were his keys to success.

He also told me that he got to bed early enough so he wasn't tired when he got up in the morning. This, he assured me, had been the most difficult part of getting his life in order. But once he had formed the habit of going to bed at the right time, everything else actually came quite easily. Every once in a while, he admitted, something came along that prevented his getting to bed as early as he wanted. And when it did, the following day would not go as smoothly and he would not be as effective.

Getting enough sleep over the long run is critical.

The second major activity is:

Spending Time with God

We talked about this in Chapter 2, so we won't spend a great deal of time on this subject now. But it is one of the day's major activities and is of extreme importance. I would say that all of the other major activities will flow from a combination of the first two — getting enough sleep and spending quality time with God on a scheduled, daily basis. Do both of those things and you've got an unbeatable combination.

As you begin the process of of dedicating quality time to God on a regular daily basis, you first have to deal with existing habits. This time has probably been spent habitually doing something else. You may be spending it sleeping, watching television, reading the newspaper, or in any of numerous other ways. What needs to be done is to convert your existing habit into a new habit of prayer and Bible reading.

Much of the process of translating an old habit into a new, good habit has to do with attitude. It's very difficult to develop a good attitude about changing an old comfortable habit. You have to want to do it. In this instance any energy expended or pain experienced will be more than worth it since spending time with God on a regular basis will absolutely revolutionize your life and make its quality so much better than it is without it.

If you're already in the habit of spending this quality time with God, you know how important it is to you. In my own life this is something I could never give up now that I know the advantages it includes.

Taking Time for Yourself

It may sound selfish to place time for yourself ahead of time with others, but in order to effectively meet the needs of others, your own needs must first be met. Not your *wants* or your *desires*, but your *needs*.

If you don't have anything, you can't give anything. This is true of many things, including spiritual vitality. It's important to get your own batteries charged so you can be of service to others.

There are a number of ways in which this time for yourself can be spent. And, in fact, much of the need for time for yourself will be met by spending quality time with God regularly. The more time you spend with God, the more your own needs are met.

If you were to consciously divorce God from time for yourself, that would be counterproductive. But in addition to consciously planning time with God, you need time to consciously plan and organize yourself. My experience is that most people wouldn't argue with that assertion — they just never get around to setting time for regular daily planning and organization.

Unfortunately, there are some who will argue with the basic assertion, who cannot see the value in or need for systematic planning. If you lean in this direction, I would encourage you to try it for thirty or sixty days and then make your judgment.

If sufficient time is set aside for sleep, spending time with God, and planning and organization on the personal level, most of the needs that should be included in the "time for self" category will be taken care of. Those needs will vary with the individual, as will the amount of time required to meet them.

For example, consider reading. On one extreme, one person may not have a "need" to read anything other than the Bible. On the other extreme, there may be a nearly insatiable desire to read, in which case some reading should probably be included under the "needs" heading.

What are your personal needs? Have you taken the time to think about what they are and then sought to build sufficient time into your day so those needs are met? Keep in mind that your needs will change with time. So the key is not necessarily to develop a checklist of needs and meet them, but rather to set aside sufficient time regularly to first identify needs and then to be sure they are included in your plan.

Time for Family

The fourth major activity is that of devoting time to family. Now we're getting into areas that contain more variables and so are potentially more complicated.

As I mentioned earlier, with fairly rare exceptions most people need between seven and nine hours of sleep daily. And probably an hour a day with the Lord meets most people's sense of the amount of quality time He wants to have with them one on one.

But it gets much more complicated when we talk about how much time you should spend with your family. That depends on a number of variables. You as an individual, the complexion of the family, and the needs of individual family members will all influence the decision as to what constitutes sufficient time. And once we've considered all those things, we'll have to talk about the *quality* of the time spent with the family. All too often the time spent with the family does not meet the minimum daily requirement for either quantity or quality.

For example, I counseled one man who knew that he wasn't spending enough time with his wife and children and wanted to improve in this regard. So he pledged to stop working long hours at the office and spend his evenings with his family.

Not too long after this I discovered that he was often carrying home a briefcase full of papers, and he'd spend the evening working on them. His wife and kids were there in the same room with him — but he might as well have been a thousand miles away. That is most definitely not the sort of "spending time with the family" we're talking about here.

Now suppose you're a single adult. Depending on your age and previous marital history, the "family" time may consist of time spent with parents or close friends. It may mean time spent with small children, teenagers, or adult children. It may be influenced by future hopes and aspirations for marriage.

What if you are a married adult? The variables here are that you will need to spend time with your spouse, children, grandchildren, parents, grandparents and even great-grandparents if they are living.

Another variable is geography. Are you close enough that your time for family can be spent in personal visits, or is the distance so great that it must out of necessity include long-distance phone calls and letters?

Another variable is age. Obviously an infant or dependent senior will require much more time than an involved teenager.

The most reliable way I know to assess what is sufficient time is to first determine the perceived needs of each individual. A husband should ask his wife how much one-on-one quality time she feels she needs. A father should ask his children the same question, and an adult child should ask his or her parent(s).

Once you get an understanding of what everyone else feels is necessary, that can be compared to the total time you have available for spending with your family.

The fifth major activity is:

Exercise

This is another key in developing the peaceful life. I have to admit that I have only recently discovered for myself the importance of exercise, even though I have taught its importance for years. As modern technology frees many of us from physical exercise as a necessity of daily living, there is more and more of a need to compensate for that freedom. In fact, if we fail to compensate for it, it becomes the opposite of freedom. Our bodies can become prisons.

From the time I was fifteen years old, I have had a chronic lower back problem. I had exhausted all reasonable means of discovering a solution to periodic attacks which have landed me in bed for up to eight days at a time. More recently, my left arm began to lose strength, as did my grip in both hands. My right shoulder became increasingly painful, and I began to experience some new difficulties with my back.

After some prayer and a little unsolicited advice, I decided to take a class in weight lifting. That decision has probably changed the course of my life. The most difficult part of the process was deciding that I could find time in my busy schedule. Since the class I was interested in was only offered at certain times, it was then or never. So I made a quality decision to register. Then I discovered that I had to spend two or three times as much time outside class as I did in class if I wanted to get the full benefit from it.

Then I got enthusiastic. Now I spend as much as six hours a week doing physical exercise, and I'm trying to find ways to afford more.

I'm learning to stretch in productive ways. I look forward to relearning swimming techniques and water-related exercises. And my back is feeling much better.

While I've known for years, and taught for some of those years, that God expects us to give priority to caring for our "temples of the Holy Spirit," I lacked the motivation to do something concrete about it. Now I wish I had gotten started on it years ago.

MAJOR ACTIVITIES

Indicate how much time is needed for specific daily activities.

ACTIVITY	HOURS PER DAY OR PER WEEK
Sleep	8 hours/day
Time with God	30 mins/day
Time for self	2 hours/day
Time for family	2 hours/day
Planning and organization	15 mins/day
Physical exercise	30 mins/day
Job	52 hours/week
Dealing with areas of procrastination	4 hours/week

Figure 4—See Form 4 in back of book

ANCHOR ACTIVITIES

Now that we've talked about major activities, let me tell you about anchor activities, which I define as five specific activities that need to occur at the same time every day.

You will be on your way to discovering the benefits of a peaceful and productive life if you learn to build your day around these five activities, which are:

1) Getting up in the morning.
2) Going to bed at night.
3) Starting the workday.
4) Ending the workday.
5) Taking a midday break.

Getting Up in the Morning

As I counsel, I often ask the question, "When does God want you to get up in the morning?"

Most people get blank expressions on their faces. They've never given it any thought. They have never even considered the possibility that *God* wanted them to get out of bed at a routine time every day.

So now let me ask you that question: "What time does God want you to get up in the morning?" Be honest with yourself. The question isn't, when can you get up? It is, when does *God* want you to get up? As I've been saying throughout this book, being obedient to His will is *the* most important thing you can do in any area of your life.

I can guarantee you that if you begin to arise each day when God wants you to do so, you'll be better positioned to receive blessings from Him — blessings that you may have no idea even exist.

To answer the question of what time God wants you to get up each weekday morning, you need to take a quick survey of the things you presently do in the morning. Make a short list of what they are. Next, ask yourself what you're not doing in the morning that you should be doing. Then make another list of those things that you are doing in the morning that could be done another time, a different way, or not at all.

For example, things that you are not doing that you should be doing might include more quiet time, taking time to eat breakfast, etc. Things that could be done differently might be reading the paper later in the day or reading a news magazine at night instead of the paper in the morning. You might decide to shower the night before.

Once you've examined what your morning should consist of, you're ready to begin to address the question of when to get up. Remember, the question is *not* how you can get everything done that you want to do in the morning, but what *God wants you to do* in the morning.

Once you've gone through that process, you can figure out what time you need to get out of bed. It may not be easy for you to change your schedule so that you get up at the time you feel God has set for you. It is often harder to be obedient in this area than in most areas. If you aren't conscientious in this area, you are bound to find that "little things" keep coming up which prevent you from getting to bed early enough to get the sleep your body needs. And if your body hasn't had sufficient sleep, it is going to find it very difficult to get out of bed in the morning. But if you've consciously decided it is God's will for you to get up at that time, it should become easier to avoid rationalizing. Give yourself a four-week trial. Determine that no matter what, during that time you'll be obedient in getting up when God wants you to.

Of course, it's much easier to do that if you're obedient in the second anchor activity too, which is:

Going to Bed at Night

In order to realistically hope to get up consistently when God wants you to, you must determine *when* you should go to bed and *how* to go to bed at that time.

Once you've determined what time God wants you to get up and how much sleep He wants you to have, just subtract the number of hours from your getting-up time and you'll have your going-to-sleep time. Then for your going-to-bed time, go back an extra half-hour, for two reasons: one, you won't always get to bed on time, and, two, you won't always get to sleep as soon as your head hits the pillow.

Now that you know when your bedtime should be, you have another set of decisions to make. If you're typical, you probably will see that your ideal bedtime is much earlier than you've become accustomed to. So make a list of all the things you now do with your time between your optimum bedtime and the time you've been going to bed. You're probably going to see one of two things. Either you're seriously overcommitted, or you've been wasting time.

You may not be able to immediately eliminate all the activities that conflict with God's time for you to go to bed routinely, but what you can do now is to establish a plan that will enable you to disengage from those other activities and commitments over the next six months. However worthwhile those activities may be, if they force you into disobedience in this area, they cannot be God's best for you.

Starting the Workday

If you work outside the home, or from a home office environment, it's critical, in my opinion, that you identify when your workday should begin. I'm not talking about when your employer expects you to start. What I really mean, as in all of these areas, is, when does *God* want it to begin? If you're a homemaker it's also important that you know when your workday begins, but this will most often be determined by the routines of other family members. In one sense your workday begins as soon as you get up in the morning, and in another sense it begins when everyone who is going to leave the home has left for the day.

If you're employed outside the home, chances are good that you should be in the office, on the job, or at least out of the house well before your employer requires you to be. You should have time to do personal planning and organization each morning, unless you have done it the evening before. Also, you may decide to spend your quiet time at work or somewhere on the way to work.

After you have determined when you should actually begin work, and after you have decided how much before that you should arrive at work, you can decide when to leave home to go to work. To do this, make a list of every-thing you should be doing in the morning at your office or before beginning your job. Include travel time, personal planning and organization, and per-haps even job-related planning. Should you be in an office Bible study or other regular morning Bible study? What about exercise or a fellowship group?

Remember, just because something has a higher priority in the overall scheme of things doesn't necessarily mean it should come first chronologi-cally. For example, you may give extremely high priority to spending an hour with your spouse every day. But that can come in the evening instead of the morning. You may have to make the decision to commit some quality time for an activity with your son or daughter on Saturday instead of dropping him or her off at school each morning.

The important thing is to decide first when God wants your workday to start and then devise a plan that will help you follow His will in the matter.

And in some instances it takes a real commitment to begin following through on this aspect of daily life.

I remember counseling a woman who told me that as hard as she tried, she just never could seem to get to work on time. She had the best of inten-tions, but morning after morning something came up at the last moment that delayed her and kept her from following through on those intentions.

As we discussed this situation, the problem suddenly became apparent. Here was a woman who was reluctant to be early.

When I first suggested that, she resisted the idea, but then she began to see that I was right. Each morning just as she was about to leave she would look at her watch and think, "If I leave now I'm really going to be early." Following that, she'd say, "Maybe I'll just take another five minutes to stick a load of clothes in the washer or make a bed." Whatever it was she was going to do, she'd soon find that five minutes stretched into ten — or fifteen — and now she was no longer early, but racing to be on time. I have found from personal experience that in order to be on time, you need to *plan* to be early. You'll do well to anticipate the unexpected in terms of interruptions or delays and plan accordingly.

Ending the Workday

As we move on to the fourth anchor activity, I'm certain you can begin to see clearly how closely connected they are. If you get to bed when God wants you to, you can certainly get up when He wants you to. And the same is true here. If you follow His plan when it comes to starting your workday, it's going to be much easier to follow it in regard to ending the workday.

To decide when your workday should end, you first need to decide when you need to arrive home. If you're married, just ask your wife or husband. Once you know when you should arrive home, then decide when to leave work so you can get home with time to spare. That means you'll have to decide when to begin wrapping up the day's business, getting your desk in order, and so on in order to be ready to leave before it's time to leave. Then you can attend to last-minute details without having to rush to leave on time. Don't overlook the fact that travel time may be a factor and that your employer also has a voice in all of this. On the other hand, your employer also has an obligation to be reasonable, and if that is not the case God may want you to work for someone else.

If you're not married, and if you don't have family priorities to consider, you can be more flexible in this area. But don't lose sight of the fact that God has a best time for you to leave work, and you should know when that time is.

Midday Break

This is the fifth and final anchor activity. Now don't misunderstand and think I'm saying that everyone has to eat lunch. You may or may not decide to use part or all of this time for eating, but I believe everyone should have a specific time on a daily basis to divide the morning from the afternoon. The amount of time you use for your midday break can vary from thirty minutes to two hours depending on your situation.

You can use your midday break for errands, a quiet time, a Bible study, plain old relaxation, or building relationships or cultivating clients for your business.

What is important is not so much how you use that time as the fact that you know when you begin work in the morning that you will have a midday break. It will help you organize your day if you visualize *before* midday and *after* midday. You will find that certain things will fit better into your daily plan and schedule if you see them as things that should be done either before or after that break.

Your Anchor Activities Schedule might look like the sample on the following page.

DIVIDING THE DAY

Dividing up the day into before and after the midday break isn't the only way you should divide it.

ANCHOR ACTIVITIES SCHEDULE

Indicate at what time you do or plan these specific activities.

ACTIVITY	WHEN/WHAT TIME
Getting up in the morning	6:00
Going to bed at night	10:00
Starting the workday	8:30
Ending the workday	5:00
Taking a midday break	12:30

Figure 5—See Form 5 in back of book

I suggest that you divide each day into six parts:

1) Early morning.
2) Morning.
3) Midday.
4) Afternoon.
5) Dinner.
6) Evening.

Why should you divide up your day in this way? Because it makes it easier for you to decide when you're going to do the things that need to be done within the day. In this way you are establishing regular routines that will become second nature to you, and this will allow you to make maximum use of your time and will add a tremendous amount of flexibility to your life.

Once you have established regular times and routines for these parts of your day, you can begin to anticipate a life that is a pleasure to live from the time you get up in the morning until you go to bed at night. You will begin a process that will permit you to have time for everything you should do and everything you really want to do. Get ready to live the life God has designed for you.

Let's take a closer look at each of these parts of the day.

Early Morning
This is the time for grooming and possibly taking a bath or shower, unless you decided to do this the night before. If you eat breakfast before you leave home, your early morning would include time for that. If you have your quiet time before you leave home, it would also include that.

How you decide to spend your early morning will set the stage for the rest of your day. If you establish a routine for spending your early morning as God wants you to, you'll have made a giant step toward spending the rest of your life as God wants you to. Since each day is determined to a large extent by how the first few hours are spent, and since it's generally easier to establish a routine for early mornings, you have a golden opportunity to begin to live a new life just by adjusting your routine for this part of the day. It is by far the most critical part of the day.

Evening

What? Evening comes after early morning? In terms of importance, yes. Unless you work evenings or shifts, this is your next segment of the day to plan.

How you spend your evening generally determines how you spend your early mornings. If you don't have an evening routine that supports your going to bed in time to get sufficient sleep, you won't have as effective an early-morning routine. And if you're married and a parent, evening is the part of the day you'll most likely prefer to spend with your spouse and children.

It is very difficult to have a godly balance in your life if your evening schedule does not consistently include your being home well before bedtime most of the time in order to provide at least some time with the family.

Which brings me to what I consider the third most important part of the day.

Dinner

This includes the time between arriving home from work and clean-up after dinner, and it is such a high priority because it is all too often the only daily anchor activity in which all the members are together. If you're single, or if the kids are grown and gone, it's not as necessary to give it any more significance than you want to. But if there are children at home, I believe a very high priority should be attached to the entire family being present at the dinner table. This should be an important time for family communication, strengthening relationships, gentle correction and discipline, and spiritual growth.

I know from personal experience that it's difficult to have a regular dinnertime with all the family members present — and that there will occasionally be situations which prevent this. But the routine of having dinner together needs to be given a very high priority.

When Pat and I got married, we decided to establish a regular dinner hour for ourselves and her two children who were then living with us.

When we announced the beginning of this new routine, it didn't attract much attention. No one gave it much thought except Pat, who was going to have to change her rather flexible approach as to when dinner was served. I knew there would be some built-in challenges, but saw no need to draw attention to them any earlier than necessary. We set 6:30 as dinnertime and asked everyone to give it a high priority. The first couple of days were uneventful. Then Kelly stayed late for a drill team practice, and when she got home dinner was over. She felt badly about it, but Pat gave her something cold and we didn't make a point of it. Then Eric was late getting away from Little League practice, which made me late since I picked him up every evening.

The next night Eric was late getting out of practice again, so I waited for the coach and explained our emphasis on having dinner together. I asked him if it would be possible for Eric to be through with practice no later than 6:15. He said he understood, and we both told Eric, who said he'd forgotten to mention it to the coach. Eric's practice always finished on time after that, and the other parents were as pleased as I was.

The following evening we were together at dinner when the phone rang. I answered it and told Kelly's caller that we were having dinner and that I would have Kelly call back when she was through. Well, Kelly took it pretty well, although she had not expected me to do that. Afterwards we talked about interruptions and agreed that the kids would tell their friends not to call during our dinnertime. In the meantime, we gave them the choice of taking the phone off the hook or just understanding that we wouldn't answer it if it rang. They were sure they wanted to hear it ring if it did, so that's the option they chose.

And ring it did.

It rang constantly during dinner for the next two weeks. Pat and I were pretty sure the kids' friends were calling to test the system. Before long the kids realized that if it was important, whoever it was would call back.

About a month later my son Kennie dropped by for dinner. He is one of those free spirits who would rather drop by than let you know he's coming. When the phone rang, he jumped to answer it. I asked him not to, and he looked at me as if I had taken leave of my senses. He couldn't believe I wasn't kidding or that everybody could just sit there and eat dinner while the phone was ringing.

Eventually those phone calls during our dinnertime became less and less frequent, as all of our friends and the children's friends came to understand how important this time together was to us and that we did not want to have it interrupted.

And it paid off too in terms of interpersonal relationships and spiritual growth.

Our rule about the phone may sound extreme to you — but that is how high a priority we assigned to this part of the day. By the way, now that it's just Pat and myself, we decide on a call-by-call basis whether to let the telephone interrupt us.

Midday Break

The next important part of the day is the midday break, which, as you already know, is also an anchor activity. As I said before, your day will be more effective if you decide which of the things you need to do will be done prior to the break and which will be done after the break.

You might set aside your mornings for going through the paperwork that is piled up on your desk, for instance, and reserve the afternoons for meeting with clients or potential customers. The important thing is that you have a break that allows you to subdivide your day into segments that are more easily kept under your control.

Morning and Afternoon

Now we're down to scheduling the morning and the afternoon. If you've developed a routine for your early morning, your evenings, your dinnertime, and your midday break, you'll find that arranging your mornings and afternoons is really a piece of cake. You can now relax and enjoy doing what you're supposed to do during the day, knowing that your life is in order, or is at least heading rapidly in that direction.

If you haven't done so during the early morning, you might want to begin your mornings with planning and organizing, both for your personal life and your job. Plan to do the most important (and often least exciting) things first and work toward the more "fun" things in the afternoon.

End your afternoon with a "clean up and get ready to start again" time. Clear your desk, organize your tools, do whatever needs to be done so you are ready to go when you come in the following day — and do it early enough that you don't risk leaving work late, which would throw your evening routine out of kilter.

If you work a rotating shift or follow a somewhat irregular routine, you may be thinking that our discussion of dividing the day does not apply to you. But even though your midday break may come at 3 A.M. or your dinner hour at the time when most of us are thinking about breakfast, it will still be profitable for you to divide your workday in this way. We will discuss shift-work and other irregular work patterns in greater detail in the next chapter.

Now we're almost to the point where we're ready to begin drafting a written schedule.

Now, a schedule is simply a plan which illustrates how we plan to spend our time, just as a budget is a plan which illustrates how we plan to spend our money. In other words, a schedule is a "time budget." There is only one major difference between time and money, and that's that we *can* borrow money and we *can't* borrow time. And that's good, because I'm sure a great many of us would be in terrible trouble if we could borrow time. But because we can't we have just one chance to spend every minute. Once time is gone it's gone, and there is no way to get it back. When we're out of time we're out of time, and there's nothing we can do about it. Because there's no way to borrow more, we need to learn to spend the time we have wisely.

The more things we have to do, the less time we have for each of them. That forces us to prioritize — to pick and choose the things that are most important to us — and a schedule is the centerpiece of that process.

When we write down in advance how we expect to spend our time, we're much more likely to spend it that way. Yes, things will come along that will change our plan, but we are more likely to achieve those things we consider most important if we have taken the time to schedule them.

While we're talking about what a schedule is, let me take just a moment to explain what it is not. It is not a rigid, inflexible imposition on our time. If we design our own schedule we are in charge of our time much more than if we let other people or random circumstances dictate our schedule to us.

IF HOURS WERE DOLLARS

Have you ever fantasized how you would spend your money if you had more of it than you knew what to do with? Suppose someone gave you $2,400 today on the condition that you had to spend it. If you didn't spend it, your donor would never give you any more money. If you did spend it, your donor would give you $2,400 the next day, the day after that, and so on for the rest of your life. The only condition is that you must spend every cent of it and you can't skip a day.

For a while it would be great. You could buy all the food and clothes and

DIVIDING THE DAY

SEGMENT OF THE DAY	SPECIFIC TIME	ACTIVITIES FOR THIS SEGMENT
Early morning	6:00 to 8:30	Arise, shower, quiet time, exercise, breakfast, leave for carpool
Morning	8:30 to 12:30	Travel, planning, begin work
Midday	12:30 to 1:30	Lunch, errands, exercise, nap, relax, read
Afternoon	1:30 to 6:00	Return to work, review day's progress, fine-tune remainder of today's plan, work, clean up, leave work, travel, arrive home with time to relax before dinner.
Dinner	6:00 to 7:00	Time to relax before dinner (unless you're the cook!), family discussion time, Bible-based conversation, Bible memory exercises, quality time for all family members
Evening	7:00 to 10:00	Time with family, homework, exercise, reading, meetings, recreation, relaxation, chores, areas of procrastination, television (?), bath, bed..

Figure 6—See Form 6 in back of book

houses and cars you wanted. You could travel and eat out and play golf and do whatever you wanted to. Medical and dental bills wouldn't be a problem, and neither would gifts and educational expenses. But sooner or later you would either have to sit down and develop a plan or begin to throw that money away.

Now let's convert those dollars into hours — $100 for every hour God gives us in a day, to use as we choose. Children and new Christians probably waste most of those minutes and hours. But as we mature, God holds us to a greater and greater standard of accountability for how we spend that time — and that's why a schedule, a time budget, is so important.

MAJOR ACTIVITIES SCHEDULE

ACTIVITY	SPECIFIC TIME
Time for sleep	10:00 to 6:00
Time with God	6:30 to 7:00
Time for self	7:00 to 7:30
Time for family	Breakfast, Evenings
Time for planning and organization	8:30 to 9:00
Time for physical exercise	8:00 to 8:30
Time for job	9:00 to 5:00
Time for areas of procrastination	Thursday evenings

Figure 7—See Form 7 in back of book

Years ago I discovered a very simple way to minimize my disobedience to God. During my planning time one day I realized that my mornings were not very productive. When I looked at my calendar for the several weeks preceding that day, I noticed that my office appointments were often in the morning. They were also scattered throughout the day with no real rhyme or reason. In fact, there was no plan for determining when I would see people. It just happened.

At the time my law practice was at a low ebb. I had plenty of time to do everything I had to do, and there didn't seem to be any reason to have a more structured schedule. After all, why should I be rigid and inflexible unless I was so busy that I had to be? That morning God gave me an insight that changed my life. I realized that if I kept my mornings free of appointments, and if I exercised the discipline to plan my work and my life during those morning hours, I could seize control of a lifestyle that up to that point had been very disorganized and undisciplined.

I had fun establishing a plan for afternoon appointments. I decided to schedule my time in one-hour segments, figuring out how many I could handle in a week. Before long I realized that my whole life was there, to be discovered in advance, through a schedule. That discovery revolutionized my life and my law practice.

Perhaps you haven't already experienced the benefit of developing routines and following a schedule, but I know this would do the same for you.

A SCHEDULE CAN AID YOUR CHRISTIAN WALK

Among the many benefits of keeping a written schedule is the fact that it can help you surrender control of your life to Christ.

Every Christian professes the intention to make Jesus the Lord of his or her life. But how many of us are actually doing that? How many of us are surrendering our will to His? What many Christians never discover is that the more control they surrender, the more freedom they will receive. If we'll just do a few things God wants us to do when He wants us to do them, He will give us the ability to do many things that *we* want to do the way *we* want to do them. As you seek God's will for your life, you will begin to uncover the things He wants you to do. Then, as you build them into your schedule, you will be more apt to translate those things into concrete action. As the New Testament book of James says, "Do not merely listen to the word, and so deceive yourselves. Do what it says." And, "the man who looks intently into the perfect law that gives freedom, and continues to do this, not forgetting what he has heard, but doing it — he will be blessed in what he does" (1:22, 25).

Of course, the heart of a Christ-centered schedule is Christ. We all need to spend the time with Him that He wants us to. We also need to obtain the proper amount of rest that our minds and bodies need. As we keep those two commitments, God promises to lead us to the fulfilled life and to help us unfold a plan that He has designed and which contains all we ever thought of wanting for ourselves and our lives.

BUILDING YOUR SCHEDULE

Before we move on I want to briefly tell you four things you need to keep in mind as you begin the process of constructing a schedule for your life.

They are:

Start Small

It will work better for you to keep your first attempts at scheduling as simple as possible. Scheduling is a technique to be learned, and the more you become accustomed to it and the better you become at it, the more thorough your schedule can become. Some people try to start off with too complete a schedule, with the result that they soon become discouraged and decide to discard the entire scheduling process. Scheduling can and will work for you, but be careful not to overwhelm yourself by cramming too many things into your first schedule.

Memorize

Even though we've discussed the importance of writing it down, the basics of your schedule should also be committed to memory. Although you can refer to your schedule periodically, you don't want to have to get it out every few minutes to see what you should be doing next. After a while many of the routines that are built into your schedule will become second nature to you, and you will find your life developing a momentum and a rhythm that carries you forward.

Revise Frequently

Remember that your schedule exists to serve you, not the other way around. If you find your schedule isn't working, get out your eraser and change it. Especially during the learning process you are likely to find that your schedule requires frequent modifications. That's all right, because it's all part of building the schedule that works best for you.

Be Persistent

Although in the beginning you may be frequently revising and fine-tuning your schedule, persistence is important too. Make up your mind that you are going to build and follow a workable schedule, and make sure you are making every effort to follow the schedule once it has been constructed. Ask yourself, when you fail to follow your schedule, whether the schedule was unrealistic or whether there was a lack of persistence and follow-through on your part. Merely building the schedule is not enough to win any battles. Follow the schedule once you've committed it to paper, or revise it so you can follow the revision.

SOME COMPONENTS OF YOUR SCHEDULE

To design your first schedule, let's begin by referring to Figure 4 (Major Activities). Using Form 4 in the back of this book, determine how much of your time you think should be devoted to each of these activities.

Next, refer to Figure 5 (Anchor Activities). Using Form 5 in the back of this book, decide what time you think you should *plan* to do each of the activities indicated. Remember, this is only a plan and is subject to change as you experiment with what works best for you now.

Your next step is to refer to Figure 6 (Dividing the Day). Using Form 6 in the back of this book, fill in the specific time for each segment of the day, using the following as guidelines:

Early Morning: From the time you get up in the morning until you leave home. If you are a homemaker and are going to remain at home, then treat your early morning as ending when everyone who is going to leave home has left. If your office is in your home, then early morning would end at the time you plan to enter your home office and begin work.

Morning: From the time you leave home (or at the end of your early morning as explained above) until the beginning of your midday break.

Midday: From the time you plan to break for lunch until you plan to return to work. Remember, you don't necessarily have to plan to eat lunch in order to plan this break. The midday break helps divide the morning from the afternoon regardless of how you spend the time.

Afternoon: From the time you end your midday break until you plan to arrive at home. If you are a homemaker, it would usually end at the time you plan to begin the evening meal preparation. If your office is in your home, it would end at the time you make a transition from work to family activities and should end at least thirty minutes before the evening meal is scheduled.

Evening: From the time you arrive home (or at the end of your afternoon as explained above) until you plan to go to bed.

Your next step is to refer to Figure 7 (Major Activities Schedule). Using Form 7 in the back of this book, fill in the specific times that you will plan to do each of the activities shown. If you're not sure, put in approximate times or some indication of when you think you might do it.

Now you're ready to begin to fill in your first weekly schedule. You'll find various typical schedules in the next chapter that should prove helpful. Referring to each of the foregoing illustrations and forms that you have filled out, fill out the Monday column on the appropriate form (see Form 12) in the back of this book. You may find it helpful to make one of your own using this form as your guide, and if you do, just be sure to keep it to one page. Use one- and two-word descriptions for each activity you fill in.

After you have completed Monday, use it as a guide for the remaining weekdays. Try to schedule the things you will repeat on other weekdays at the same time on each day you will repeat them. You will find that it is much easier to establish the habit of doing them consistently if you do them at the same time on each day that you repeat them. Weekends are usually different from weekdays, and you can fill them in as you go along.

The first things that will go on your schedule are: the time you have decided you should go to bed (at least Sunday through Thursday) and when you will get up. Next indicate when your workday starts, when your midday break is, when you will end your workday, and when dinner will be. Refer to Figure 6 and Form 6 (Dividing the Day) for this information.

Now by referring to the work you have done on Forms 4, 5, and 6 (Major Activities, Anchor Activities, and Major Activities Schedule), you can fill in your time with God, your planning time, time for physical exercise, time for spouse, time for children, and time for dealing with such things as procrastination.

Once you've divided the day in this way — once you've incorporated the major and anchor activities into your schedule — you're ready to turn your attention to other activities and matters that ought to be included on a daily or weekly basis. I'm sure you can think of many of these: church on Sunday, Bible study during the week, school- or child-related events such as plays, concerts, games, etc. Some of these events occur on a regular basis and can easily be plugged into your schedule week after week. Other special events may be added as you find out about them.

If you want to get serious about managing your time God's way, you must learn to see certain activities in your life as repetitive and subject to systematic scheduling. (Remember Ecclesiastes 3:1 — "There is a time for everything, and a season for every activity under heaven.")

As an example, consider all those household chores and projects that have piled up. Suppose you are able to set aside two evenings per week for "chores and projects." At this point you don't even have to think about what chores and projects you'll do — just set aside those two evenings a week, perhaps between 7:00 and 9:00 P.M., to deal with them. Once you've picked the best two evenings and eliminated whatever conflicts there are, you can begin to think more specifically about what you're going to do during that time.

As you spend time thinking ahead to these evenings, you'll begin to see the order in which those chores and projects need to be handled. This will enable you to prioritize them and thus begin to build a more complete schedule with regard to them.

What if you do the same for those undone things at the office? What if your children had a routine time to do their chores or their homework? My point is, if you have decided at the beginning of each week what you will do as a matter of routine, you can have a plan that will enable you to remember what to do during those times.

And when something comes up it's always a simple matter to check your schedule and say, "I've got another important engagement that night. It looks like I won't be able to make it," or "Can we do it another time?" On the other hand, if it's a higher priority you can schedule it in place of whatever you did have planned. Just remember to reschedule whatever you need to.

In the next chapter, I'm going to give you some examples of typical schedules for people in various walks of life. But before we get to that, let me tell your four important events I work into my schedule on a weekly basis.

Errand Day

I set aside part of one day each week to run all the errands for the coming week. During my time for personal planning and organization, I keep a list of the errands I need to run. During the day, if I think of something else I write that on my list too. I may need to drop off dry cleaning, pick up a few items at the hardware store, and make a few other stops in town. Whatever those errands are, I then arrange them in the most logical and convenient sequence. Putting all the errands together in this way saves a tremendous amount of time.

Parents' Day

In my schedule, one afternoon a week is designated as time to be spent with my mother. This may not be possible for you, depending upon whether you live in the same community as your parents, but your schedule should include time for them if they are living. If you cannot see them in person, set aside time for phone calls or for writing letters. On occasion I combine my time for errands with time for my mother. She enjoys going along with me, and we have plenty of time to talk.

Date Night

I believe a married couple should set aside at least one afternoon or evening per week for a date. That date may be dinner and a movie, a concert, or simply a walk in the park. It doesn't really matter what you do as long as you spend some quality time together. It is also important that you both enjoy the activity. A husband who loves to fish — but who has a wife who doesn't — is not fulfilling his obligation to her if Date Night finds them at the river wearing hip-boots and waiting for the trout to bite.

Family Bible Study

Perhaps you will want to schedule a family devotional every night, and if you can do that, wonderful. It is more likely that one night per week is the best you can do when it comes to getting everyone together for a sufficient amount of time for effective Bible study. This is a time when the members of your family will grow closer to each other and to God — and I highly recommend it to you.

I'm sure you can think of other important activities that you want to schedule on a regular basis. Perhaps there are some things you've wanted to do for quite some time, but you just haven't gotten around to them. If so . . . start scheduling them, start experiencing them, and enjoy the changes that come into your life as a result!

When you get to Chapter 7, you'll find some more things to include in your schedule, At first you may very well feel totally overwhelmed. But don't give up. What you are really in the process of doing is discovering just how overcommitted you really are. No wonder you experience anxiety!

Instead of giving up, just take a deep breath and begin to prepare yourself for the race. It took you a while to get where you where, and it will take you a while to get out of it. Purpose to take one step at a time. Don't bite off more than you can chew at any one time and you'll do just fine. And just try to imagine how nice it will be to have time to do everything that is important and to know that whatever there is not time for, God does not intend for you to do — at least not now.

PRACTICE SCHEDULING

1) Of the various routines suggested in this chapter, which ones do you believe God wants you to establish?

2) What are some problem areas in your life that could be improved upon if you had a schedule?

3) If you are a parent, what routines should you begin to build into your children's schedules?

4) If you are married, what evening should you and your spouse agree to spend together?

5) If you are single, what routines should you establish that are not specifically suggested in this chapter but which you know you need to plan?

6) Draw up a weekly schedule which should be modified at least once each week for the first several weeks.

$$\overline{6}$$

A Look at Some Typical Schedules

In this chapter I want to take a look at some schedule examples from people in various walks of life. Before getting to the first of those, I want to briefly describe one very good way to visualize the use of your time — and that's to think of it in terms of percentages.

For example: there are 168 hours in every week. If you spend about eight hours per night of those hours sleeping, that leaves a net of about 110 hours per week for everything else. You can decide in advance what percentage of that time should be spent in each of the four priorities of life — God, Family, Job, and Service to Others. (We'll discuss these in more detail in Chapters 9-11.)

Let's assume that 10 percent of your net time, after deducting time for sleep, should be used for God-related activities. While I know of no Scripture to support that assumption, I think it's certainly reasonable and can arguably be justified as returning a tithe of our time to the Lord. Ten percent of 110 hours is eleven hours per week. If you spend three hours in church and church-related activities on Sunday, and another couple of hours for a week-day church service or Bible study, you only have five to six hours left for your remaining time with God during the entire week — enough for perhaps an hour a day of quiet time with Him.

If you have one full-time job with no overtime, and if you live in a major metropolitan area, you may spend as many as fifty-two hours per week in job-related activity, including travel. That amounts to 47 percent of your 110 hours per week (after deducting time for sleep). If you're a full-time home-maker with children, you'll need to be extremely well disciplined to hold your work-related time to fifty-four hours a week, or 50 percent of your waking time. And if you have small children it will be far more. Remember, the tighter your time constraints, the more important it is to protect your time with God. Don't make the mistake of letting your work-related time steal your God-related time from you. If you do, things are likely to just get tighter.

In the example we're using, you might still have as much as forty hours left after sleep, quiet time, and work. Since most of us will spend at least ten to twelve hours per week bathing and grooming and meeting our own basic needs, that leaves around thirty hours for family members and service to others, most of which usually needs to be reserved for family. In my opinion, that represents a fairly good balance for the normal family situation. The more time that goes into work-related activity, the less time there is for family and ministry or service to others, especially if you continue to give your quiet time the highest priority.

SCHEDULE FOR A HUSBAND/FATHER

Now let's talk about how some specific individuals might schedule their time. Let's start off with Bill, who is married to Pat and has several children. He is employed on a full-time basis, is a committed Christian, and desires to become the person God wants him to be. He is not particularly well organized, but he is intelligent and knows he can make better use of his time.

Pat has been increasingly vocal about the impact his lack of organization is having on her life. The pressure in the office is getting worse, and Bill is beginning to feel a little anxiety because there's not enough time to do what has to be done.

He knows he should be spending more quality time with the kids, but when? And although he hasn't really focused on it, the fact is, he no longer has a regular quiet time.

Pat finally got him to attend a Christian Stewardship Ministries Life Management Seminar, and now he's motivated. He knows where to begin — with his schedule.

Over the last several years Bill has gotten into the habit of watching the 11:00 news before going to bed. He reads the morning paper and *U.S. News & World Report*. At the seminar, Bill realized that he really doesn't *have* to watch the late news; he's just formed a habit of doing that. The problem is, he should be getting up earlier. He's known that, subconsciously, for a long time, but he was just too tired. It was bad enough getting up when he had to, much less earlier!

When he takes a realistic look at his life, he decides he should be in bed every night by 9:30 and asleep by 10:00 so he can be up at 6:00. His plan is to shower immediately, then spend thirty minutes in quiet time.

The next night Bill is in bed at 9:30. He has trouble getting to sleep, but when he does he sleeps well and wakes up before the alarm. He showers and shaves, then goes downstairs to the family room for a refreshing thirty minutes with the Lord. He prays about the day ahead and asks God to help him with an upcoming deadline at the office. There's some anxiety there, but he feels much better this morning than he has in a long time.

At 7:00 Bill has breakfast with the kids and Pat, and at 7:30 he is off to work. He still has to fight traffic, and there's a problem waiting for him at the office, but it's going to be a good day. He can feel it in his spirit.

Bill gets to the office a half-hour earlier than usual and settles back with a cup of coffee, using that time to plan his day. He's not even sure what he's supposed to plan, but he's there, he's got his coffee and his desk calendar, and he's ready to start.

Before he gets very far, Bill begins to focus on the problems of the day, and as he does so he comes to realize that he has big problems. It's not that the problems are new — it's just that he's never taken the time to sit back and look at them. He's just dived into the day and worked busily at whatever needed his attention the most. But as he begins to list his projects and his daily tasks, he realizes he is very far behind on a number of projects.

Thinking back to the seminar he attended, Bill remembers just to make his list, not to begin working on it. Then he decides to set up a meeting with his boss to discuss the overload. As he reflects on that process, he remembers his quiet time this morning and his asking God to help him at the office. He remembers the assurance he felt that God had heard that prayer. All of a sudden the crisis is under control.

Before completing his planning time, Bill decides that no matter how hectic things are at the end of the day, he'll clean up his desk at 4:30 and be ready to leave at 5:00. He's going to be home thirty minutes before dinner tonight no matter what.

The rest of the day is no picnic. He works as hard as he can all day, and when 4:30 comes he doesn't stop for a second. But at 4:35 he begins to think about his time with God that morning. He remembers his promise to clean up at 4:30 and leave no later than 5:00. He also realizes that he could work all night and still not catch up. He might as well do something right. So he cleans up his desk, organizes his files, and puts everything away. He still has

TYPICAL SCHEDULE— HUSBAND

	SUN	MON	TUE	WED	THU	FRI	SAT
4:00							
4:30							
5:00							
5:30							
6:00		Shower	Shower	Shower	Shower	Shower	
6:30		Bible	Bible	Bible	Bible	Bible	
7:00	Bible	Breakfast	Breakfast	Breakfast	Breakfast	Breakfast	Bible
7:30	Breakfast	Travel	Travel	Travel	Travel	Travel	Breakfast
8:00	Shower	↓	↓	↓	↓	↓	Shower
8:30	Church	Planning	Planning	Planning	Planning	Planning	Planning
9:00		Work	Work	Work	Work	Work	↓
9:30							Family
10:00							
10:30							
11:00	↓						
11:30	Family	↓	↓	↓	↓	↓	
12:00		Lunch	Lunch	Lunch	Lunch	Lunch	
12:30		Work	Work	Work	Work	Work	↓
1:00							Ministry
1:30							
2:00							
2:30							
3:00							
3:30							
4:00							
4:30		Clean-up	Clean-up	Clean-up	Clean-up	Clean-up	
5:00		Travel	Travel	Travel	Travel	Travel	
5:30		↓	↓	↓	↓	↓	↓
6:00	↓	Family	Family	Family	Family	Family	Family
6:30	Dinner	Dinner	Dinner	Dinner	Dinner	Dinner	Dinner
7:00	↓	↓	↓	↓	↓	↓	↓
7:30	Family	Family	Family	Family	Family	Family	Family
8:00							
8:30							
9:00	↓	↓	↓	↓	↓		
9:30	Bed	Bed	Bed	Bed	Bed		
10:00						↓	↓
10:30						Bed	Bed
11:00							
11:30							

Figure 8

a few minutes left, so he quickly outlines what he wants to get done the next morning.

Pat can't believe it when Bill walks in the door at 6:00, and when he offers to spend time with their preschooler her pleasure is obvious. He hears her humming to herself as she goes about preparing dinner. Bill will perhaps never know just how much of Jesus had walked in the front door with him that day. Dinner is a real joy, and after dinner Bill takes the kids out for ice cream. They are thrilled and so is he.

Things are still not perfect at work, and Bill knows that. But he also knows he's on the right track, and everything will soon be under control.

As for Pat, she is so impressed with the changes in Bill that she decides to make some changes in her life too.

SCHEDULE FOR A WIFE/MOTHER

The first thing in Pat's life that needs attention is her time with the Lord. She used to be faithful in prayer and Bible reading every day. But as the family grew and the children got older, she started making exceptions, and now she doesn't read or pray much anymore.

Come to think of it, there was a relationship between Bill's going to bed later than he used to and Pat's letting her quiet time slip away. She had gradually let his bedtime become her bedtime. Then she had to get up earlier because of the kids, and there just wasn't time to spend with God. Now that she's thinking about it, she sees that's when other things began to change too — things like time to talk to Bill about the day . . . their commitment to spend an evening together each week . . . and whatever happened to a regular dinnertime?

Pat feels overcommitted with housework and chores. She's president of the PTA because everyone thinks she's so well organized. She has the soccer team . . . and the Scouts . . . she's on the Fellowship Committee at Church . . . and she's in charge of the carpool and has to drive twice a week because she hasn't had time to replace the mom who dropped out.

She knows that the beginning of the solution lies in regaining the habit of spending time with the Lord. Since Bill has now started to go to bed at 9:30 and has his quiet time at 6:30, maybe she can take advantage of his new schedule. If she also begins to go to bed at 9:30, she can get up at 6:00 and have at least a half hour with the Lord. Then she can get breakfast ready and have everyone taken care of by 8:00.

Now, what about all those commitments? Are there too many of them?

First off, she decides she will say no to everything new that comes her way for a while. No matter what, she has to get some breathing room. She'll try to live with her existing commitments, but will not add any new ones until she has the big picture. Those evening meetings mean she won't always be able to get to bed by 9:30 — but with God's help she'll do her best to stick to her schedule.

The next thing Pat has to do is find a regular time for planning and personal organization, and she finally decides to try doing it mornings from 8:30 to 9:00. She'll put her preschooler in his room, and just let him begin to expect that every morning.

Now that she has decided when to spend her time with the Lord and when to do her daily planning and organizing, she has the keys to reestablishing order in the other areas of her life. Her next step is to make a list of everything else that needs attention. She decides to use her planning time to begin this process. There are those areas of overcommitment that she's already begun to think about — meetings and committees and housework and chores. But there's another area — things she's not doing that she should and would really like to be doing.

Pat realizes that to some extent she has to wait on some of those things or she'll just add to her overcommitments. She can't take on more projects, even though they may be more deserving of her attention, until she's able to get rid of some of her existing responsibilities. But she can at least make the list.

She also realizes that she needs to make a weekly schedule. In order to do that, she'll have to make a list of all her existing time commitments. She also needs a list of the things she should be doing that she's not doing. There will also be a list of all family members — Bill and each of the kids — and what their needs are.

After that, she needs to make a list of her own needs, including those things she believes God wants her to do beyond her own family. Pat begins to realize she's got a lot of thinking to do and lists to make before she can really begin to *do* anything. After she's made all the lists of all the things she needs to do, Pat knows that the next step is to prioritize — to decide what to do now, what to do at a definite time in the future, and what to leave to the indefinite future.

Now for a plan of action. In order to have time to do anything besides what she's already doing, Pat needs a plan for shedding some existing commitments. She's had the carpool for two years and it's time for someone else to take over, so she decides to give notice. As of thirty days from now, she'll be available to drive one day per week, but someone else will have to serve as coordinator or there won't be a carpool.

Her term as PTA president is about over, and she will not accept nomination for another term. Maybe Bill can help share the Scouting Committee, or she might even resign from that. She'll talk to Bill about it.

She also acknowledges a need to be better organized in some of her household chores. For example, there's the matter of dinnertime. She's been harping on the need for a regular dinnertime for years, but now that Bill's coming home regularly at 6:00, she hasn't been consistent with having dinner on the table at 6:30. From now on she's going to begin dinner at 5:00, and it's going to be on the table at 6:30.

The other family need that Pat decides to plan for involves helping the kids with their homework. She decides to encourage them to do homework right after getting home from school. Then she and Bill can plan to be available from 7:30 to 9:00 to help as needed. Maybe they can even work in a family Bible study on Sunday evenings.

The only thing remaining for Pat to do is plan her daily and weekly routines. She makes a list of all the things her job as a homemaker should consist of, then fills out a weekly schedule that shows when she'll do what.

On Mondays she'll do her planning at 8:30, right after the kids leave for school and the youngest is in his room. Then she'll get dressed, do a load of wash, and do housework until 11:00. After a thirty-minute break she'll fix lunch, and while the toddler naps she can rest and read. (Thank goodness she had the foresight to get him on a schedule.) If there's additional work to be done for her family-related outside commitments — for example, PTA and Scouts — she can work on those then too. The kids will be home from school at 3:30, and she'll talk to them about their day, then get them started on homework. Then she'll start dinner by 5:00, so it can be on the table consistently at 6:30.

Tuesday and Wednesday will be the same routine except that on Wednesday afternoon she'll do her Fellowship Committee things and try to spend some quality time with her unsaved neighbor. Thursday morning, instead of housework, Pat will use her planning time to make a list of her weekly errands. Then she'll spend the morning doing them. Friday will be the same as Tuesday, and Friday night the family will attend a Bible study at

TYPICAL SCHEDULE—WIFE IN THE HOME WITH SMALL CHILDREN (ONE UNDER 6)

	SUN	MON	TUE	WED	THU	FRI	SAT
4:00							
4:30							
5:00							
5:30							
6:00		Prayer	Prayer	Prayer	Prayer	Prayer	
6:30		Work	Work	Work	Work	Work	
7:00	Bible						Bible
7:30	Breakfast	↓	↓	↓	↓	↓	Breakfast
8:00	Dress	Plan	Plan	Plan	Plan	Plan	Dress
8:30	Church	Dress	Dress	Dress	Dress	Dress	Work
9:00		Laundry	Laundry	Laundry	Errands	Laundry	Family
9:30		Housework	Housework	Housework		Housework	
10:00							
10:30		↓	↓	↓	↓	↓	↓
11:00	↓	Self	Self	Self	Self	Self	Work
11:30	Family	Cook	Cook	Cook	Cook	Cook	
12:00		Lunch	Lunch	Lunch	Lunch	Lunch	
12:30		↓	↓	↓	↓	↓	
1:00		Self	Self	Ministry	Self	Ministry	
1:30							
2:00							
2:30							
3:00		↓	↓	↓	↓	↓	
3:30		Family	Family	Family	Family	Family	
4:00							
4:30		↓	↓	↓	↓	↓	
5:00		Cook	Cook	Cook	Cook	Cook	↓
5:30	↓	↓	↓	↓	↓	↓	Cook
6:00	Cook	↓	↓	↓	↓	↓	↓
6:30	Dinner	Dinner	Dinner	Dinner	Dinner	Dinner	Dinner
7:00	↓	↓	↓	↓	↓	Clean-up	↓
7:30	Clean-up	Clean-up	Clean-up	Clean-up	Clean-up	Church	Clean-up
8:00	Family	Family	Family	Family	Family		Family
8:30	↓	↓	↓	↓	↓		↓
9:00	↓	↓	↓	↓	↓	↓	↓
9:30	Bed	Bed	Bed	Bed	Bed		
10:00						↓	↓
10:30						Bed	Bed
11:00							
11:30							

Figure 9—See Form 12 in back of book

the church. It's been quite a while since they've been able to do that regularly as a family, but with Bill coming home at 6:00 it should work just fine.

Saturday? That will be a day of work and family activities, and then Saturday night is her night out with Bill. She's so grateful for her husband — and for his new commitment to the family. And for the way her life is coming together!

SCHEDULE FOR THE SINGLE ADULT/STUDENT

There is a world of difference between the single who has never been married and a person who is single by virtue of divorce or death of a spouse. The most visible variable is experience. The never-married single is often younger than the previously married single, though that is not always the case.

For our purposes, let's assume that our single has not been married, is under the age of thirty, and has completed his or her schooling. This person is typically focused on career and marriage, though not always in that order. Our single may still be searching for direction on what career or vocation to pursue, or that decision may already have been made. If it has not been made, the biggest single point of pressure or anxiety in his or her life is likely to be the need for direction. If it has been made, the pressure point often involves striving to succeed.

One of the biggest problems for the single is that he's often in too much of a hurry and doesn't want to slow down and take time to find out what God wants. At this point, that's the most important thing he can do. Once he's determined that, he'll find relief from the fast pace. God is often speaking, but the single may be too busy to hear Him.

The highest priorities for the single should be time with God and time for parents. Another relationship that needs to be given a high priority if you are a single is a relationship with one or more Christians of the same sex, a relationship with an element of accountability.

It is often most effective to form this relationship with someone with whom you can share your victories and defeats, who enjoys your confidence, who cares for you and will give priority to helping you. Actually everyone should have someone besides a spouse to share with, but for the young single adult it may be an even more critical need.

Sometimes a natural parent can fulfill this need, and often that is probably the ideal, but be sure you have *someone*. Have a routine meeting time which occurs at least weekly and allows sufficient time to communicate at a casual pace. In other words, the time should be viewed as more than just a meeting. There should be opportunity for the free exchange of ideas, as well as for just "catching up."

If you have time for listening to God, time for your parents, and time for fellowship and holding yourself accountable to someone else, you're well on the road to success as a single adult.

There is one other very important way singles use their time, and that is in dating — looking for a life-partner. There are many single people who are quite content to remain single (the Apostle Paul was apparently one of these — see 1 Corinthians 7:1-7), but most of us want to be married —to love and be loved by one special person for the rest of our lives.

How much time should a single invest in dating? Certainly not so much that there is no time left for relationships with God, parents, and others of the same sex. In many instances dating also can be combined with other activities, such as attending a singles group function at your church. The primary consideration here, as everywhere else, is to listen to what God is telling you — and to realize that He loves you and wants to give you the desires of your heart. If one of those desires is to have a loving husband or wife, trust Him to lead you to the right person.

As a matter of fact, if God desires that you be married, you can be sure He had your husband or wife picked out for you before the dawn of time — and He will bring that person into your life at the proper moment. Your job is not so much to find the mate He has chosen for you as it is to discover what changes God wants you to make in your life so you can be ready for marriage.

Frankly, I have known singles who were nearly consumed by the search for a mate. And I admit that it is sometimes hard to wait on the Lord, especially if you have been "looking" for several years. But I encourage you to build your relationship with the Lord to the point that you have confidence that God will lead you to the person He has selected for you. And He will do it.

Now, what about the student? So much time is wasted by students who have never been shown how to maximize their potential by scheduling their activities and commitments. I realize that a large part of the student's schedule is dictated by the classes he needs to take, but even here there are things he can do. For example, if you are a college student, you might look for early classes. There is usually less demand for the first class of the day, and it will

TYPICAL SCHEDULE—
COLLEGE STUDENT

	SUN	MON	TUE	WED	THU	FRI	SAT
4:00							
4:30							
5:00							
5:30							
6:00		Shower	Shower	Shower	Shower	Shower	
6:30		Bible	Bible	Bible	Bible	Bible	
7:00		↓	↓	↓	↓	↓	
7:30		Breakfast	Breakfast	Breakfast	Breakfast	Breakfast	
8:00	Shower	Class	Plan	Class	Plan	Class	Shower
8:30		↓	Study	↓	Study	↓	
9:00		Plan	Class	Plan	Class	Plan	Class
9:30		Study	↓	Study	↓	Study	↓
10:00	Church		Study		Study		Study
10:30		↓	↓	↓	↓	↓	
11:00	↓	Class		Class	↓	Class	
11:30		↓	Lunch	↓	Lunch	↓	
12:00		Lunch	Class	Lunch	Class	Lunch	
12:30		↓	↓	↓	↓	↓	↓
1:00	Study		↓		↓		
1:30		Work	Study	Work	Study	Work	
2:00							
2:30			↓				
3:00			Lab				
3:30	↓						
4:00	Finances		↓				
4:30	↓	↓		↓	↓	↓	
5:00							
5:30							
6:00		Dinner	Dinner	Dinner	Dinner	Dinner	
6:30							
7:00		Study	Study	Study	Study		
7:30							
8:00							
8:30							
9:00							
9:30		↓	↓	↓	↓		
10:00	Bed	Bed	Bed	Bed	Bed		
10:30							
11:00							
11:30							

Figure 10—See Form 12 in back of book

enable you to make better use of your time — if you *want* to make better use of your time.

After your class schedule is known, determine how many hours of *out of class* study you should devote to each course. A good rule of thumb is three hours of study for every hour of class, but make sure you spend at least two to one. Next, prepare a weekly schedule. Enter your class schedule and your daily quiet time. Then enter when you will get up each morning (it's much better to make it the same time each weekday) and when you'll go to bed at night (which should also be the same time Sunday through Thursday nights).

Following that, enter your study times and time for planning and organizing each day. If you have a part-time job, show that next. Then schedule all the other things you want to do or feel you should do, including your primary recreational times. While you should have the freedom to be flexible and move with the flow of daily events, if you don't plan to protect the times that are important, they'll often get away from you.

Plan for the unexpected by allowing unplanned time. Remember to have time for organizing and keeping track of your finances, for redoing your schedule regularly, and for all those things that make life worth living — for example, wasting time in the student center.

SCHEDULE FOR THE WORKING MOTHER/SINGLE PARENT

There are several variables which will affect the typical schedule for the working mother or single parent. If the mother is married, the father's or stepfather's schedule will definitely impact on her schedule. If the mother is separated or divorced, the father's proximity and interest in the children will be a big factor. If the mother is close to her parents or other family support, her schedule will differ from a mother's who does not have that support. The age and number of children and the age of grandparents and other relatives are all variables that will affect the mother's schedule. Where the mother works, when she works, how much she earns, and how much money the husband or non-custodial father provides are all factors that influence her schedule. By far the most difficult lifestyle in which to establish a Christ-centered balance is that of a working single mother of small children.

The most obvious difference between the schedule of a mother who is not employed outside the home and one who is is the necessary compromise on the amount of time that can be spent on family members. An outside job carries its own rewards and liabilities. Some mothers work because they want to, others because they have to. It's much easier to adopt a balanced schedule if one is working out of desire as opposed to necessity. Just knowing you have an option provides relief and freedom not available to the mother who feels she has no choice.

By establishing routines and planning in advance how her time should be spent, a working mother who is not ruled by circumstances can make a much better decision on whether she should work outside the home, and a mother who must work can at least rest in the knowledge that she's making the very best use of the time she does have available in the home.

In addition to insisting on getting sufficient sleep and having a quiet time, the working mother must exercise close control over her children's schedules. Very often a single working mother will not be able to carve out quiet time in the morning because of the family schedule. The children's schedules will be such that she must rise early to meet their needs, as well as prepare to go to work herself. The only significant time to spend any quality time with them and do housekeeping is at night and on weekends. Quiet time often becomes an evening activity, or even midday, perhaps during her lunch hour.

Her children may need to be in bed earlier than they'd like or, depending on their ages, at least be home early enough at night so she can responsibly plan an appropriate bedtime for herself. They almost certainly will need to assume responsibility within the home for as much as they are capable of doing. The children's social life may well be affected, both because of their additional responsibilities and the financial constraints. Very often the responsible single mother has little or no recreational outlet. There should be time set aside to be away from her children, for their sake as well as hers.

An example of a typical weekday might be to go to bed at 10:30 in order to rise at 7:00. After showering and dressing and breakfast, it's off to work until 5:00. Lunchtime is devoted to errands and maybe a little time for self. Then she goes home to fix dinner. After clean-up comes an hour or so with the children, a half hour for light cleaning, quiet time, planning and organizing for the next day, and bed. Weekends are typically devoted to housework and family activities and needs, as well as church and perhaps some church-related activity. Hopefully Friday or Saturday evenings can be devoted to some form of recreation.

TYPICAL SCHEDULE—SINGLE PARENT/ WORKING SPOUSE WITH CHILDREN

	SUN	MON	TUE	WED	THU	FRI	SAT
4:00							
4:30							
5:00							
5:30							
6:00							
6:30							
7:00		Shower	Shower	Shower	Shower	Shower	
7:30		Dress	Dress	Dress	Dress	Dress	
8:00	Bible	Breakfast	Breakfast	Breakfast	Breakfast	Breakfast	Bible
8:30	Dress	Job	Job	Job	Job	Job	Dress
9:00	Work	↓	↓	↓	↓	↓	Work
9:30	↓	Planning	Planning	Planning	Planning	Planning	↓
10:00	↓	Work	Work	Work	Work	Work	↓
10:30	Church	↓	↓	↓	↓	↓	↓
11:00	↓	↓	↓	↓	↓	↓	↓
11:30	↓	↓	↓	↓	↓	↓	↓
12:00	↓	Errands	Self	Errands	Self	Errands	↓
12:30	Work	↓	↓	↓	↓	↓	↓
1:00	↓	Job	Job	Job	Job	Job	↓
1:30	↓	↓	↓	↓	↓	↓	↓
2:00	↓	↓	↓	↓	↓	↓	↓
2:30	↓	↓	↓	↓	↓	↓	↓
3:00	↓	↓	↓	↓	↓	↓	↓
3:30	Family	↓	↓	↓	↓	↓	↓
4:00	↓	↓	↓	↓	↓	↓	↓
4:30	↓	↓	↓	↓	↓	↓	↓
5:00	↓	↓	↓	↓	↓	↓	↓
5:30	↓	↓	↓	↓	↓	↓	Cook
6:00	Cook	Cook	Cook	Cook	Cook	Cook	↓
6:30	Dinner	Dinner	Dinner	Dinner	Dinner	Dinner	Dinner
7:00	Clean-up	Clean-up	Clean-up	Clean-up	Clean-up	Clean-up	Clean-up
7:30	Bible Study	Family	Family	Family	Family	Family	Family
8:00	↓	↓	↓	↓	↓	↓	↓
8:30	Work	Work	Work	Work	Work	↓	↓
9:00	Bible	Bible	Bible	Bible	Bible	↓	↓
9:30	Prayer	Prayer	Prayer	Prayer	Prayer	↓	↓
10:00	Planning	Planning	Planning	Planning	Planning	↓	↓
10:30	Bed	Bed	Bed	Bed	Bed	Bible	Bible
11:00						Prayer	Prayer
11:30						Bed	Bed

Figure 11—See Form 12 in back of book

WHAT ABOUT THE SHIFT-WORKER?

Is there a systematic way people who have unconventional jobs can live and order their lives, or are they destined to chaos just because most of the world operates on a different schedule? Does God have a plan for each of these occupations that includes the same consistent approach to scheduling as the more typical man or woman who goes to work every morning and returns home every night?

Absolutely! As we discussed back in Chapter 4, there is no reason why the person who works a rotating shift cannot draw up a consistent and work-able schedule. Many people who work nights or shifts don't realize that they can be just as consistent and well organized as their counterparts who have "normal" schedules. In fact, their job-related schedules are consistent. Most know well in advance when they are to work and when they're off, and that allows them to use the time in between to set up regular routines, just like anyone else.

Let's assume that our shift-worker works a rotating eight-hour shift. He works midnight to 8 A.M. for two days, 8 A.M. to 4 P.M. for two days, 4 P.M. to midnight for two days, and then a day off. This is the most difficult com-bination of shifts that I've come across. The longer the period that a person works the same shift, the easier it is to plan around. But our hypothetical worker in this example doesn't have very many days that are the same.

Assuming that our hero needs seven and a half hours sleep and that he can get up, dress, have his quiet time and get to work in two hours, his sched-ule could be like this: On Mondays he would get off work at 8:00 A.M. and have until 4:00 P.M. to do the things he would do during non-work hours. On Thursdays and Fridays his free time would be from 8:00 A.M. until going to work at 4:00 in the afternoon. Saturday would be like one of our normal Saturdays until 6:00 in the afternoon, which would be nap time prior to going to work at midnight.

In other words, Tuesday and Wednesday would look very much like any-one else's normal days, with a bedtime of 10:00 P.M. and a workday from 8 to 4. Sundays would be the most unusual, with bedtime at 2 in the afternoon. The other four days would be somewhere in between.

One of the keys to success is letting the body adjust to a longer cycle than just twenty-four hours. In this example, everything repeats itself every 168 hours instead of every twenty-four hours. It's critical that bedtimes be estab-lished and maintained. If that happens, everything else will fall into place.

TYPICAL SCHEDULE—SHIFT-WORKER

	SUN	MON	TUE	WED	THU	FRI	SAT
5:00	Work	Work	Sleep	Sleep	Sleep	Sleep	Sleep
5:30			↓	↓	↓		
6:00			Shower	Shower	Shower		
6:30		↓	Bible	Bible	Bible		
7:00		Daily	↓	↓	↓		
7:30	↓	Routine	Plan	Plan	Plan	↓	↓
8:00			Work	Work	Daily	Shower	Shower
8:30					Routine	Bible	Bible
9:00						↓	↓
9:30						Plan	Plan
10:00	Church					Daily	Daily
10:30						Routine	Routine
11:00							
11:30	↓						
12:00		Nap					
12:30		↓					
1:00		Daily					
1:30		Routine					
2:00	Bed						
2:30							
3:00							
3:30			↓	↓	↓	↓	
4:00			Daily	Daily	Work	Work	
4:30			Routine	Routine			
5:00							
5:30							↓
6:00							Nap
6:30							
7:00							
7:30							
8:00							
8:30							
9:00							
9:30	↓	↓	↓	↓			↓
10:00	Shower	Bed	Bed	Bed			Shower
10:30	Bible						Bible
11:00	↓				↓	↓	↓
11:30	Plan						Plan
12:00	Work						Work
12:30							
1:00							
1:30							
2:00	↓	↓	↓	↓	Bed	Bed	↓

Figure 12—See Form 12 in back of book

In our example, bedtime on Monday, Tuesday and Wednesday nights is at 10:00 P.M. On Thursday and Friday nights it's after work at around 2:00 A.M. Saturday requires a four-hour nap in the evening, and Sunday requires going to bed at around 2:00 in the afternoon. Within that framework, quiet time for as much as an hour at a time can be scheduled soon after rising at 6:00 A.M. on Tuesday, Wednesday and Thursday, at 8:00 A.M. on Friday and Saturday, and before going to work at midnight on Sunday and Monday mornings.

Discipline must be exercised in getting up at the right time, not only to protect quiet time, but to retain the balance between hours awake, so that when it's time to sleep the body is ready to sleep.

So there you have some typical ways you can begin to establish your weekly schedule, whether you're a husband, a wife, a single adult, or someone who works an unusual shift.

Coming up next, we're going to spend some time talking about the four priorities of life — what they are and the benefits you will derive by bringing your life in line with them. But first, take some time to put into practice the things we've talked about in this chapter. It will be well worth the investment of your time and energy.

PRACTICE MAKING A SCHEDULE

1) If you believe God wants you to develop a written schedule, are you willing to do that? If so, fill in the blank: I will plan to sit down on _____ (day of the week) at _____ o'clock and make my first effort to apply what I have learned up to this point.

2) If you are married, and if you believe God wants your spouse to become more organized, will you ask him or her to read this book by a certain date? What date?

3) If the answers to question 2 are yes, would it be helpful to discuss the book between yourselves after you have both read it? If so, when?

4) If you are a single parent or a working spouse, are there things about your schedule that you feel need to be addressed that are not addressed in this book? If so, will you write to Ken Smith and give him the benefit of your thinking, including possible answers? If so, when will you write him?

7

How to Break Free from Overcommitment

Have you ever thought about all the things you have to do and said, "How in the world did I get into this mess?"

Most of us have had thoughts like that at one time or another. It is easy, especially in this high-pressure era, to find ourselves overcome and overwhelmed by overcommitment from which it is seemingly impossible to extract ourselves.

Well, it's *not* impossible. It may take some time, and it's certainly going to take some effort on your part, but you *can* be set free from the problems and pain that overcommitment brings.

One of the first steps necessary in the fight against overcommitment is to establish some regular routines so that everything you do becomes part of your overall approach to life.

I first met a particular friend of mine when he asked for help in his struggle with overcommitment. He was a real estate broker with a successful business, but the economy had taken a downturn, and he had been forced to reduce his overhead and staff. The more he cut back, the more he had to do. He finally concluded that his problem was overcommitment, and that's when he came to me.

After we talked a while, I agreed that he was overcommitted, but I thought he might be able to handle the problem by establishing some routines instead of having to decide what he had to stop doing. He said he was willing to try anything. His anxiety level was such that he knew he couldn't go on the way he had been going, but he was afraid to cut back on his business activities for fear his income would drop even further.

First of all, I asked him if he was getting enough sleep. He said no, that he used to, but anxiety had been keeping him from sleeping. Furthermore, he was going to bed later and trying to get up earlier. When I asked if an earlier bed-time would help, he said no, that he would just have that much longer to roll and toss. He felt the answer was to have less to worry about, and that if he tried to *do* less, he would just worry more about what was being left undone. I asked if he spent time with the Lord regularly, and he admitted that he didn't because he just didn't have the time. He knew it ought to be a high priority, but the way his life was going it would be just one more "duty" he'd have to worry about.

I finally suggested to him that a few simple routines would help him find the beginning of the answer to his problem. We agreed as a matter of prin-ciple that he should have sufficient time with God and sufficient time to iden-tify and plan the solutions to his problems. He also agreed that God had a plan for his life and that his job was to discover what that plan was rather than continue to try to develop his own solutions. With those two facts clearly in focus, we agreed on the following:

1) There was a best time and place to regularly meet with God.

2) There was a best way to discover what God's plan was.

He felt that 6 A.M. was the best time for him to spend time with God in prayer and Bible reading, and in order for that to happen he had to get up and shower at 5:30. He felt he needed seven hours of sleep (it later turned out to be eight), which meant he needed to be asleep by 11 the night before (which later became 10). That, in turn, meant he had to give up watching the 11 o'clock news, which he didn't like at all, but he agreed to try. He agreed to follow that routine for one month and report his progress — or lack of progress — to me at the end of that period.

When we met just a month later, he was on his way to becoming a new man. His problems hadn't disappeared, but he had a much better outlook on them, and his life was in much better shape. He had a more accepting atti-tude regarding what he couldn't figure out a way to change and much more enthusiasm about what he felt he could change. He was getting more sleep, sleeping better when he slept, and hadn't given much thought to the fact that he was missing the nightly newscast.

Now, years later, he is still in business, although his company is smaller and has fewer employees than in its heyday. On the other hand, he makes just as much money as he did before, has more quality time to spend with his fam-ily, and experiences anxiety much less frequently. He told me recently that through that early decision to establish a few routines, he had discovered the overall value of routines and has built many more of them into his life.

WHO IS SUBJECT TO OVERCOMMITMENT?

The kind of person who is most subject to overcommitment is often the same person who most reflects much of the fruit of the Spirit, as listed in Galatians 5: love, joy, peace, patience, kindness, goodness, faithfulness and gentleness. A misguided desire to serve and to exercise those traits may also be the path to unrighteousness through overcommitment. Such people are trying to be Christian by doing too much — more than God wants them to do.

In Luke 14:31 Jesus says, "Or suppose a king is about to go to war against another king. Will he not first sit down and consider whether he is able with ten thousand men to oppose the one coming against him with twenty thousand?" Jesus is saying, "Before you say you'll do something, sit down and count the cost." Failure to do that will lead to a number of very serious problems for you, including overcommitment.

You may have noticed that the one fruit of the Spirit that I didn't mention is self-control. That's because the person without self-control or self-discipline (which is really Holy Spirit-directed discipline for a Christian) can have all the attributes of a Spirit-led Christian and yet be rendered almost totally ineffective. Lack of self-control, even though combined with all kinds of good traits, can often neutralize those whom God could most use.

Another kind of person who is often guilty of overcommitment is the one who is so self-centered that he wants it all *now*. This person constantly strives for success in a secular sense. He's afraid there won't be time to accumulate all the wealth he wants, acquire all the knowledge, or achieve the greatest position of power. This person basically suffers from greed, and for him *everything* wouldn't be enough. Then there are the rest of us. We're at neither of the extremes mentioned above, and yet we find ourselves overcommitted because we haven't been through a process of learning what we should say no to. And basically that's what brings on overcommitment — saying yes when we ought to say no. We haphazardly say yes or no, more because of the circumstance of the moment than because of any planning.

SOME SUGGESTIONS ON HOW TO OVERCOME AND AVOID OVERCOMMITMENT

1) Practice Saying No

The first problem here is that most of us aren't organized enough to know when we should say no. Secondly, most of us don't want to say no. Thirdly, most of us don't know how to say no. And lastly, most of us don't understand what it is we should say no to.

Let's look at an example. When someone comes up to you at church and asks you to assume a responsibility, what is your reaction? If you're already so overcommitted that it is creating anxiety, you may say no in a completely inappropriate way. You may be defensive or angry about it instead of politely thanking that person for thinking of you and explaining that your schedule simply won't allow for another responsibility at the present time.

If you are not already feeling anxiety due to overcommitment, you may go to the other extreme. Although you know you shouldn't say yes, you do anyway — even though you're churning inside because it's the last thing you want to do. For you, this is where overcommitment begins.

The answer is to practice saying no when you need to say no, and doing it in a firm but gracious manner. A no doesn't have to be impolite or rude, and you certainly don't have to feel guilty about using the word more often. In the meantime, you need to know how much you can handle. If someone asks you to do something, and you are honestly not sure whether or not you have the time, the best thing to do is to be completely candid. "Let me check my schedule and I'll get back to you."

However, be sure to get back to the person. Check your schedule, and if you find this extra activity would be too much of a burden, say no to it. If you find upon reflection that you could easily work it in, and it's something you'd like to do, then a yes may very well be appropriate.

I would go so far as to suggest that you should form the habit of never saying yes until you've had time to reflect and pray about it. When someone asks you to do something, give him a time within which you'll have an answer. Make a note of the request, and take it before the Lord in your quiet time the next day.

Realize that God is seldom, if ever, in a hurry. Even when you know your answer will be yes, don't say yes immediately. If it's important to God, it'll wait at least one day. You'll be surprised what a difference a one-day delay will make. You may very well still say yes, but you may have much more insight into the matter. For example, it may be that the completion date should be different, or that someone else should also be involved in the project.

But what can you do now when you realize you've already said yes to far too many projects and other time-consumers?

Certainly there may be some projects you feel unable to extricate yourself from. It may be that God didn't want you to say yes to something, but you did, and now other things have occurred which require you to follow through on the commitment. You may not have the option of saying no now although that's what God wanted you to do originally.

But there are things you've said yes to that you must now go back and say no to, even though the cost may be high. It's difficult to break commitments, and it takes courage to go back and say, "I know I said I'd do this, but I really can't." But if that's what God wants you to do, then of course you'd better be willing — not necessarily tickled pink, but at least willing. Ask forgiveness for failing to keep your commitment, and make restitution where appropriate. Make up your mind to say no to begin with the next time and save yourself some pain and embarrassment.

2) Establish Priorities

For instance, when you have an opportunity to advance your career, there's almost always a cost attached. Suppose you are given a chance to move up, but it means you'll have to devote 75 percent of your time during the next year to travel.

If you haven't set goals and priorities for yourself and your family, you have no rational basis on which to turn the opportunity down. (We'll discuss the establishing of priorities in more detail in Chapter 9.) You probably know instinctively that it will cause problems for you at home, but you have no way to analyze the consequences, and the truth is that there will always be something you don't want to do if you want to advance!

But if you *have* set goals and established priorities, there may be a definite conflict that will give you the ability to make the right choice as to whether to say yes or no.

3) Be Accountable

Another major reason we find ourselves overcommitted is lack of accountability. If you are married, make a habit of asking your spouse before you make commitments. I have a friend who has spent half his life making unrealistic commitments and the other half undoing them when his wife found out about them. Some people seem *never* to learn!

If you go back to the book of Genesis and read about Adam and Eve, you'll see that God created Eve to be Adam's helpmate. Husbands and wives bring strength to each other, and that means they should consult one another on all major decisions and strive always to be accountable to one another.

There are other important areas of accountability as well — and of course it is especially important that you strive to be accountable to God. We will discuss accountability in much greater detail in Chapter 13.

4) List Your Current Activities and Commitments

I remember the first time I decided to make a list of my current activities and commitments. I hardly knew where to start. I wasn't organized enough to have anything to go to for reference. I started with my appointment book, but all that told me was that I had appointments, and I already knew that. So I just carved out some uninterrupted quiet time and began to think about all the things I did with my time. I made a list of my current caseload, I mentally reviewed how I had spent yesterday and the day before, etc.

Once I had reviewed the way I spent my time at work, I moved into my non-work-related time. I spent quite a bit of that time reading the Bible, in prayer, attending church, and visiting my mother. I didn't have the distractions of a family because they had left me five years earlier. I didn't yet have all of my Christian singles activities. That meant that what other time I had was spent on such worthwhile things as watching television or feeding my tropical fish. My life had been reduced to just about the irreducible minimum, and it was pretty boring.

Most of you who are reading this book won't have that problem. One of the things that probably motivated you to pick up this book in the first place was the sheer number of things you have to do. You're looking for ways to do less, not more. You'll have family-related commitments, business and social engagements, church- and community-related activities, and so on. You'll have twice as much to do as you feel you have time to do it in.

How do you handle that?

The first thing to do is to remember that you have to develop an attitude that is pleasing to God. He needs to know that you wish to make things right with Him, and you need to know that you are willing to do things His way.

Once you are willing to make things right with Him, the next thing to do is to identify all the possible areas of disobedience. To do that, first make a list of all the things in your life that you're presently committed to. It might help to break it down by priorities: God, family, job, and service to others.

Next, make a list of all those things you should be committed to but you're not. For example, what about all those things around the house that you should be doing that have just piled up? Husbands, if you have any difficulty making this list, just ask your wife for a little assistance.

You'll find that you have been disobedient in two ways: you've been doing things you shouldn't do, and you've not been doing things you should do.

After you have as complete a list as possible of everything you are committed to and should be doing, decide which ones should definitely be done, and mark them with an A. Then choose the ones that don't need to be done, and give them a C. Everything else gets a B. Some of the items on your list are likely to be commitments you never should have made in the first place and from which you will need to extricate yourself. You may see that you made agreements you never should have made, promises that you can't possibly keep — and if so, this is the time to free yourself from those commitments as gracefully and honorably as possible.

Ask God to give you grace and favor, and then honorably break the commitments which must be broken and delay the commitments which must be delayed. Following that, the next step is to develop a plan for doing everything else in timely fashion. Remember that your goal is not to please people but to be obedient to God.

Once you've got a plan for doing everything on your commitment list, you'll feel a freedom that too few people ever experience. Getting out of overcommitment is much like getting out of debt or losing weight. You don't realize how much of a burden you're carrying until it's gone! In fact, much of your load will lift once you've developed the plan and before you accomplish your objective.

Don't Commit Until You've Sought God's Will

Now the question becomes, how long will it last? How long will it be before you are again overcommitted and anxious?

The answer lies in how serious you are in your relationship with the Lord. If you really desire to be obedient, you will learn to seek His will for more and more areas of your life. You will become less likely to become overcommitted. God is a God of order, not of confusion (1 Corinthians 14:33). The first eight verses of the third chapter of Ecclesiastes tell us that He has established a time for everything to be done in its turn. If you try to do everything at once, you will continue to be overcommitted. But if you seek God's will and do things according to His timing, you can have increasing peace and freedom from overcommitment.

Remember the axiom, "if in doubt, don't." Work on forming the habit of resolving to not agree to something until it's clear to you that God wants you to do it.

HOW LACK OF PATIENCE LEADS TO OVERCOMMITMENT

Most Americans are not very patient people. We're used to rushing around, doing everything in an instant. We have instant potatoes, instant coffee, and microwave ovens so we can cook our meals in a fraction of the time it used to take.

Lack of patience can be a terrible problem, one that leads directly to overcommitment.

Patience can be defined in many ways, but in Scripture it's linked with endurance. Proverbs 16:32 says, "Better a patient man than a warrior, a man who controls his temper than one who takes a city." Webster defines it as "the capacity, habit or fact of (1) bearing pain or trials calmly or without complaint; (2) manifesting forbearance under provocation or strain; (3) not hasty or impetuous; and (4) steadfast despite opposition, difficulty or adversity."

I remember back in the days when I was active in politics, I was constantly setting short-term goals and convincing other people to do what was necessary to achieve those goals. Usually I could achieve the goal by virtue of the tremendous amount of energy I put into accomplishing it. As often as not, however, the goal itself proved not to be worth the effort expended, and very often the cost was great — both in terms of wasted time and in damaged or broken relationships. I realize now that if I had exercised more patience in both setting goals and in achieving goals once they were set, the cost would have been less to me and those around me, and the results would likely have been more lasting.

Patience is an important ingredient in a life of peacefulness and a key to avoiding overcommitment. But how do we obtain it?

The first step is to ask God for it. Pray that He will give you patience in a particular area of your life, and then be ready to face the challenges that will come your way as He answers that prayer. As each challenge surfaces, surround it with prayer so you will have the right attitude.

The second step is to try to see the big picture. When a challenge associated with impatience comes your way, try to see how that challenge fits into the things God wants you to learn through it.

The third step in developing patience is to resist discouragement. Discouragement will certainly come your way — and the key to success is recognizing that it's just part of the program. The more obedient you are in doing what God wants you to do, the more equipped you are to resist discouragement. The more serious you are about acquiring patience, the more serious the Enemy becomes in bombarding you with discouragement. The more obedient you are to God, the less vulnerable you will become to the Enemy's bombardment.

Now it's time for you to start taking the initiative. Up to this point we've been talking about doing the things that will build patience in you. Now let's talk about how you can begin to apply those lessons. Step four in gaining patience is learning to consciously decide not to do the things you want to do until the flow of circumstances supports your doing them. This means that instead of rushing to pursue the next good idea that comes your way, give it a little while to simmer. If it continues to look like a good idea, pursue it a step at a time until you meet with resistance. At this point consider the possibility that God wants you to exercise patience. It may be that He wants you to press on and overcome whatever the point of resistance is, but it may also be that He wants you to recognize the resistance as an indicator to slow down until the flow of circumstances supports your continuing the effort. At this stage you're usually no longer struggling with whether to do something, but with when to do it. It becomes a matter of timing.

By the time you reach this stage in acquiring patience and learning to use it, it is very likely that you have struck a good balance between being too busy and not being busy enough. You've learned to spend time with God and seek His will in whatever you decide to do.

So . . . how are you doing? Are you trying to move too fast? Are you trying to do things God does not want you to do, or to do them before it's time to do them? Do you have the big picture? Do you know what God wants you to do today and what He wants you to leave until tomorrow? Are you exercising the discipline necessary to say no and resisting the impulse to say yes when you know you really shouldn't?

If you're too busy to answer these questions, or if you can't answer them as God would have you do, it might be a good idea to pray, "Dear God, please give me patience."

If you will pray that prayer, and keep on praying it, there will be pain in the short run, but you'll become more obedient in the long run. And the more obedient you are, the more peace you'll have in your life and the less you'll struggle with overcommitment.

Coming up next, we'll talk about how to bring organization into your home!

CURRENT COMMITMENTS & ACTIVITIES INVENTORY

List randomly all of your present commitments and activities that involve the use of your time. Using the same system of prioritizing that you have already learned (A-C-B, 1-3-2), determine the relative importance of each commitment and activity. Now estimate how much time you presently spend per week on each item, and how much time you think you should spend (including 0).

COMMITMENT/ACTIVITY	PRIORITY		HOURS/WEEK	
	A-C-B	1-3-2	PRESENT	PLAN FOR
Truro Singles Ministry	A	2	4	same
Seminars	A	1	4	same
Radio Program	A	1	10	same
Counseling	B	2	2	same
Business consulting	B	1	4	same
Saturday morning men's group	C	1	3	0
Monthly bridge game	A	2	4/mo.	same

Figure 13—See Form 8 in back of book

PRACTICE OVERCOMING OVERCOMMITMENT

1) Make a list of as many things as you can think of that you are committed to doing.

2) Make a list of the things you should be doing that you are not doing.

3) Of the things you are committed to, make a list of the ones that you cannot justify doing on the basis of time available to do them.

4) Outline a plan for extricating yourself from each of the commitments in Exercise #3.

5) Decide *when* you should begin doing the things in Exercise #2 so that you do not become overcommitted all over again.

PROPOSED COMMITMENTS & ACTIVITIES INVENTORY

List randomly all of those things that you ought to be doing that you are not presently doing, and all of those things that you want to be doing that you are not presently doing. Determine the relative importance of each of these things by using the same system in prioritizing (A-C-B, 1-3-2). Now estimate how much time is needed for each of these things.

COMMITMENT/ACTIVITY	PRIORITY		HOURS/WEEK	
	A-C-B	1-3-2	PRESENT	PLAN FOR
More time with Pat	A	1	6	12
More time for biking	A	3	0	6
More time for reading	C	1	0	6
More time for grandchildren	A	3	3	6
Time to work with homeless	A	2	0	4/mo.
Time with godchildren	A	2	0	4/mo.
Time with delinquent teens	B	1	0	4/mo.

Figure 14—See Form 9 in back of book

REVISED COMMITMENTS & ACTIVITIES INVENTORY

After reviewing the two previous forms, decide which commitments and activities should be eliminated from your schedule and which new ones should be added. Any activity that you are able to eliminate immediately, just do so. Now list on this form all remaining present and proposed activities and commitments that you feel must be or that you wish to be part of your immediate future. Since it will probably take a while for you to extricate yourself from some of the things to be eliminated, use the Begin/End Date column on this form to indicate the date by which you plan to terminate any particular commitment. Likewise, you may not be able to immediately commence a new commitment, so indicate the date you plan to commence anything new.

COMMITMENT/ACTIVITY	PRIORITY		BEGIN/END
	A-C-B	1-3-2	DATE
Saturday morning men's group			4/1
Biking with Pat two Sats./mo.			4/1
Grandchildren one Sat./mo.			4/15
...dchildren one Sat./mo.			4/22
Begin reading on Sunday afternoons			3/26
Breakfast with homeless Wed. mornings			3/22

Figure 15—See Form 10 in back of book

8

Organizing the Home

There was a time when I was an organizational disaster.
I had no system for determining the order of things that came to my desk, or what I did with them once they landed there. I would just look around my desk and act on what seemed most urgent. Part of the price I paid for that was that, as a lawyer, I lived in a state of semiconscious terror that I would miss a statutory deadline, which would open me up to a malpractice suit.

I am grateful to God that in His mercy I no longer live that way.

But I have found that even those who seem to be very well organized when it comes to the office may be completely disorganized at home. If you want to live a peaceful life with a minimum of anxiety and stress, it is important that your home life be as orderly and organized as possible.

After all, many aspects of your home life are very similar to what goes on in a business. There are financial matters to take care of, maintenance to be kept up, family members' needs to be met, etc.

In this chapter we're going to talk about some concrete steps you can take to make your home the peaceful all-is-under-control place it should be.

Keeping the home organized takes effort, whether you are a single or a family of twelve. But of course it takes more effort to keep the larger family organized, so our discussion in this chapter will be broad enough to cover the family that includes children.

ESTABLISHING A SCHEDULE

As in your personal life, there are certain things pertaining to the home that should be done regularly at the same time, and often in the same place, on a daily or weekly basis. You first need to identify what those things are and then decide when they should be done.

The first activity you should schedule on a regular daily basis, in addition to your quiet time, is time for planning the day. You also need a regular time once a week for planning the week, and your subsequent daily planning time will build on the weekly plan.

Some of the activities that you will be scheduling include mealtimes, cleaning time, shopping and errand time, project and chore time, time for child-related needs, and time for your own needs as well as those of your spouse.

First, let's take a look at mealtimes. When should they be? That will depend on who's eating and what that person's schedule *should* be (not necessarily what it is presently). For example, lunch may be dictated by a child's schooling commitments or by his nap time. The dinner schedule is dependent upon a working spouse's arrival time, as well as commitments of older children. And so on. Often the working spouse and older children will need to conform their schedules to a more appropriate dinner hour. The one who prepares the meals should not be subject to everyone else's whims in the matter. Having a prearranged time for meals each day is helpful to everyone in the family. There is a very best time, and it's the responsibility of the head of the family to determine when that is, and to implement it as a high-ranking priority.

Another example of an activity that can be routinely scheduled is cleaning time. Rather than being driven by what is most in need of cleaning, you can set up a schedule for cleaning on a routine basis. Dishes and beds are examples of daily routines that should best be done at the same time each day. Dusting and vacuuming might be done twice a week, ideally on the same days and at the same time on those days. Kitchen and bathrooms might be done on a weekly basis, again at the same time on the same day each week. Windows, floors and closets can also be regularly scheduled at appropriate frequencies.

Having a complete inventory of what needs cleaning and when is very helpful. It breaks the cleaning process down into bite-size pieces so you don't find yourself overcommitted one or two days a month — and it keeps you from putting off the more unpleasant parts of the job so long that they become painful points of procrastination. The same is true of grocery shopping. To make this aspect of life easier, choose a day of the week and a time for obtaining each week's major supply of groceries. During the week, as things come to mind that you need, they should be written on a pad or other paper that is used only for that purpose. It should always be in the same convenient, accessible location and have a pen or pencil attached to it.

You can even develop a checklist by saving your lists for a month or so and then listing alphabetically or by category all those things you buy. Then, whenever you think of something you'll need to get the next time you go to the store, just put a checkmark next to that item on the list. Checklists are also available commercially.

You should also have a regular errand day, or perhaps two days, each week. Every time you think of something you need, just put it on an errand list, knowing you'll have it before you need it.

For example, let's say Thursday morning is errand day each week. Beginning on Friday during your planning time, you'll start thinking about the things you need in order to get certain projects done. You may see that you need items from the hardware store, drugstore, paint store, etc. You will continue to build your list each morning during your planning time.

Then on Thursday, during your planning time, organize all those things you need for your projects and draw up the most efficient plan for running all the errands and making all the needed stops.

WHO'S IN CHARGE HERE?

There are a number of other components that go into getting the home organized, and in order to get a handle on all of them there has to be one person who is in charge — not in the sense that he or she is the "boss" of the home, but in the sense of being the "chief organizer."

Deciding who in the family is going to fill that role is a giant step toward organization.

Keep in mind that it is very difficult to organize anything if the person in *charge* of organizing it isn't *inclined* toward personal organization. That's not to say that he or she needs to be well organized, but they do need to have a *desire* to be organized. It's just as important that everyone else in the home is willing to let that person be in charge of overall organizing and is willing to cooperate with him or her.

The organizer may be the husband or wife, it may be the single parent, it might even be an older child. Things often work best when it's the father, as opposed to the mother, but if it is the mother, then the father needs to designate her as the organizer, and he needs to cooperate. She needs to have the authority to get the job done, and he must be careful not to undermine her authority.

Once the person who is to be the organizer has been clearly identified, you can begin the process of organizing your home just as God wants it organized. In order to do that, there are several things to do and keep in mind. They include:

1) Gathering input from other family members.
2) Fostering a spirit of compromise.
3) Establishing a system of accountability.
4) Following through consistently.
5) Dividing and conquering.

We're going to briefly discuss each of these areas.

GATHER INPUT FROM FAMILY MEMBERS

If you have been chosen as the organizer for your family, you need to begin the process of putting together a plan for your household. And it's always best, when you're making a plan that affects other people, to get input from the people affected. Depending on many variables, such as the number and ages of family members, you should decide whether you want to get input from everyone at once or have each individual tell you what is important to him or her. It is absolutely critical that each person in the family feels he is part-owner of the ultimate plan. That way he or she will be more inclined to cooperate.

If you're not good at conducting meetings, you might start with individual conversations. Begin slowly and work toward sensing and developing a consensus. When you feel you know what's particularly important to each person, then you might hold a meeting to let everyone hear from each other what you've already heard from each of them individually.

FOSTER A SPIRIT OF COMPROMISE

Be prepared for some friction and controversy, and don't feel that you have to resolve all the apparent conflicts that surface. Your job at this point is to facilitate communication, not to solve the problems. Assume the attitude of a mediator. Be quick to make suggestions if ideas occur to you, but look primarily to the antagonists to resolve their touchy points between themselves.

Depending on the size of the family and the ages of the children and other family members, this stage can get complicated. Just remember, God has a plan, and you're trying to lead your family members through the process of discovering it. It is not your job to come up with all the answers.

As your family members work through compromising their interests with each other, God's plan will begin to emerge, and everyone will begin to get a larger view of the family's world.

Begin to bring organization to the family on the basis of the points where there is the greatest degree of agreement. As you implement things that are not controversial and as everyone sees them working, it's easier to attack some areas that may be more sensitive and more difficult to organize.

ESTABLISH A SYSTEM OF ACCOUNTABILITY

Once everyone has seen the importance of having the home organized and is willing to help the family move in that direction, it is important to have a system in which all family members can be held accountable for their actions. Whatever form that system may take is entirely up to you, but its purpose is to eliminate confusion and to see that no one's rights are being violated.

For example, when Pat and I got married, her two youngest children were still in the home. Despite my requests and complaints, whenever they needed a tool they just took it. As a result, many times when I went to get a tool, it wasn't where it was supposed to be. There was no effective way of knowing who took it or where it was.

After a while I realized that the real problem was accountability. When a tool was needed, it was only natural to take it. The problem came in not remembering to return it. After it was used, the tool got left in a bedroom, loaned to a friend, or whatever. What I needed was a way to establish some accountability.

So I made up a form and attached it to the tool box with some directions. In order to be able to take a tool, the borrower had to write down the date it was taken, what tool it was, and who took it. It was agreed that until the tools borrowed on one occasion were returned, no more tools could be borrowed.

That worked for a time, but then things got comfortable again. Tools began to disappear with more frequency as everyone got older and into cars. My solution finally was to lock the toolbox so that whoever wanted to borrow a tool had to plan far enough ahead to ask me when he wanted something. At that point it seemed easier for the borrowers to buy their own tools. Pat and I gladly helped, and before long there was another toolbox with a complete set of tools, and the problem was solved.

The key to success was not in designing the plan, although that was certainly necessary. The key to success was *enforcing* the plan, which brings us to the next point.

FOLLOW THROUGH CONSISTENTLY

It is the husband/father's responsibility as head of the family to see that consistent follow-through is part of the family's fabric. If the wife/mother is better equipped in this area, then authority can and should be delegated to her. But a husband/father's investing this authority in his wife does not mean his responsibility ends.

In fact, it increases. Not only does he still bear the ultimate responsibility for the smooth running of the family, but he now has the responsibility of supporting his wife in her follow-through role. When a child fails to follow an agreed-upon plan, the mother should be able to rely on the father to be the disciplinarian. The mother can be consistent in rewarding the child, but if discipline is indicated, the father should be prepared to step in. Otherwise he does a disservice to the child, his wife and himself.

Lack of consistent follow-through will affect everyone in the home. When child #1 is obedient to the plan, but sees child #2 not being held accountable for his or her misbehavior, child #1 is adversely affected. Remember that setting up the plan is never enough. It takes constant maintenance, and that means follow-through to keep things running smoothly.

DIVIDE AND CONQUER

What exactly falls into the category of organizing the home? Many things. It can run the gamut from reorganizing the entire house and all its routines to just refining what is already in place. It can include dealing with excessive clutter, organizing the paperwork relating to the home, changing the use and purpose of individual rooms, and so on.

It's very easy to become overwhelmed by it all.

But it will not seem like such a difficult task if you will divide it into smaller compartments. Create areas of bite-size dimensions, and then prioritize them. Start with things that are not dependent on someone else. Enjoy some successes before you risk failure because someone else won't cooperate.

It's also important that, for the sake of your own peace of mind, you learn to accept for now those things that only prayer will change. And then start praying!

DIFFERENT PERSPECTIVES ON ORGANIZING THE HOME

Let's take a brief look at organizing the home from two different perspectives — that of the wife/mother and that of the husband/father. My purpose is not to give an in-depth look at the way different family members would look at organizing the home, but rather to show that there are different viewpoints — or spheres of influence — at work here that go into the integrated whole of an organized home.

For example, the wife/mother is usually the person most interested on a day-to-day basis with having the home well organized. One of her primary needs might be to have her kitchen better organized. If space is a problem, that needs to be addressed. Additional shelves or cabinets may be necessary.

Her cookbooks and recipes should be organized and easily accessible. If you are the wife/mother, you will find that preparing weekly menus will greatly simplify your life and can be very useful for controlling expenses.

The husband/father's view of what's needed to have an organized home may differ considerably from his wife's view. He may focus more on *responsibilities* — on seeing that everything which *should* be done *is* done.

Household rules should normally be established and enforced by the husband/father as the head of the home. As we noted earlier, the husband can serve the wife by being the disciplinarian with the children — not with the attitude of being a tyrant, but with the realization that it is much easier for the father to consistently enforce the rules in a normal situation.

If the husband/father sees himself as a servant, he can meet two other great needs: he can do those things which his wife needs done to enable her to better organize; and he can teach the children, by his example, how to be the helpers God wants them to be.

CONTROLLING THE PAPER FLOW

One of the biggest aspects of keeping the home organized is controlling the paper flow. Even in this age of electronic communications, there is still a need to keep track of a tremendous amount of paperwork — hundreds of pounds of it every year.

There are important papers to file away, receipts to hold onto, and bills that have to be paid. And someone has to keep track of all these. Also, some-one has to go through all of the paper in order to decide what must be kept and what can be thrown away.

Have you ever needed an important paper and couldn't find it anywhere? You went through all your boxes, your desk drawers, your filing cabinets, everywhere you could think to look, and you just couldn't find it. I'm sure you have. We *all* have. But it doesn't have to happen again, and you don't have to drown in a sea of paperwork. You can keep the paper flow under control.

The need to organize the paper flow covers many dimensions, and it all begins when a piece of paper comes into the home. The initial decision or action required is how to get it to the person it needs to go to.

And then, once that person has it, what should happen to it? Should it go to someone else in the home? Should it be sent to someone outside the home, or perhaps stored for future retrieval? And who should be making those decisions?

1) It Begins at the Mailbox

The most common way paper comes into your home is via the United States Postal Service — which means your plan for organizing the paper flow in your home should begin at the mailbox.

The first step is to have a specific place for putting the mail every day once it's brought into the home. It may be the dining room or kitchen table. It doesn't really matter, as long as everyone knows where it is. From there, either have each member of the family responsible for getting his own mail or have several designated places to which the mail will be distributed. For instance, the husband's mail could go on the desk in his office, the teenage daughter's mail could go on the nightstand in her room, and so on.

There are four major categories of mail: bills, mail requiring an answer, mail to be read and discarded, and mail to be discarded unopened. The unopened bills should go directly to the person responsible for paying them. Junk mail which does not need to be opened should be discarded immedi-ately. Mail to be read and discarded should go to the person who should read it or to a place where it can be read at leisure. Mail to be read and responded to should also go to the appropriate person, and that person should have a system for responding in timely fashion.

Encourage everyone to discard all paperwork as soon as it is not needed. If it must be saved, there should be a central location that everyone recognizes as the filing system in-box. Whenever anyone has papers to be filed, they would be deposited in the in-box. The person in charge must then periodically clear out the box by filing everything. That person should also have discretionary authority to discard rather than file, or at least to return something to its owner for another look to make sure it needs to be filed or dispose of it in another way.

2) Create a Home Filing System

The important papers would then be added to the home filing system. The first step in getting such a system together is to obtain some manila file folders and something to hold them — either a filing cabinet or some boxes that are the right size. Having done that, choose the location where you are going to maintain the filing system. Have an area that everyone will recognize as the logical place.

Understand that every single piece of paper needs to have a place, and most of the time that's either the trash can or a file. Realize that it's going to take several hours per month for several months to perfect this filing system. No matter how well you've planned in the beginning, the very nature of a filing system is such that it must be changed and modified over a period of time to accommodate all those things that make up the paper in our lives.

The home filing system is not the place for books, magazines or newspapers. If you feel that you must save bulky items, have a separate system. Bookcases are much better able to handle them. When it comes to your home filing system itself, a bulky file is a signal that it's time to subdivide the file by breaking it down into subcategories. More about that in just a moment.

Depending on whether you've already got a filing system of sorts or whether this is your first attempt, you need to gather together all the paperwork that needs to be filed. If you have existing files, include them, but realize that some of their contents may need to be reorganized.

Go through everything and throw away as much as you possibly can. There's no need to organize and store what's already obsolete. Then make notes regarding the things you decide to keep. Don't worry about organizing these notes — just write down enough information so you can remember the kinds of paperwork you have. These notes will come in handy when you get to the point of making the index to your system.

Remember that what you're doing at this stage is figuring out what categories of papers you have and not where you're going to put them. That comes after you have made an index. Remember, patience and perseverance are the keys.

3) Create the Index to Your Home Filing System

The key to a meaningful filing system is its index. If you have a good index, you'll have a good system. If you don't, you won't. You can really set up your index any way that suits you, but I have found the following categories work very well:

HOME FILING SYSTEM

I. Administration
    A. General
        1. Filing system index
        2. Vacation plans
    B. Correspondence
        1. Family
        2. Friends
        3. Miscellaneous
    C. Automobiles
        1. First car
        2. Second car
        3. AAA
    D. Insurance
        1. Automobiles
        2. Home
        3. Hospitalization
        4. Life
    E. Planning — objectives and goals
    F. Spiritual — family Bible study
II. Financial
    A. General — benevolence requests
    B. Budget
    C. Taxes
        1. Income
        2. Personal property
        3. Miscellaneous
        4. Receipts

    D. Financial statement
        1. Assets
        2. Liabilities
    E. Bank statements
        1. Household account
        2. Tithe account
        3. Savings account
III. Legal
    A. General
    B. Parents' estate
    C. Home purchase
    D. Children
    E. Wills
IV. Household
    A. General
    B. Home inventory
    C. Appliances
        1. Small — general
        2. Large — general
        3. Small — kitchen
        4. Large — kitchen
        5. Home furnishings
        6. Personal care
    D. Home entertainment — games
    E. Personal purchases
        1. Clothing
        2. Jewelry

F. Tools & equipment
  1. Air conditioner
  2. Camping
  3. Furnace
  4. Household
  5. Lawn & garden
  6. Recreational
  7. Sports
V. Mementos
  A. General
    1. Birthdays
    2. Weddings/anniversaries
    3. Miscellaneous photographs
    4. Other occasions

B. Children
  1. First child
    a. Preschool
    b. Grades 1-3
    c. Grades 4-6
    d. Grades 7-9
  2. Second child
    a. Preschool
    b. Grades 1-3
    c. Grades 4-6
  3. Third child
    a. Preschool
    b. Grades 1-3

Give the creation of your index some good quality mental time and it will pay rich dividends. I know it sounds like quite a bit of effort is necessary to get your home filing system into proper working order. But I guarantee you, it's more than worth it.

After you have at least the beginning outline for your index, you are ready to make files and begin placing papers in them.

Next up, we'll discuss the very important process of building a weekly schedule for your life.

PRACTICE ORGANIZING THE HOME

1) List five routines you would like to establish during the next year in your home.

2) Decide when it would be wise to try to schedule a family meeting to discuss this chapter.

3) Decide when you should do the following on a routine basis:
- Errands
- Vacuuming
- Kitchen cleaning
- Closet reorganization (until they're all done)
- Bathroom cleaning
- Laundry

PART THREE

GETTING YOUR PRIORITIES IN ORDER

9

What's Important in Your Life?

In this section we're going to talk about the four most important aspects of your life.

Before going any further, let me remind you that in order for your priorities to be right, you must first lay the foundation of a personal relationship with Jesus Christ. We talked about this in the Introduction to this book, but let me take the time to urge you again, if you haven't already done so, to stop right now and acknowledge Jesus Christ as your Lord and Savior.

There is no good reason for anyone to refuse to receive Christ. That is the Number One priority of life and the most important thing you could ever do.

If you've never done this, all you need to do is: 1) admit your need ("I am a sinner"); 2) be willing to turn from your sins (repent); 3) believe that Jesus Christ died for you (on the cross), and 4) through prayer invite Jesus Christ to come in and control your life (receive Him as Savior and Lord).

After you've done that, and *only* after you've done that, you are ready to move on with setting the other priorities for your life.

How often during the day can you be heard to say, "I don't have time to do" something or other? Whether it's a matter of "I don't have time to read the Bible," or "I don't have time to pray" or "I don't have time to" anything else, when you say that, you're really saying that the subject under discussion is not a high enough priority. If something is a high enough priority for you, you *will* find the time to do it, and it really is that simple.

If you will establish priorities for your life that are in line with what God wants for you, you will see your life come together in a wonderful way. What we are talking about here, as well as elsewhere in this book, has to do with obedience to God. It is obedience to Him that will bring about the peaceful, joyful, fulfilled, and organized life that we all seek, whether we consciously realize it or not.

SEEKING GOD'S PRIORITIES

What are God's priorities for your life?

> 1) God-related activities.
> 2) Family-related (and self-related) activities.
> 3) Job- or career-related activities.
> 4) Ministry-related activities — which I usually refer to as service to others.

In this chapter we're going to take a look at what I mean by "God-related activities." Then in Chapters 10 and 11 we'll discuss the other priorities in the order of the importance God assigns to them.

Remember, this list of priorities is not something I thought up by myself, but is based on my understanding of God's Word and His will for the lives of His people. For example, the Bible tells us over and over that God wants us to put Him first in our lives (see Exodus 20:3-6). We can also see that His second priority for us is our families (including ourselves) (see 1 Timothy 5:8 and Ephesians 5:22-33). Would your husband or wife and children know that in priority they are second only to God? And when it comes to your career, do you subordinate your job-related activities to your God and family obligations? Many people confuse their family-related responsibilities with their career-related duties, or their career even assumes the Number One spot on the list. Others confuse the fourth priority, which is ministry or service to others, with the first priority. They become so busy doing things *for* God that they don't spend sufficient time *with* Him, getting to know Him as a friend and as a Father.

Have you ever heard it said that God doesn't want anything you have — He wants you? Well, it's true. He desires to have fellowship with you, to commune with you on a one-to-one basis, Father to child, friend-to-friend. Revelation 3:20 tells us that Jesus is standing at the door and knocking, and that if anyone will open the door to Him, He will come in and fellowship with that person. In a nutshell, that is what the first priority is all about: establishing, strengthening and maintaining an intimate friendship with God.

DOING WHAT GOD WANTS YOU TO DO

On occasion there may be a conflict between what God wants you to do and what you feel prepared or equipped to do. But here, as everywhere else, your priorities need to line up with His will for your life.

For example, when I was a practicing attorney the last thing I wanted to do or felt comfortable doing was public speaking. I enjoyed speaking and arguing in court on a subject with which I had become familiar, but the idea of conducting seminars was very close to the last thing I would ever have chosen to do. I had no training and felt ill-prepared. My first seminar was done without so much as an outline to follow. But God sent people to listen, and afterward many of them told me it had been a life-changing experience. I decided that if God could do that much with that little, I would strive to give Him more to work with.

And so I applied myself to the task, not because I enjoyed it, but because I knew God wanted me to do it. And even though I sometimes felt as though I was stumbling and fumbling, God used me, lives were changed, and I began to feel better and more capable regarding my seminars and other speaking engagements. Later the same became true of my response to His direction in writing.

Whatever God calls you to do, apply yourself to do it, then watch your quality of life improve.

What more could one want than to have an ongoing, one-on-one relationship with the Creator of the universe? Anyone who strives to develop such a relationship and to continuously improve upon it will not be disappointed. Let's talk about some ways to develop that relationship and to ensure that God is the Number One priority in our lives.

THE IMPORTANCE OF WORSHIP

In addition to the need for a quiet time, which we have already discussed at length, another way of ensuring that you are making God your Number One priority is to spend time worshiping Him. We do this both corporately — that is, with other Christians — and individually.

The Bible is clear that God wants our worship. Luke 4:8 says, "Jesus answered, 'It is written: "Worship the Lord your God and serve Him only."'" Most Bible-believing Christians agree one day a week should be devoted to corporate worship. There may be differences with respect to which day and what all might be appropriate to include on that day, but the principle of corporate worship on at least a weekly basis is widely accepted and Biblically based. Acts 20:7 tells us that the first-century Christians had the habit of coming together "on the first day of the week" for corporate worship.

There is also the matter of individual worship. While in some churches this might not be as widely practiced as corporate worship, as far as I know there is no serious disagreement with the proposition that God desires that we worship Him regularly on an individual basis. Disagreement crops up on the question of what is included in worship. Is it limited to singing psalms and hymns and spiritual songs, or does it include all the activities that are normally associated with producing a church service?

Does worship include the collateral activities that are also an integral part of organizing and running a church? What about serving on a board of elders or a vestry? What about teaching Sunday school, serving on a church committee, or singing in the choir?

In my opinion, worship should not be deemed to include activity that is not directly related to a person's one-on-one communication with God or His communication with them. All of the activities necessary to *produce* that worship experience, however important, should not be considered a substitute for or part of the activity of worship itself.

THE IMPORTANCE OF FELLOWSHIP

Other activities I would include in the first priority are some types of fellowship, such as those that result in serious personal accountability or that seek to apply Scriptural principles to daily life.

The worthwhile fellowship or accountability group that may be considered a God-related priority is one that establishes specific measures of a person's needs and proposes solutions to meet those needs. There should be conscientious follow-up and a determination made that the person being held accountable is making and following through on commitments designed to improve his or her relationship with the Lord. If there is no way to establish or measure progress, the chances are very good that none is being made that would justify including the time involved as a God-related priority.

Another God-related priority activity is group Bible study. In this case, the measure of whether the activity should qualify as God-related is that the time spent be tied to Scripture. Obviously this can encompass a number of approaches, and the quality of the discussion will almost invariably be tied to the quality of preparation. Nevertheless, if God's Word is central to the discussion, I would consider it one of the God-related activities deserving of the highest priority in your life.

THE SPIRITUAL RETREAT

The last activity we will include in our discussion of God-related activities is the spiritual retreat, or as it is referred to in some quarters, the spiritual advance.

The spiritual retreat has a solid Scriptural base. Christ Himself often sought out a place where He could be alone to fellowship with His Father (See Mark 6:46; John 7:53 — 8:1). And after the Apostle Paul's conversion he went on a spiritual retreat of sorts that lasted for three years (Galatians 1:15-18)! The thought behind a retreat is that it provides an opportunity to withdraw or to shelter oneself from the normal activities of life and devote a significant amount of time to communing with God, free from the interruptions of normal daily life. A retreat can be undertaken by a single individual, a couple, or a group of any size, ranging from a family on up to a large group from a church. The key to success lies not in the number of people involved, but in planning and preparation for the retreat and in hearing God at the retreat.

If the goal of the retreat is to hammer out an answer to an individual's problem or to target some aspect of an individual's relationship with the Lord, it's probably best for that person to go on the retreat by himself. If the objective is for a husband and wife to address their relationship with each other or with the Lord as a couple, both should be present. And so on.

Once the objective is clearly established, a fairly detailed plan should be designed. This will range from location and duration of the retreat to all the logistical details. Since the location is often chosen for its remoteness in order to discourage interruptions, it's helpful to build a list over a period of time that will anticipate all the things that will be needed for the retreat. Your list should include Bible and study materials, linens, food, utensils, clothing and cash. It can also include other reading materials, equipment and supplies. The more thought you put into your list, and the less you forget, the more enjoyable and profitable your retreat will be.

Another thing you can do to make your retreat as productive as possible is to have an agenda or written plan on how you plan to spend your time. If you are the leader of a group, an agenda is essential. But even if you're by yourself or with another person, it's very helpful to reflect on how you will spend your time before you get to the retreat. You may not end up spending it the way you planned, but if you have a plan, you at least have a framework from which to depart.

My last suggestion is that before the retreat ends you have a follow-up plan. You should determine just what you have learned and accomplished and what you need to do to realize God's potential for you as a result of the retreat. If you don't take this last step, you should look at what you've done more as a vacation than a retreat. There's a purpose to be served by both, but they shouldn't be confused. A retreat is to obtain spiritual direction, a vacation is a vacation.

In the next chapter we're going to talk about God's second priority — your family and yourself.

PRACTICE PUTTING GOD FIRST

1) If you have not asked Christ into your life as Savior, or if you are unsure, would you like to do that at this point?

2) Based on your understanding of this chapter, list the things you now do that are included in the first priority (God-related activities) of life.

3) List the things you do *not* now do that you believe God wants you to do that are included in this first priority of life.

4) If you believe it would be helpful to you to schedule a retreat, when do you think you should plan to go, and where do you think would be a good place to go? Should anyone accompany you?

5) Do you attend church regularly? If not, list several churches you will attend over the coming weeks to determine which church family you will attend and eventually join.

10

Finding Time for Yourself and Your Family

If you're like most people, you wish you had more time to spend with your family. Well, you can have that time if your priorities are in order. And if they *are* in order, you will put time for God first, and time for yourself and your family second.

By the way, if you're single, you still have a family you should be spending time with on a regular basis, even if that family does not consist of blood relations. The single person's family may be his parents and his brothers and sisters. But it may also be his or her Christian friends. Anyone who feels he doesn't have a family should ask God to show him who his family is.

TIME FOR YOURSELF

I believe that unless our own basic needs are met, we are not well positioned to attend to the needs of others. The fact is, we all have certain needs, certain basic requirements, which must be met in order for us to get our focus off ourselves and onto those things God has for us to do. Another way of looking at this is that we need to have our present needs met so we can become the person God wants us to be. As you mature in your relationship with God, you may find that you have fewer needs and that the needs you have are changing, perhaps dramatically. But at each stage of maturity, you will continue to have certain basic needs which must be met.

For example, I have a friend who used to own his own construction company. He had a nice house, a big lawn, expensive cars, and so on. At that point in his life his material possessions demanded his attention before he was able to look beyond himself and his family to the needs of others. That's not to say he needed the possessions, but as long as he had them, he felt the need to have them. Later his business failed. He lost everything, and he, his wife, and their daughters decided to enter the mission field. Now, ten years later, their needs are quite different. They need food, shelter, and transportation. They no longer need to assume responsibility for a house and lawn and expensive cars. Their felt needs are significantly different, but they still have needs, and unless those needs are met they cannot minister effectively.

STAYING WITHIN YOUR COMFORT ZONE

Whether he has much or little in the way of material possessions, each person has a comfort zone. The comfort zone can be modified, but it can't be totally ignored. When the comfort zone is violated, the result is first discomfort, then worry, and finally anxiety. If too much happens too quickly to disturb this comfort zone, even for good reasons, the result can be counterproductive. Each person needs to determine what areas to change voluntarily, and then to recognize that God will change other areas through circumstances. There is a very fine line between wants and needs, but there is a minimum level of need below which you are not presently prepared to slip without having it adversely affect your ability to meet the needs of others.

You should, however, devote yourself to working on voluntarily reducing that level of basic need to the point to which God wants it reduced. Maintain an awareness that God has His own timetable for your progress in this department; if you're not sensitive to that timetable, you may find painful circumstances affecting your progress. Or worse yet, you may fail to progress and as a result miss much of what God has for you as you fail to reach your potential in Him. Jesus may never say to you, as He did to the rich young ruler, "Sell everything you have and give to the poor" (Luke 18:22), but you should work on getting to the point that you'd be happy to do so if He asked you to.

SPENDING TIME WITH YOUR SPOUSE

If you are married, time spent with your spouse is the highest-priority, family-related activity, second only to the time you spend with God. It's critical that you understand God's plan for the use of your time as it relates to time with your spouse.

If your relationship is healthy enough, simply ask your mate what you can do, time-wise, to improve the relationship. Each of you should make a list of the other's perception of ways the relationship can be improved by changes in how you spend your time *with* and *for* each other.

If communications between you are poor, it might be better to start by doing something that you already know is a priority but that you have been neglecting, or stopping something you shouldn't really be doing — especially if it is something that takes away from the time you have to spend with your spouse.

It's important that you plan to spend time with your spouse on a regular basis. Do you have one afternoon or evening per week carved out for the two of you to spend time together? You don't have to spend money, but between you, you should be able to plan quality time together that is within your means.

But don't think that one afternoon or evening a week is sufficient, or that you can ignore your spouse the rest of the time. You should be spending quality, one-to-one time with each other on a daily basis. When Pat and I married in 1981, we established a regular time in the evening to be alone together for thirty minutes. The kids were told we were not to be interrupted, and after the first month or so they got used to the idea. They then even looked for ways to protect us from outside interruptions. They saw it was a priority for *us*, so it became a priority for *them*. They developed their own methods of making clear to callers and visitors that when we were together alone, it was much too important to even consider interrupting us.

During that time, we prayed, read the Bible, and just talked. We still have the routine, but now that the kids are gone, we don't have to hide out in the bedroom to protect it.

My time alone with Pat is very precious to me. It has strengthened my relationship with her as surely as my regular quiet time has strengthened my relationship with God.

When Pat and I were married, she and her children were living in my house, and I had lived in a rented townhouse nearby. So after the wedding and honeymoon, I moved back into a house that had been mine alone for ten years. But now it was full of other people's things. About the only space I could find for myself was one-half of the medicine chest and a closet.

I was having trouble adjusting, and Pat was having difficulty adjusting to my adjusting. So I felt somewhat isolated, and she felt rejected. Same facts but different perspectives. I decided that time together in prayer and Bible study would be a good way to attack the problem.

I suggested that we use the bed as our prayer rail, with me kneeling on the floor on one side and Pat on the other side. For our first few times together, it was usually the case that I prayed and Pat listened. I found out later that she was really so hurt by her perception of my rejection that she didn't know how or what to pray for. But as I began to talk to the Lord in front of her about my regard and love for her, she began to see that my attitude was one of really wanting to please her. So she was more willing to openly talk to Him in front of me about our "problems" from her perspective. Both of us were coming to see that we weren't really in disagreement — we just needed to learn to communicate more effectively with each other.

After our prayer times together, we began to find it easier to talk to each other about our feelings. We found ways to say things that didn't cause a reaction. Before long we were communicating very well. That's not to say we were in agreement on everything because we weren't, but we could talk about things and work together to meet whatever challenges came along. We both look back on that time as a real foundation-block in our marriage.

The Christian family that lives according to the plan found in Colossians 3:18-21 will prosper:

> Wives, submit to your husbands, as is fitting in the Lord.
> Husbands, love your wives and do not be harsh with them.
> Children, obey your parents in everything, for this pleases the Lord.
> Fathers, do not embitter your children, or they will become discouraged.

YOUR FAMILY COMES *BEFORE* YOUR JOB

Some people — especially men — make the mistake of thinking their jobs should take precedence over their families. That's not true. Your family, and especially your spouse, must come first.

I remember when a friend of mine, Don, came to me for help on the use of his time. There just wasn't enough time in the day for him to get his work done and still have time in the evenings and on weekends for his family. Donna, his wife, was a long-suffering, seldom-complaining type, but Don knew he was sacrificing his family's needs for his job. With the help of Don's boss, Casey, who was also a Christian, I devised a form to help Don keep track of his time.

The next week Don put in sixty-two hours on the job and complained because there were so many more things he had to do. But as I looked over the form he had filled out, it became apparent that he was spending the bulk of his time on things he enjoyed doing, all of which were related to using the computer, and then scrambling to get everything else caught up. He also complained about numerous interruptions from coworkers, including Casey.

I recommended to Casey that he give Don a separate office with a door which could be shut so he would not be interrupted by coworkers casually dropping in to chat. I also asked him to give Don his daily instructions in writing and advised him to do his best to avoid interrupting Don when he was in his office. Furthermore, Don was not to be allowed to work on the computer until 2 P.M. each day.

Don wasn't overly happy at first. He felt he was being treated unfairly, especially with regard to the computer situation. But as time went by, good things began to happen. He began to get more done in less time. As for Casey, he discovered he had formed a habit of interrupting those who worked for him and giving them additional work to do. And even though he shouldn't have, he realized now that he often assigned that new work a higher priority than it ought to have been given. This had only decreased the productivity of his workers.

Pretty soon Don reported that he was getting out of the office by 5:30 and was no longer working weekends. He used his mornings and early afternoons to handle tasks he wasn't all that crazy about and generally couldn't wait until 2:00 every afternoon so he could use the computer. Finally I got the call I was hoping for. It was Donna, saying that Don was now spending quality time with her and the kids on a regular basis. I knew then that a life-changing event had taken place.

You see, if you're too busy to spend time with your spouse — and the rest of your family too — your priorities are out of order, and you need to spend some time working on them.

A good friend of mine is a medical doctor. I was immediately impressed with his dedication and interest in the people he treats, but I didn't know at the time that he wasn't giving the same sort of loving attention to his family.

It all started when I got a call from my son, Kennie, who told me he had just come out of emergency surgery. It turned out that Kennie had been feeling poorly for a couple of days and had finally gone to a doctor — one he had just picked out of the phone book. That night he had come down with an extremely high fever and called the doctor's emergency number to see what he should do.

After they talked, even though it was around midnight, the doctor came to Kennie's room, picked him up, and took him to the hospital. He had correctly diagnosed a staph infection which could have been fatal. Naturally I was grateful for what this doctor had done, so the next time I needed a physical I decided to go and see him. From the waiting room I could see him going from one patient to another and from one file to another, and he was moving as fast as I've ever seen anybody move. When I had a chance to talk to him I told him that I was a time management expert, and I asked him if he was tired. He surprised me with his candor. He was exhausted, he said, and never got enough sleep or had quality time with his wife and children.

I gave him my card and told him to call me if he wanted to do something about it.

Months later I was in his office again. He still had my card and said he was ready to take me up on my offer. When I met with him and his wife, I found out that he was overextended, overcommitted, and definitely out of control. His wife said she never saw him, the kids never saw him, and they had given up on hoping it was ever going to be any other way. In addition to his office practice, he was on call at three hospital emergency rooms and he was physician for a high-school football team.

When I advised him to leave emergency medicine he yelled like a stuck pig. He loved emergency medicine and couldn't bear the thought of giving it up. Nevertheless, I stood my ground. I said that unless he was willing to close his general practice and earn his livelihood solely from an emergency practice, he must stop. It was killing him, and his family was growing up without him. It was during this same time period that he asked Christ into his life.

Several months later he and his wife invited Pat and me out to dinner. When we arrived at the restaurant, I couldn't believe we were looking at the same couple. She looked years younger. The tension was gone from her face. She was relaxed and had us laughing all evening.

He had taken my advice. He had resigned from the staff of all the emergency rooms. He had put an assistant in charge of the football team and had hired an administrator. This out of control doctor had turned his life around, and his practice was making more money than it ever had before.

He had drawn up a goal statement which had read, "I will spend no more than sixty hours per week on medically related activity and will spend at least ten hours a week in quality time with the members of my family."

Here was a man who didn't think he had time for his family, but he did. He had to come to understand that family is always a higher priority than career, then rearranged his schedule to reflect that.

TIPS FOR HUSBANDS AND WIVES

Let's take a look at some things husbands can do to maximize the potential for a super relationship with their wives.

1) Help Around the House

Just ask your bride to present you with a list of those things you can do that are her highest priorities. Then set aside some dedicated time on a regular basis to deal with your honey-do list. Specific evenings or parts of weekends generally work best. Even if you never exhaust the list, she will appreciate your demonstrating that she's a priority by carving out time to help her.

2) Establish a Regular Time That You Will Be Home in the Evening, and Then Be Faithful to That Commitment

Let the exception be just that — an exception.

3) Make a Weekly Date with Your Wife

Set aside a specific time in your schedule on a weekly basis that she knows is her time with you. Try to spend that time the way she wants to spend it, even if you're not particularly enthusiastic about her choices.

4) Observe Special Occasions, Especially Her Birthday and Your Anniversary

They are very important to her, and if you're attentive to her pleasure, you may enjoy them more yourself.

5) Schedule Regular Time Together for Prayer and Bible Study

Practice praying in each other's presence and watch your communication improve dramatically.

6) Make a Commitment to Listen

Just as you may want her to listen at the end of the day, she needs you to listen — attentively, carefully — and not halfheartedly while your head is buried in the newspaper.

Now, because turnabout is fair play, let's look at this from a wife's perspective. What can she do to improve her relationship with her husband?

1) Don't Nag

It's totally counterproductive and will only serve to frustrate your husband. At best it leads to arguments, and at worst it leads to silence. Whatever the solution is, it is *not* to endlessly reiterate your husband's shortcomings. Once you've made your point on any given topic, leave it up to God to remind and motivate your husband.

2) Pray for Insight

Ask God to show you what you can do (as opposed perhaps to what your husband can do) to reinforce the relationship.

3) Be Willing to Act on the Insight God Gives You

For example, you may need to relinquish some of your expectations for your husband.

4) Make a Commitment to Be Pleasant in Appearance

If you need to establish a time for exercise, do so. If you need to lose weight, give that a high priority. It's difficult for your husband to have pride in you if you have low self-esteem.

5) Make a Commitment to Listen

Your husband needs to be heard, and if you're not there to listen, you may be very sorry.

SCHEDULING TIME FOR YOUR CHILDREN

If you have children, you should decide how to schedule quality time with each one of them. That decision will be a product of how many children you have, what their ages are, and other demands on your time. If you have twelve young children, you'll obviously plan differently than if you have one or two. You may need to double up or make it a monthly schedule rather than a weekly one. If you have teenagers, this commitment may translate into making yourself available. If they don't choose to spend the time with you, you can always use it for something else.

Remember, though, that each child should have some one-on-one time with you. Don't just schedule "time for being with the kids," but schedule time individually for each one of them.

Here are some other things you, as a parent, should do for your children.

1) Be Sure They Know Jesus

Do all you can to cultivate and encourage their relationship with God and their spiritual growth.

The most important thing a parent can do is to see to it that his or her child knows and loves Jesus Christ as his Lord and Savior. You can do this by taking the time to talk to him about the Lord, by making sure she is in church and Sunday school, and also by having a weekly family Bible study, with all family members participating.

You can design this so it's fun for everyone. Depending on the number and ages of the children and their depth of commitment, you can range from playing games to serious study.

You might want to devote the evening meal to spiritual matters. You can rotate responsibility for a short devotional and give everyone Bible verses to memorize.

Another thing you can do is encourage a regular daily quiet time with God. Give each of your children a suitable Bible and encourage them to read it. Talk to them about prayer, and make sure they understand that it is just as important to listen to God as it is for them to make their requests known to God.

2) Involve Yourself in Your Child's Schoolwork

Perhaps the most important contribution you can make to your child's well-being as a student is to see that he acquires good study skills. If you don't know how, get some good advice. There are people who teach study skills, and your child is being cheated in today's world if he is not being taught how to study.

Establish a schedule for your child and help him understand that the time he spends studying on his own is every bit as important as the time he spends in school. As a parent, you may also need to revise your measure of success. I suggest that you measure your child's success by the time and effort he has invested in trying to learn rather than in the grade he receives.

In other words, reward effort, not result. A smart student can ace all his subjects and still not be pleasing to God. Teach your child what success in school really is — becoming the student God wants him to be and reaching his potential in Christ as a student.

3) Help Your Children Find Good Friends

It's important that you know your children's friends. One of the ways you can get to know them is by including them in family devotions and Bible studies when it's practical to do so.

Encourage your children to discuss their friends with you. Pray for them and their families when they need it, and take a stand with regard to unwholesome friends. If your child is associating with people you would not want him to have as friends, show him through Scripture how dangerous such relationships can be. If he won't listen to you, seek God's wisdom and do nothing to encourage the relationship.

Always keep in mind that the best defense is a meaningful offense. Find a way to encourage wholesome relationships, perhaps by getting your child involved in activities he will enjoy and where he will meet godly children.

Finally, pray that your child will be able to find friends who will be an encouragement and a support rather than a stumbling block.

4) Help Your Children Plan for the Future

Another very important thing that you as a parent can do is to help your child understand what lies ahead of him in life. You can do this by taking note of those things he does well and trying to encourage his development in those areas. Be sensitive, too, to those areas your child has an interest in, even if he or she is not terribly proficient in them. On the other side of things, note those areas where your child is not particularly adept and where there is a definite lack of interest.

Instill within your child appreciation for the fact that God has a specific plan for his life. God has a certain vocation in mind for him that will be more fulfilling than anything else he could do. The key to all of this is for the child to know and understand God so that he is always motivated to be obedient. Help your child to understand that obedience is the road he must take if he wants to discover God's plan for his life and receive the benefits attached to that plan.

TAKING TIME FOR PARENTS

Another valuable contribution you can make to your children is to encourage close and regular contact between them and their grandparents.

Society has changed so dramatically over the last fifty years that it's no longer possible in many families to have grandparents and grandchildren living in proximity to each other. Nevertheless, maintaining such a relationship should in my opinion be an objective of most Christian families.

God's plan for raising children includes a very definite and necessary role for grandparents. Parents are busy trying to keep it together on a daily basis, and no matter how hard they try, they'll never have the leisure time or the attitude that will permit them to fulfill the role that grandparents can play in the lives of children. So to the extent that it's possible, we should give a very high priority to establishing a close relationship between our children and our parents.

As our parents grow older (and wiser), we also assume a greater and greater responsibility for their well-being. I was close to forty years old when I began to realize what God meant by "honor your father and your mother." Since mine were divorced, it required more effort, but I determined to become obedient to that commandment. My mother lives near me, so I reversed a lifelong habit of independence and ignoring her needs and began to visit her every week. I carved out Thursday afternoons, and more than ten years later we still spend that afternoon together regularly.

I lived in Virginia, and my father lived in Florida and was in a nursing home — so I began calling and writing him. I dictated cassette tapes to him and told him things about me and my relationship with God. I also took trips to visit him. Now, my father was a heavy-drinking, foul-mouthed, blasphemous Texan who had never said anything positive about God for as long as I could remember. He cursed God at every opportunity.

But in 1978, two years after I asked Christ into my life, God told me to go witness to my father, who was then partially paralyzed and seventy-four years old. While I saw no earthly reason to do so, I flew to Florida to join my mother, and we met at his nursing home in Tallahassee. My parents had not seen each other for twenty years.

We sat together, the three of us, in a big, bright room, and I presented the gospel to my father. I then asked him if he would like to ask Jesus into his life, and with tears running down his face he said, "Yup." So we prayed together.

I never saw my father again, but quite contrary to what I always thought would happen to him, he now waits for Mother and me in a place called Paradise.

REPAIRING RELATIONSHIPS

Are there relationships within your family that need repairing? Perhaps it's your relationship with your brothers and sisters, your parents, children or friends. Wherever the severed or strained relationship may be, it's well worth any time and energy you may invest to get it repaired.

I encourage you to look for opportunities to revitalize your relationship with blood relatives and long-time friends. In the case of non-Christians, be prepared to share Christ with them. You're no friend if you're not willing to at least share *your* experience with them. With respect to your Christian relatives and friends, it's important to realize that, like you, they're not perfect, just forgiven.

The older I get, the more impressed I become with how critical good relationships are to God and to ourselves. It may take some time to restore the bad relationships of the past, and it's possible that not all of those relationships can be restored. Each of us has within his own province, however, the ability to do all *we* can to restore those relationships. If the other person won't cooperate, then that ultimately becomes his or her problem.

I had a friend in college who looked up to me. When he got out of the Navy, he sought my advice and I encouraged him to go to law school. He met his future wife through me and often stayed in our home. I named my first son after him and another friend with the same first name.

Then I did something that greatly offended him. He actively hated me for almost twenty years. I became a Christian, and not long after that I asked my friend to forgive me. He cursed me instead. I made several attempts over the years, but was always rebuffed.

In 1984 my twenty-two-year-old son, who was named after my friend, killed himself. I called my friend to tell him of his namesake's death. He said he didn't have time to talk, and that he would call me back, but he never did. I know I've done all I can for that relationship, except to pray, which I do regularly. I believe that God will restore the relationship one day, but until He's ready I can do no more.

In the multitude of relationships we all have, we need to identify those that are primary to God and work to bring them to their maximum potential.

What can *you* do? Make a list of all your relationships that need repair or reconstructive maintenance. Then establish a plan for improving each of those relationships. Gain the assurance that you've done everything God wants you to do. Don't try to do more than God has for you to do, but for any that need additional work commit yourself to prayer until that relationship has been brought back up to speed. The more progress you make, the better positioned you'll be to receive God's best.

A LOOK AT SOME OTHER FAMILY PRIORITIES

After you've addressed the matter of relationships in the family — your own needs and the individual needs of other family members — you're at the point of attending to all those things that life consists of as they relate to *family*.

I'm talking about things such as budgeting and financial planning, an area that affects virtually every other aspect of the family. Remember, it's not how much money you have that will determine your family's quality of life, but how obedient you are in managing what you do have. God is perfectly capable of providing as much money and creature comfort as you need or even desire as long as you're putting God first. But how you conduct yourself with regard to what you have will very likely influence that provision. The key to your conduct is dedicating sufficient quality time to managing your financial affairs. Unless you take the time to identify and adhere to God's plan for your finances, can you seriously expect Him to assume responsibility for your financial well-being?

Other activities included within the family priority level include household chores, home maintenance, children's activities and commitments, vacation planning, recreation, projects, and even family meetings.

Remember, no matter how tight your schedule may be, you *can* find time to spend with your family. In fact, you cannot afford not to.

Next, we'll discuss the third and fourth priorities in life — your career and your ministry (service to others) respectively.

PRACTICE PLEASING YOUR FAMILY

1) Make a list of your basic needs that are not being met. What can you do to improve the situation? What is beyond your control and requires insight through prayer?

2) Make a list of the things you need to do to meet the needs of your spouse . . . your children . . . other family members. Develop a plan for how you will do this.

3) If you are married and have children, ask each of them to make a list of their unmet needs. Use these lists in compiling your own list.

4) Do you have a budget? If not, contact Christian Stewardship Ministries for a budget workbook and forms. Perhaps you can even take the initiative to schedule our Life Management Seminar in your church or business. You might also contact Larry Burkett at Christian Financial Concepts in Gainesville, Georgia (404/534-1000).

11

Looking at Your Job and Your Ministry

I n this chapter we're going to discuss the third and fourth levels of priority — your job or career, and your ministry or service to others.

THE THIRD PRIORITY: CAREER/WORK

First, we'll take a look at your lifestyle as it relates to your job. The Bible makes it clear that God expects man to work. Genesis 2:15 tells us that as soon as God created Adam, "The Lord God took the man and put him in the Garden of Eden to work it and take care of it." "Work" has been with us from the very beginning of creation. We've already seen that 1 Timothy 5:8 says that a man who does not work and provide for his family is "worse than an unbeliever," and Ephesians 4:28 promotes the work ethic when it says, "He who has been stealing must steal no longer, but must work, doing something useful with his own hands, that he may have something to share with those in need." There can be no doubt that God approves of work.

Basically there are three classifications of job-related activity: income production, homemaking, and education. Education should be directed at preparation for one of the other two categories.

Income production is most easily divisible into categories commonly known as white-collar and blue-collar jobs. White-collar jobs are usually associated with an office environment, and blue-collar jobs are usually associated with manual labor. Neither is superior to the other; both are essential.

Homemaking is the art of providing an environment within which the marriage relationship can prosper and where children can be reared in the fear and admonition of the Lord. Education is the process of being taught, preferably through the experience of others. While the focus of formal education is often not on income production, eventually the individual should move from a mode of primarily learning to primarily applying what has been learned and eventually to teaching others. The path of life is such that very few of us remain in the student class. We become either income producers or homemakers or both.

The Role of the Homemaker

Let's discuss each of these job classifications, beginning with the homemaker.

Let's assume for the point of our discussion that our homemaker is a wife with children still in the home. There is no more diverse a job than that of a homemaker. She must be extremely well disciplined because the job description encompasses all levels of management and labor. In the case of a single mother of several children, it can be absolutely overwhelming.

It's difficult from a time management perspective to plot the exact line between job and family-related activity for a homemaker. In one sense the job begins daily at about the moment the first family member awakens, or even before that. In another sense, her workday begins after all who leave for work or school leave the house. Either way her job-related activities quite often end only after the last family member is in bed. Somewhere in between all those demands lies what we would like to think of as family time — that is, quality time with each member of the family — ideally one-on-one and without the pressure of job-related responsibilities (housework, meals, shopping, errands and the like).

In order for the homemaker to protect her family-related priorities from her job-related priorities, she must have a supportive husband and must be extremely well disciplined. She needs to have a clear understanding of when her job-related priorities end and her family-related priorities begin. The two most logical times to devote to meeting the needs of self and family are often during the middle of the day and in the evening after dinner.

In my opinion, it is practically impossible for a wife and mother of small children to strike a Christ-centered balance between family and job if she must also work full-time outside the home. It may be difficult to find an alternative, but I don't think she or her family are likely to discover God's best balance as long as she is not free to be a full-time homemaker. Husbands, unless your wife feels strongly that she should or must work, I encourage you to find an alternative to her doing so.

The Role of the Wage-earner

In order for the full-time wage-earner to establish the balance between job and family that represents God's best, he or she must decide how much time should be devoted to the job, and then take steps to establish the job within those limits. If you have a job that is taking up all of your waking time, you may need to have your job redesigned, or you may need to eventually find a job that permits the proper balance. Remember, God has the plan, and your task is to discover what that plan is.

Now if your job is the kind that permits you to bring work home, don't deceive yourself by working at home and thinking of it as time with your family. There's nothing wrong with bringing work home — just be sure it's included in the total amount of time you *should* be spending in job-related activity.

There's a tendency on the part of many people to see other jobs as more desirable than the one they have. But the real key is to ask whether the job you have now is the one God wants you to have — at least for now. If it is, you owe it to yourself, your family, and God — as well as your employer — to do your very best in it.

I counseled a woman several years ago who was working as a secretary to support herself and an invalid husband to whom she was devoted. Her employer was a wealthy retired industrialist. She worked long hours for a meager wage and was required to work overtime on a regular basis without receiving additional compensation. She had no fringe benefits and received no vacation time, and the place she worked had no retirement plan. Her husband's retirement plan included continuing medical care for him, but not for her.

Ann was concerned for her husband. She needed time to care for him, and she needed more income than she was making to support the two of them. She was sixty-two years old, so finding another job was not going to be easy.

My advice was to give her stingy employer two weeks' notice immediately. She had no reason to stay in that difficult situation but could not better her situation until she decided to leave.

Ann took my advice and applied herself full-time to finding another job with retirement benefits. She happened onto a Christian ministry which was looking for a telephone receptionist. She got the job, which she immediately loved. It met her needs, including a retirement program, and she enjoyed networking with the people there, both personally and over the phone.

Ann is not the only one who benefited from the change, because she is one of the world's best receptionists. She solicits prayer concerns from callers and makes them feel like she and her organization consider them the most important person in the world. She's an absolute delight and is clearly in the right job. God has honored Ann's devotion to her husband and her confidence in His provision for her.

Now if you're unhappy in your present situation, it may be that the only way God will lead you to a better job is if you do your very best where you are. And part of doing your best includes maintaining a godly balance. You should not invest more time in your job than God wants you to, but you should make the very best use of your job-related time.

If you have a job that does not have fixed hours or a required routine, you may be the beneficiary of a blessing or the recipient of a curse. A job with a definite time in and out is often not fully appreciated. Many people have struggled to be set free from that stable environment only to discover an unstable environment for which they are not well suited.

The biggest disadvantage of a job with flexible hours is that such a job is often perceived as producing more money and creature comforts. For some reason man equates creature comfort with success. While I believe God wants us to have creature comforts, I'm afraid that all too often we seek to acquire them independently of God. Instead of conducting ourselves in obedient fashion and permitting Him to provide them as we "seek first" His Kingdom (Matthew 6:33), we set our course and then perhaps remember to ask Him to bless it.

If you have a job in sales or own your own business, chances are good that you have much greater control of how you spend your job-related time than would a person who is employed in an office or in skilled or unskilled labor. At least in theory! But do you really? Have you taken the time to plan your steps? Do you have regular work hours and a regular routine that permits you to be effective? To focus on achieving your potential? Remember, you can make a great deal of money and still not be a godly steward of your time or your money.

If your job requires that you be on the road much of the time, you absolutely must carve out time for planning and organization. You must also establish a schedule that your family can rely on. If your work keeps you away overnight or longer, you must have compensating times when you are home — and your family needs to know when that will be. If you do establish the discipline to manage yourself in a flexible job environment, the rewards can be great, not only financially, but also in peace of mind and a sense of fulfillment. Just remember who is providing the peace and realize that unless it comes as the result of an obedient lifestyle, it's likely to be very fleeting.

The Role of the Student

The last classification is that of a student, and for the purpose of our discussion we'll confine ourselves to college students. Today many students are employed part-time or full-time, and many are well established in their careers, or have even retired from successful careers. With that kind of diversity, it's difficult to generalize, but there are several valid points to make.

1) If you are a full-time student, realize that your status is very temporary. Your purpose should be to learn, to become equipped to do the work God has planned for you. College is not a game or a form of recreation. As with any job, you should be able to have fun doing it. But recreation is not the purpose.

2) It is extremely important for the student to protect his time with the Lord. I'm not sure exactly why — it's probably a combination of maturity level and stress — but time with the Lord often falls victim to the student's busy schedule. Just remember, the more important it is for you to succeed as a student, the more important it is for you to succeed in your relationship with God.

3) Keep a regular schedule as much as possible. Because of the unstructured nature of campus life, it becomes increasingly important to impose structure on yourself. Have a regular time to go to bed and a regular time to get up regardless of when your first class meets. Schedule study time between classes and your quiet time before the day begins. Plan to do your long-term assignments systematically, and avoid the crisis living that seems to devour so many students. Be the student God wants you to be, so you can be the person He wants you to be.

THE FOURTH PRIORITY: SERVICE TO OTHERS/MINISTRY

The fourth priority of life is service to others, which may also be referred to as ministry. Every Christian ought to be involved in ministry of some kind. In the twelfth chapter of 1 Corinthians the Apostle Paul says that each Christian has been given at least one spiritual gift which should be used for the benefit of other believers. In verse 27 he writes, "Now you are the body of Christ, and each one of you is a part of it."

You have special gifts and abilities which God expects you to use in ministry, just as much as in your job and the other areas of your life.

When I talk about ministry some people get the wrong idea. They envision clerical collars and years in seminary. That is not what I'm talking about. Ministry is that area of your life through which you serve the needs of others beyond yourself and your immediate family. That would include church-related activities, service to and through Christian organizations, and secular charities as God leads you to get involved in them. It includes service within the neighborhood and the community and the thousand and one things upon which the charitable underpinnings of this country are founded.

There is a real difference between the first priority (time with God) and this fourth priority. Unfortunately, some people get them confused.

I remember a fellow named John, one of the nicest guys I ever met. It seemed that he was as spiritual and hard-working as it is possible for a man to be. I never heard anyone say a bad word about him.

One day John happened to mention to me that he had no quiet time. I was surprised because I knew that he spent time witnessing to his employees and that he would even remind other people to make sure they were having a quiet time with God. But he was "too busy" being about the work of God to spend time with God!

He spent much of his time doing church-related things and even spent more time at the church than some of the paid staff. He wasn't an elder, but he may as well have been because he enjoyed everyone's confidence, and if anyone had a problem, they knew John would listen and dispense solid, Biblical advice.

At a women's retreat one weekend my wife Pat met John's wife, Jean. As the two of them talked it became apparent that Jean felt her husband did not really love her. He was everyone else's friend, but he spent almost no time with her. She was lonely and angry and desperate for things to change.

With Jean's permission, Pat told me about their conversation, and I decided to talk to John about his responsibilities toward his wife. It turned out that he was horrified. He loved his wife deeply and had no idea he had been hurting her. He said he would start spending more time with her immediately, and he did.

About two months later, I asked him if his quiet time was any better. When he said it wasn't, I asked why he was willing to make the decision to set aside time for his wife but not for the Lord. I asked him if he ever considered the possibility that the Lord was just as upset about their relationship as Jean had been. He looked at me as if he had just seen the devil.

He told me later that when I told him of Jean's misery, it had almost destroyed him, and when I compared that incident to his relationship with the Lord, it occurred to him for the first time that he had offended God in much the same way. Before that, he had seen the time he spent helping others as compensation for not spending time with God. Now, through Jean's eyes, he saw it differently.

From that time on John was a different man. He was still popular, he still did things for people when he could, but now his marriage was also terrific, as was his relationship with God. He now realized that those two aspects of his life had to come before everything else.

That shows what a difference it can make when you confuse the first priority with the fourth priority.

Another point of confusion arises when the third and fourth priorities — job and ministry — are mixed up. While it may be true that a person's job contains elements of service to God and/or man, it is still his job and not his ministry. If it is a source of income, it is a job. If it is not a source of income but rather something someone does because he wants to be of service to others without compensation, it is a ministry. In other words, even someone whose job is totally service related — a pastor of a church, for example — should have a ministry beyond his income-generating occupation.

In my own life there was a time, when I was a practicing lawyer, that what I now do for a living was my ministry. I helped people get their lives in order, and I did that through free counseling and seminars and the like. I still do that, but it is no longer my ministry — it's my job. It is my only source of income, and I must do it to support my family.

On the other hand, my ministry — my service to others — is now fixing coffee at my church between services. It is evangelizing friends and neighbors who don't yet know Jesus in a personal way. It also consists of serving on church committees.

Generally speaking, a person with a family and a full-time job only has about six hours per week for service to others. As the children get older and leave the nest, and as retirement becomes a factor, more and more time becomes available for it. There's nothing more fulfilling than to see a husband and wife in their retirement years, engaged in "full-time" ministry and doing what they both enjoy.

Your service to others may take the form of hosting a neighborhood Bible study, or working for the Red Cross, or serving as a volunteer for a Christian ministry. It may involve being a witness at work just by putting God first in your life and reflecting His glory. Just be sure that whatever your ministry is, you have a proper balance in your life — meaning that you have set aside sufficient time to be with God and your family and that your job-related commitments are attended to.

If you are a long-time Christian, deeply rooted in the faith, one of the best ways you can be of service to others is to be available to someone who is not as mature as you are in the Lord. The Book of Acts contains the story of Barnabas, an older, more mature Christian who discipled a convert named Paul (Saul) and helped him to mature in the faith so that he (Paul) was able to disciple others. To a great degree, because of the investment Barnabas made in the life of Paul, Paul was able to become the most effective evangelist the world has ever seen. The things he said and the things he did became the basis for Holy Scripture, inspired by God for the reproof and correction of thousands of generations to follow.

One of the people Paul invested himself in was a young Christian named Timothy. Paul took Timothy under his wing and nurtured him, just as he himself had been nurtured by Barnabas. And Paul saw that the chain continued when he told Timothy, "the things you have heard me say in the presence of many witnesses entrust to reliable men who will also be qualified to teach others" (2 Timothy 2:2).

Unless you are a brand-new Christian I believe you should also have a Timothy — someone you can get to know and care for and encourage and disciple.

Ask God to show you who your Timothy might be. And when you identify him (or her), ask for direction in how to become his Paul.

You might take him to a Bible study that you attend. You might begin a one-on-one Bible study. You might even begin by just being there to listen. You can pray with him and show by your example how to begin to become the person God wants him to be. I guarantee that as the teacher you'll learn at least as much as your student.

HOW CAN YOU BE OF SERVICE?

What other areas of service to others is God calling you to? In order to answer that question, you should first ask yourself three other questions:

1) How Much Time Do I Have?

Determine in advance how much time you have available for ministry-related activity without shortchanging the other priority areas of your life. If you have two jobs, you probably have no time. If you are already committed to several people or organizations, you may already be fully committed or overcommitted.

2) What Are My Strengths?

God has given you certain areas of strength which He expects you to use for His purposes. When something you are especially good at comes your way, it's nice to be able to recognize the opportunity. Take inventory of the things you like to do and believe you do well. You might ask others — and especially your spouse if you are married — what they perceive your primary strengths to be.

3) What Are My Weaknesses?

There are bound to be some things you'll never be good at no matter how hard you try, and it may be very painful for you if you become involved in them. Of course, if you hear clearly from God that He is calling you into a particular area of service, you should obey — even if it's something you are not sure you are particularly well suited for.

Moses didn't think he was cut out to be the leader of the Israelite nation, but that's what God called him to, and he proved capable with God's help. Don't rule something out just because you think you are not good at it. But remember, it is at least as likely that God will use you in an area where you already have demonstrated strengths.

Once you've answered the three questions above, you must also be able to recognize the right timing and understand the flow of circumstances.

When it comes to learning to recognize the right timing, the best advice I can give is that if you feel impatient or anxious, instead of speeding up, slow down or stop until you're able to proceed with peace.

Understanding the proper flow of circumstances is closely related to the matter of patience. When things are not flowing smoothly, you may need to exercise patience, or you may need to press on. There's no substitute here for experience. I would say that when it comes to ministry-related activities, it's usually safer to be slightly behind God than to get ahead of Him.

THREE TYPES OF MINISTRY

There are basically three ways you can bring your ministry to the Church and/or the world. The first is, as we've already discussed, person-to-person. The second way is through Christian organizations. The third is through secular organizations.

It can be very fulfilling to invest time in an individual, and I believe that is where most of us can be used most effectively. But there is also the need to invest in organizations which God uses to meet the needs of individuals. The first of these is the Church itself, and there are many ways you can be of service to others through a local congregation of believers. You may teach a class, serve as a deacon or elder, be on a committee, or serve in any number of other ways. There are also numerous other organizations, some religious and some not, that do worthwhile things. Many evangelical Christians are active in non-profit Christian ministries. God does many necessary things through those ministries, and I believe they are a necessary and integral part of the fabric of society today.

That does not mean, however, that every Christian should spend or invest time in Christian organizations. Very often the only ministry-related time a person has should be devoted to serving in his or her local church. It may be that God's plan for the individual includes spending ministry-related time working for a secular charity or even a for-profit organization.

Assuming that time is available, the primary question for a Christian considering what to do with that time is: What would be most reflective of God's will for me at this particular time in my life? God isn't nearly as interested in what we get done as He is in our doing what He wants us to do. Obedience is the name of the game, and those of us who learn to put God's will before our own will prosper naturally and spiritually, both now and in the world to come.

MINISTER THROUGH WHO YOU ARE

Another way to view ministry is to see ourselves as God's image in the eyes of the world. Be and act like someone whom it is desirable to know. As people in an unbelieving world are drawn to us because of who we are rather than what we do or believe, we will become much more effective in accomplishing our primary task — winning souls to Christ and discipling them in their relationship to Him.

The key to being the person God wants you to be in order to win and disciple souls is a direct product of the quality time you spend with Him. And the time you spend witnessing about Him simply by being who you are is much more likely to occur during your time with family members or on the job than while you're serving the needs of your local church or a Christian ministry. So on one hand we need to guard the time we commit to so-called ministry (service to others), and on the other hand we need to see ourselves as full-time ministers. Maintain God's balance in your commitments, and you will be God's witness wherever you are.

THE IMPORTANCE OF WITNESSING FOR CHRIST

Jesus tells us in Matthew 28:19 that we are to "go and make disciples of all nations, baptizing them in the name of the Father and of the Son and of the Holy Spirit, and teaching them to obey everything" that He has commanded us. Now, that's a rather large order. How do we make disciples of nations? How do we teach them to obey all His commandments?

It all begins with our own commitment to obedience. If we know Christ as Savior and are committed to Him as our Lord, we have all we need to begin discipling the nations. As you concentrate on becoming the person God wants you to be, you *will* be given the opportunity to introduce someone else to Christ. Your job is *first* to learn to recognize the opportunity and *second* to be willing to be obedient. God will do the rest.

Now before you tune me out because you know you're not an evangelist, let me tell you that neither am I. My strength is not leading people to Christ. I'm not very good at it. What I *am* good at is helping them move from where they are *after* they've made a commitment to Christ. But I have a responsibility, a mandate from God, to introduce certain people to Him. If I don't, someone else may, but I'll miss the blessing God has for me. Not only that, but I have to contend with the possibility that if I don't talk to them about Christ, it could be that no one else will. The fact of the matter is, you cannot be committed to becoming the person God wants you to be unless you're willing to present the gospel to someone else. Even if you never have the opportunity to do it, you must be willing.

If you're willing to make the commitment to witness to someone else, God will take care of the rest. Let me share with you how He did that in my life.

Soon after asking Christ into my own life in 1976, I was in my law office meeting with a prospective client and her mother. The young lady had been involved in a serious automobile accident, and her pelvis had been severely fractured. She could not walk normally, was in pain, and feared that she would not be able to have children. Both the daughter and mother were tearful and very distraught.

I knew God wanted me to share my faith with them. But if I did, I risked offending them and thereby losing a lucrative personal injury case. On the other hand, God was telling me to tell them about Him. I had no idea where to start. I didn't know the Bible; I didn't know *anything*. But there was no doubt that God was telling me to act. I really don't remember much of what I said that day, but I did share with them how I had come to know Jesus Christ and how that decision had changed my life. I didn't ask them to pray with me, but I at least planted the seed. They listened graciously and did not become angry, and I ultimately received a handsome fee from their case.

As the weeks and months rolled by, more and more unsaved clients came to me. With that experience behind me, I tried to be sensitive to when God was telling me to share my faith, and I did share it when I could. But I was always embarrassed to ask them to pray with me. Instead, whenever it got down to that, I would call one of the pastors at my church, which was just next door to my office. Then I'd take my client to his office, and he would pray with them to receive Christ.

After several months of running back and forth, the pastor told me, "Ken, you've got to start doing this yourself."

"Oh no, not me," I said.

But not long after that, I did ask a client to pray with me. I was sure he'd say no, and I was prepared for failure. To my amazement, he said yes, we prayed, and I had taken a giant step in obedience. Since then I've been able to lead dozens of people to the Lord, not because I'm good at it, but because God has sent them to me when *they* were ready.

SOME AIDS TO WITNESSING

I know many people who want to witness for Christ, but they don't feel equipped to do it. They need something to guide them.

That's understandable. For those people there are some excellent aids to witnessing that can be used with great effect. There are courses you can take, Bibles that have key passages marked, tracts and pamphlets you can read or hand out. And there are audio and videotapes that you can share.

The aid I like the best was developed by Campus Crusade for Christ and is titled *Four Spiritual Laws*. It has been copied and retitled by different organizations, but the content is the same. This little tract is designed to be read by the person witnessing and by the person being witnessed to. It explains God's plan for mankind in four easy to understand steps and reprints the Bible verses that support each of those steps. It takes about seven minutes to read through the whole thing, and it includes a prayer which can be read by the unsaved person or recited by both saved and unsaved together.

This tract is so effective that it is commonplace for people to accept Christ just by reading it to themselves. I'll never forget the time I picked up a hitchhiker in a driving rain. No sooner had he gotten in the car than he said something that led me to ask him about his relationship with God. I gave him this little tract, and he read it in the course of our short drive. When he finished, I asked him if he would like to pray the prayer at the end. He said yes, and before he got out of my car, less than ten minutes after he'd gotten in, he prayed to receive Christ. Now that's what I call effective!

There are two final questions regarding witnessing. To whom do you witness? And how do you know when the time is right for witnessing?

Part of the answer to that first question has to do with your own personality. God isn't likely to start with the most difficult person you can think of. In fact, chances are, the person will be a complete stranger to you or at best a casual acquaintance. So you don't have to start worrying about whether it's your parent or your boss.

The best thing you can do is to ask God during your quiet time with Him to show you who the person is. Once He does that — once you know beyond a reasonable doubt *who* the person is — then you can make plans for how to approach him. Remember, there is one person God most wants you to witness to first. He may show you well in advance, and He may show you with little or no warning. Be ready to be willing. As the Bible says, "Always be prepared to give an answer to everyone who asks you to give the reason for the hope that you have" (1 Peter 3:15). God will do the rest.

Remember, the first time you tell someone about Christ will be the hardest time. It will become increasingly easier after that.

Now as to the second question, timing is always critical, but I know of no one who hasn't made mistakes in the past and doesn't expect to make mistakes in the future. There are also times when we don't need to ask a person whether he wants to accept Christ. I had a man come to me recently for counseling, and he asked me, "What must I do to be saved?" It certainly didn't take any guesswork in that case to figure out *when* God wanted me to present the gospel. But that is a rare experience.

One good way to see if the timing is right is to ask a question such as, "Where do you go to church?" or "What was your family's religious background?" If a question like that doesn't lead anywhere, you might wait for a more opportune time.

Another way to judge whether it's the proper time to talk to someone about Christ is to consider what you know about what's going on in the person's life. If he or she is in the midst of a number of problems and trials, he or she may be more open to spiritual things than is immediately apparent. Sometimes a person who sounds very negative about spiritual things is actually very ready to receive the gospel. On the other hand, don't get into an argument. Bow out graciously and quickly if that's the direction the conversation is taking.

The only time I consistently risk imposing myself on another is when I think he is about to die. In that situation I would definitely not wait until later, because the opportunity may never come.

The best advice I can give on the matter of timing is to be available. God is perfectly capable of telling you *when* if He knows you're willing. Sometimes I go for months without witnessing, but I try to always be ready and willing when God presents the opportunity.

That concludes our discussion of the four priority areas of life. Coming up next, I'm going to tell you how to deal with those aggravating interruptions that can really put a crimp in your day!

PRACTICE PROPER PRIORITIZING

1) As honestly as you can, list the four priorities of life in the way you *currently* have them prioritized. What changes do you see that you need to make?

2) Do you believe your present job is representative of God's will for you? If not, what changes do you need to make in your attitude and performance that will enable God to improve the situation?

3) Are there conflicts between your family-related activities and your job-related activities? If so, what changes need to be made to strike a godly balance?

4) What special strengths has God given you that He expects you to use in service to others?

5) After you've made a list of your own strengths, ask a close friend (perhaps your spouse) to draw up a list of your strengths as he or she sees them. What does your friend's list tell you about yourself? Does it agree with the list you prepared?

PART FOUR

PUTTING IT TOGETHER ON A DAILY BASIS

12

Dealing with Interruptions

ave you ever thought of interruptions as destructive? They are, you know. They may seem to be unavoidable at times, and they are definitely necessary at times, but they are destructive. They destroy your train of thought or your course of action whenever they occur.

Many Christians seem to think it's bad or even un-Christian behavior to refuse to permit interruptions. And while there certainly are situations where refusing an interruption would be unwise or undesirable, I suspect that most attempted interruptions should be at least partially resisted.

The Bible tells us that Jesus Christ resisted interruptions. For example, He knew He had to go into Jerusalem, even though He was going to be beaten and crucified there. When Peter tried to "interrupt" the Lord's journey to Jerusalem, Christ said, "Out of my sight, Satan! You are a stumbling block to me" (Matthew 16:23). Luke 9:51 tells us, "As the time approached for him to be taken up to heaven, Jesus resolutely set out for Jerusalem." He would not be dissuaded from the task which had been set before Him — and for the most part I believe that should be our attitude with regard to interruptions that seek to keep us from doing what we should be doing. Sometimes Jesus allowed Himself to be "interrupted" by people seeking His assistance, but that was always because He had made the decision that the "interruption" was a higher priority than the task at hand. Always He sought to do what His Father told Him to do — and that must be our attitude. Later on we will talk about what to do when an interruption deserves to take precedence over presently planned activity. The vast majority of the things that interrupt us are not deserving of such a high priority.

Do you ever resent being interrupted? I know I do. While God certainly doesn't want us to be resentful, unless we take steps in advance to avoid the interruptions God wants us to avoid, we'll fall victim to them. Then not only have we not used our time as God wanted us to, but very likely we'll have to spend more time undoing the damage caused by our failure to be prepared for the interruption. We'll need to repair relationships with others, or ask God for forgiveness for the bad attitude the interruption caused in us, or sometimes both.

Do you know how you can tell people you don't want to be interrupted without offending them? It's very easy to handle almost any situation if you've given the subject a little thought ahead of time.

DEALING WITH TELEPHONE INTERRUPTIONS

When was the last time you let the telephone interrupt what you were doing? The answer probably is, the last time you answered it.

As convenient as it is at times, the telephone can be as destructive to God's plan for our time as anything I know of. No one would think of interrupting you in person at certain times, and yet they think nothing of waking you up, keeping you from getting to sleep, or distracting you during any part of the day. The person on the other end of the line can always say it wasn't his intention to interrupt when you were doing something important. After all, he didn't know what you were doing when he called. That's why it's *your* responsibility to control the interruption, not his.

The next time your phone rings at a time when you do not wish to be interrupted, remember that you have two options.

1) You Can Choose Not to Answer It

The first option is just to let it ring. Most of us would never seriously consider exercising that alternative, but believe me, there are times when you should do exactly that. In Chapter 5 I told you what happened in my house when we enforced the rule that the telephone would not be answered during dinner. It seemed strange at first, but we all got used to it, and soon we realized that there was no natural reason why we had to be slaves to Ma Bell.

2) You Can Ask, "When Can I Call You Back?"

Let's assume that you're right in the middle of your quiet time, and the phone rings. It's your next-door neighbor, and she's really upset because her husband has just told her he's leaving her. She is absolutely devastated, and you're the only person in the whole world she can talk to about it.

How's that for a pressure-packed situation? As a committed Christian, is there justification for not either spending the next hour listening to her or asking her to come right over? In fact, is there any way you can avoid the temptation of hearing all about it? She wants to talk, you want to listen, and the only sacrifice is your time with God.

What if, instead of your quiet time, you were just leaving to have tea with the President of the United States? How would you handle the interruption then? Would you be more motivated to postpone it?

Assuming that you believe God wants you to complete your scheduled time with Him, how could you handle this emergency? First, you would express your own devastation at the news. In a minute or two you would assure your neighbor of your concern for her and her situation.

Next, you might set a time later in the day that you will come over to talk to her or have her come to you. You could encourage her to spend some time with the Lord until the two of you can get together. You might tell her that you will stop everything and immediately begin to pray for her and her husband.

As long as you don't tell her what *you* are doing, it won't occur to her to be offended. It's possible she will be temporarily disappointed that she can't talk to you for an unlimited time right then, but as soon as you adjust her expectations and set up a time when you will be able to get together with her, she'll begin to look forward to that.

Don't ever make the mistake of telling the other person what you are doing with your time. If you do, you'll almost always run the risk of offending them because they'll compare *their* need with *your* priority and feel they are a lower priority. While that's not necessarily true, it will seem so. The fact is, God has a *best* time for everything, and you're just trying to be obedient to Him as you schedule *when* you will handle the interruption.

Set Up a Time for Receiving Calls

One of the keys to time management and personal organization as it relates to the telephone in an office environment may be to have a time designated for telephone calls. If you have a secretary or someone on the front lines to filter your calls for you, that's great. Or it may be that your job is such that you are expected to field your own calls from the outside. In either case, there are ways to improve the use of your non-telephone time by limiting or avoiding telephone interruptions.

First, we'll address the situation where you have a secretary. You need to decide in advance when you wish to receive telephone calls. In my case I've designated 9:30-11:30 A.M. as the period during which my staff knows

I can be interrupted with phone calls. Unless I specifically request otherwise or I'm already on the phone, all incoming calls are announced during that time period. I give a priority to taking calls during that time. At all other times during the day, I retain the freedom to take any call that comes in, but the chances are much greater that I won't have time because I've given other things priority.

If you don't have a secretary, you'll have to do the screening yourself, but the same principle applies. When you do answer during a time that you have not established as telephone time, you can be polite but brief. Explain that you can't talk right then, but that you will call them back by a certain time. Do *not* explain in detail why you cannot talk now. Your caller will form a satisfactory mental picture of why he thinks you're busy, which will probably be much better than any reason *you* can give him.

Remember, you always retain the right to talk to anyone you want to at any time. However, most of us need to establish the discipline of not talking just because the opportunity presents itself. If what you're doing before the interruption deserves priority, then give it priority, even though it means calling the person back later.

Dealing with Telephone Solicitors

Telephone solicitation is now part of the American way — and judging by the increasing number of calls I'm getting, it's proving to be quite successful.

For years I was frustrated by my inability to avoid telephone solicitors. Not only was the call interrupting something I was doing that was of a higher priority, but the caller usually offended me before I had managed to end the conversation. I tried everything. I was rude. I was silent. I would put the phone down and walk away. I would hang up. I would complain to the phone company. But mostly I was just frustrated by my inability to prevent the calls.

One day I decided to apply my basic philosophy of problem-solving to the matter of telephone solicitation. My philosophy is that what I can't do anything about, I won't worry about. With that decision made, I now set about trying to decide how not to worry about it, or more accurately, how to not let it bother me. Finally God gave me the answer.

Now I look forward to receiving calls from telephone solicitors. I'm even tempted to answer the phone during dinner, which we almost never do, just to be able to receive their calls. (Nobody ever calls us during dinner anymore, except telephone solicitors.) When I get them on the phone now, I ask for some of their time when they are through, and they always agree to that because it means they get to make their pitch. I then respond politely to all their initial questions. I let them complete their presentation before I take my turn.

After we've discussed what they wanted to discuss, I remind them that it's my turn. I then ask if they know Jesus Christ as their personal Savior. I present the gospel. If they are local, I invite them to go to church with Pat and me. I give my testimony. I offer to send them a Bible if I can have their address. I've led one person to the Lord in this way and have witnessed to many others. Who knows? The next one to be saved may be the one who calls you tonight — right after dinner.

HANDLING INTERRUPTIONS AT THE OFFICE

How can you handle people who insist on interrupting you when you're in your office trying to get your work done?

1) Put a "Do Not Disturb" Sign on Your Door

First, let's assume you've got an office with a door you can close. When you want to avoid interruptions, just put an appropriate sign or note on your door and close it. If necessary, clear the procedure with your superior. Your sign or note might be subtle (such as, "Please do not disturb until 10:00 A.M."). Or it might be more direct (such as, "Upon pain of death, do not open this door until 10:00 A.M."). The nicer you are, the less others will be tempted to test your resolve.

If someone does knock, the easiest way to resist the interruption is simply not to respond. All but the most fearless will give up at that point. If you do answer, you have just given up your greatest advantage. Now you will have to take the initiative to avoid further intrusion.

2) If Someone Insists on Coming in, Meet Him at the Door

What if your visitor either continues to knock until you answer or even opens the door without your permission? In that case, you should immediately rise from your sitting position and walk toward him. The closer to the doorway you can keep him, the better off you'll be.

Then field the question or concern as politely as possible, indicating with body language that you would like to pursue the matter no longer than absolutely necessary.

3) Move the Conversation to a Neutral Location

If you still can't end the interruption, try moving the guest and the conversation out of your office toward a neutral location such as the watercooler or coffeepot. Your aim is to quickly end the conversation there and then get back to your office — alone.

4) Explain That You Really Need to Avoid Interruptions

It shouldn't take long for everyone to understand that you're serious when the sign or note is on your door, but you must enforce your request for privacy when you are interrupted. Otherwise your request will eventually be ignored. It's okay to make exceptions, but they need to be just that — exceptions, not the general rule. Explain that you put the sign or note up because you really can't afford to be interrupted right now. And be sure to take your sign or note down when it's not needed. If it stays in place all or most of the time, it's likely to get less attention.

It's much more difficult to deflect an interruption when you don't have a door you can close, but it is possible. If you can surround yourself with some type of barrier, such as a screen or divider, that you can attach your sign or note to, you'll be much better off.

The key to avoiding interruption is first to put the world on notice that you don't want to be interrupted, and then to politely make that point again with whoever chooses to ignore your notice.

5) When You Are Trying to Have Your Quiet Time, Have Your Bible Open on Your Desk or on Your Lap

Almost no one will choose to interrupt you directly if they realize you're talking to God or even thinking about Him.

6) Always Try to Be Nice About It

The nicer you are to people, the more inclined they are to respect your wishes. Of course the nicer you are, the more difficult it is for you to run the risk of offending someone by trying to shield yourself from interruption. That's when it's helpful to have your priorities so in order that you feel confident God wants you to avoid the interruption.

7) Find a "Hideaway"

It might be that you can find a place other than your regular work station when you want to avoid interruption. See if your boss can help you. It's best to have a door to close, but just being in a different location might help send the message to others. If all else fails, your special hideaway might even be somewhere away from the office — again provided you have your boss's permission.

DEALING WITH DROP-INS

Suppose it's 10:00 on Tuesday morning, and you are a homemaker who has just established a schedule for your time. You've decided that 10:00-11:00 on Tuesday is when you'll do the vacuuming each week.

The doorbell rings. It's your neighbor, Sally, who often drops by to chat. Now you've never minded her dropping in before because you never had a schedule. But now that you do, you really want to make it work.

How do you handle this interruption without offending Sally? Well, go ahead and invite her in, but only far enough to reach your written schedule. Show her how excited you are to have a schedule and how beneficial you feel it's going to be in helping you get better organized. After you've shown her the part about vacuuming on Tuesday morning, let her down slowly. Ask her when you can schedule time to come over to her house or for her to come back to yours. Show her that she's important enough to you that you want to include her in your schedule. Since it's the first time, you might even make this visit the exception, but be careful — your own resolve might slip the next time if you're not disciplined.

If you're purposeful about your relationship with Sally and put some thought into it, you can probably accomplish much more in the relationship and in her life. She'll see that she is a priority. She'll value the time you have set aside to be with her. You'll be able to decide in advance how to spend that time.

RESISTING THE TEMPTATION OF INTERRUPTIONS

I think that many times the reason we're interrupted is because we want to be. I know that I used to look for opportunities to avoid doing what I was supposed to be doing. Almost any excuse was good enough, and there was a great deal of anxiety in my life as a result.

I have since learned that the first step in avoiding distractions is to decide in advance that you're not looking for one and that if one comes your way you'll resist it.

Another problem many people have is lack of focus. They can't seem to concentrate on what they're supposed to be doing and so constantly drift off into other things. While this lack of focus or concentration may require medical or psychological help, sometimes it's just a matter of a lack of discipline. If that is the problem, here are some suggestions:

Try to work in an interruption-free environment. Avoid radios, TVs, stereos, and the like. Resist talking to other people. Have an organized and clutter-free desk or work area. Have a written plan for how you're supposed to spend your time. Work from an outline. When reading, use a straight edge. Plan periodic breaks to get up and walk around — but don't forget to come back to work when it's time. Get plenty of sleep at night. Establish the habit of doing the same thing at the same time. Keep track of your time and how you spend it. Use a timer to break your work up into fifteen- or thirty- or sixty-minute segments.

If you suspect a medical problem because of an inability to concentrate or stay focused, have your eyes and ears examined. You may need to consult a Christian psychologist who can look at your situation from a spiritual and emotional perspective.

And don't forget to ask God's help. He can and will give you supernatural insight into what is causing you to fall prey to distractions. Is it sin in your life? Is it something that only He can reveal to you?

Being easily distracted is not something to just accept. View it as something to be dealt with, and continue to seek the solution. In the meantime, learn to compensate for it by concentrating on personal planning and organization.

WHEN SHOULD INTERRUPTIONS BE ALLOWED?

My philosophy of life generally is that God has a plan, and within that plan there are a few things subject to my influence and control. However, most of the things included within God's plan are not subject to my control.

What I can't do anything about, I don't believe God wants me to worry about. If I waste my time and energy worrying about those things I can't affect, I'm disobeying God.

As well as I can, I plan each day in advance. I know what I must do, what I'd like to do, and what there is to do if there's time left over. I'm confident that my daily plan is what God wants it to be because I spend sufficient time with Him daily for Him to let me know of any serious miscalculations in the plan.

However, I have absolutely no idea what each day will actually look like.

One of the ways God has of informing me of the differences between my plan and His is through interruptions.

As we grow in knowledge and grace, we learn how to distinguish between those interruptions God wants us to resist and those which reflect His plan for us. That's called discernment. The basic rule is that if you can't think of a way to effectively resist an interruption and still provide a good witness, then allow yourself to be interrupted.

A baby's cry is generally the beginning of an interruption that is to be permitted. So is the wail of a siren; the closer it gets, the more permissible it becomes. The unmistakable tone in a boss's voice, the terror in a child's voice, your dog's bark at midnight, and the screech of tires immediately behind you are some of the many interruptions that must be permitted at times. We all learn sooner or later to accept the inevitable.

The question is, "Is this interruption God's will for me?" If so, you'd better say yes. But if not, remember to say no, in love.

PRACTICE RESISTING INTERRUPTIONS

1) Is there one person who is the source of most of the interruptions in your life? If so, decide now how you will handle this person the next time he or she interrupts you.

2) Think back over the past couple of days and see how many times your work was interrupted. How many of those interruptions could have been avoided? What problems did those interruptions cause you? What can you do to avoid similar interruptions in the future?

3) Ask yourself if you are ever guilty of unnecessarily interrupting others. If you are, resolve that you will be more respectful of other people's time in the future.

13

Improving Your Life Through Self-discipline and Accountability

L et me begin this chapter by admitting that self-discipline is not a fun topic. And yet, you can never be or become the person God wants you to be without it. A measure of self-discipline is necessary to execute or implement the life-changing procedures and plans we've been discussing throughout this book. Self-discipline can best be achieved by understanding that we are accountable for our actions and the revelation we have received, and then acting upon that understanding.

There are areas in each of our lives in which we do exercise self-discipline, even though we may not think of it in those terms. For instance, most of us get up in the morning even when we may not feel like it — maybe not when we know we should get up, but at least in time to do what we have to do. Some of us do the things we know we should do around the house on weekends, not because we necessarily feel like it, but because we know we should, or because we know that someone else expects us to do them — and that is self-discipline in action.

But there's another way to look at this matter of self-discipline. Instead of just doing those things that others require of us or that we feel we have no real choice about, we can decide in advance what those things are that we should do and then design a process of learning to do them in a relatively painless way.

Before going any further, I think it would be a good idea to define what I mean by *self-discipline*. Self-discipline is the training and control of one's own actions and emotions, usually for self-improvement. But how can we go about doing that? Can we just decide to gain control and do it? I don't think so. What is really needed is a series of decisions, one after the other, exercising self-discipline and self-control in situation after situation. The hardest decision, I believe, is the first — when you decide that you're going to do whatever is required to become more disciplined.

SELF-DISCIPLINE FROM GOD'S PERSPECTIVE

It's impossible for a Christian to look at the matter of self-discipline without realizing that the word is really a contradiction. Ideally there should not be any such thing as *self*-discipline. God, through the empowering of the Holy Spirit, provides us with first the insight and then the ability to do the things He wants us to do. Of course, it's up to us to recognize and accept that direction, but it's there for the asking, and often we don't even have to consciously ask for it.

The first step in acquiring "God-directed discipline" is to want to have it — to be motivated to want to do the things God asks us to do. Very often that just seems to come with the territory of being a Christian. But for some people the desire to do what God wants is a real struggle. If that's the case with you, then ask God to give you the desire to be obedient to Him. Strive to be obedient to the words of Romans 12:1 — "Therefore, I urge you, brothers, in view of God's mercy, to offer your bodies as living sacrifices, holy and pleasing to God — which is your spiritual worship."

The Apostle Paul also had this to say about self-discipline: "I beat my body and make it my slave so that after I have preached to others, I myself will not be disqualified for the prize" (1 Corinthians 9:27).

And of course "self-control" is listed as part of the fruit of the Spirit in Galatians 5:22.

If you would acquire "God-directed discipline," you must maintain a relationship with God so He can provide you with ongoing direction. You need to have a working knowledge of what it means to be obedient to Him in specific situations. The only way to know consistently what God wants you to do is to spend sufficient time with Him on a regular basis. The reason for this is twofold. Not only do you need to be available to hear Him when He has something to say to you, but you also need to have the assurance that if you haven't heard from Him, He hasn't had anything to say on the subject.

In my opinion, it's that second part that produces the encouragement to walk the walk God has called us to. It's one thing to know what God wants us to do and do it, and it's quite another thing to have the ongoing motivation and encouragement to continue to walk it out even when you don't feel

God's direction in the process. If you know you've done what you needed to do to receive His direction and just haven't gotten any, it's easier to keep on keeping on. You have the peace of knowing you are being obedient.

No matter how undisciplined you think you are, you can acquire God-directed discipline through spending time with Him on a regular basis.

WHERE SHOULD YOU BEGIN?

If you have a regular quiet time and still don't know where God wants you to begin to exercise self-discipline, let me give you a few possible areas to consider.

What about your physical well-being? Are you getting sufficient sleep? Have you made it a practice to get a physical exam periodically? If so, have you followed your doctor's advice with regard to such things as weight, diet and exercise? What about your relationships? Have you exercised the discipline to hold up your part of the bargain with the family? What about your job? Have you exercised the discipline to be organized enough so you know the Lord is well pleased (not to mention your employer)? What about your responsibilities within your church? Any room for improvement there?

Just in case you are still at a loss for direction on where you might start, if you're married you might ask your wife, or even your children. If you're not married, you might ask your close friends or people at work. Your pastor or your employer might also be good points of reference.

Usually the problem isn't so much where you need self-discipline as it is a matter of getting started on one of any number of areas. It's often hard to know where to start. If that's the case with you, make a list of several areas in which you have not exercised discipline. Then pick the one that will relieve you from the most pressure. Carve out some time to decide just what the best approach might be. For instance, if it's in the area of physical exercise, you might go sign up for a weight lifting course. It's not that you necessarily want to increase your strength — you just want to establish a routine of getting regular exercise. You could as easily decide on swimming or golf. The idea is to begin somewhere — anywhere — but begin!

DON'T DAMAGE GOD'S REPUTATION

The manner in which we conduct ourselves is extremely important. When we project an image that is inconsistent with the image God wants us to project, we are running the risk of damaging God's reputation. It's not that God isn't perfectly capable of taking care of His own reputation, but when He has to overcome our own poor witness in the process, we're likely to have to suffer some consequences.

For example, one area where I struggle with self-discipline is in my diet. I'm blessed with a high metabolism, and I don't have a serious weight problem, but that's a blessing and a curse. Since it doesn't show too much, I don't have much natural incentive to eat the things I should eat and to avoid the things I should avoid. I know there are natural as well as spiritual consequences to my disobedience, but so far I've made little progress on being disciplined in this area. When I'm with others who need to exercise more self-control than I do in this area, I know I tempt them to sin because of my bad example.

The more we bring our lives under the control of God-directed discipline, the less likely we are to fail and thus be bad witnesses for Christ — although there will always be room for improvement. For instance, I have a hard time keeping my mouth shut when a stranger does something dumb, such as blocking me in the parking lot. I have a tendency to want to correct people that I perceive to be, well, stupid. I did that not long ago, and then I saw a member of my church standing there watching me. To top it off, one of the people I was correcting hadn't even done what I was correcting him for. I wasn't being a good witness for the Lord, and I was sorry. I was also humbled. All I could do was ask God's forgiveness and seek more God-directed discipline in the future in that area of my life.

HOW TO OBTAIN GOD-DIRECTED DISCIPLINE

1) Ask for God's Help
By far the most effective thing you can do to get God-directed discipline into your life is to make it a matter of regular, consistent prayer. Ask God to show you the things that will be most effective in helping you establish self-discipline where it does not now exist. For your prayer life to be effective, you absolutely must have the discipline to pray regularly and consistently.

2) Establish Regular Routines
The next most effective technique that I know of to conquer lack of discipline is to establish some habits and routines in the areas needing the most attention. Many of the problems which we see as caused by lack of discipline

are also included in such problem areas as procrastination, overcommitment, and lack of punctuality.

The best way to use a routine as a means of defeating lack of discipline is to approach it from the positive side of the spectrum. Let's say your lack of discipline involves watching too much television. You can handle it the hard way, by simply deciding to stop watching so much TV, or you can approach it from the standpoint of deciding what you're going to do with some of that TV time. For example, you may decide that you'll use the time between 8 and 10 P.M. on Tuesdays and Thursdays to catch up on those projects that need to be done around the house. Design a plan of attack so you will know what you're going to do first, second, and so on. Before you know it, you'll be so involved in your projects that hopefully you'll wonder how you ever found all that time to watch TV.

The idea is that rather than giving something up that you want to do, concentrate on something that you know is a better use of your time. This approach can apply to all areas of your life.

3) Find a Partner

Another effective technique for establishing discipline in an area is to plan to do whatever it is you're supposed to be doing with someone else. This adds the element of accountability. If you can do it with someone you enjoy being with, so much the better.

For example, you may find it hard to go on a diet. But if you have a friend who will go on a diet at the same time, the two of you will be able to give each other support and encouragement, and you'll find that the diet will be much easier to adhere to. You may not need to go on a diet — but the principle holds true in any area of endeavor.

WHAT IT MEANS TO BE ACCOUNTABLE

God-directed discipline is a necessary ingredient of the ordered and fulfilling life. Another aspect of such a life is Spirit-led accountability.

Spirit-led accountability is a process of learning to be submitted to God so we can assume the responsibility or liability He *wants* us to assume. Ironically, the more "accountable" we are according to that definition, the more we allow God to assume responsibility for our lives. We free Him to assume the liability for all those areas He wants surrendered to Him, leaving us with relatively little weight to carry.

Unfortunately, many Christians do not understand this concept at all.

Many others understand it only partially. An example is the formation of so-called "accountability groups." The typical way such a group might operate is for each member to bring his or her problems to the group for comment or advice. Everyone in the group is equal to everyone else from the viewpoint of responsibility. What that really translates into most of the time is that no one is responsible for anyone. It quickly becomes a fellowship or sharing group. Of course, there's nothing wrong with forming a group for fellowship or mutual sharing. But too often Christians are misled into thinking they are submitted to a group or to a process when the people to whom they are voluntarily submitted don't feel the responsibility. It's a circuitous street that often goes nowhere.

It's impossible to be submitted to someone who doesn't know he has that authority or who doesn't choose to exercise that authority. Remember, though, that for a Christian, Christ-centered accountability can only be voluntary. If it is imposed by others, it is no longer Christ-centered.

In my experience, relatively few Christians hold themselves accountable or, more accurately, place themselves in a position to be held accountable. The problem is that God's plan includes our placing other people above us, and too often we see that as an undesirable *infringement* on our freedom. It's really just the opposite — it's the *pathway* to freedom.

When Should We Be Accountable?

The easy answer to the question of *when* we are to be accountable is, *now*. But is it that easy? The answer to that question really depends on *what* you're doing. In those areas of your life where you're being obedient, you may not need much accountability to stay obedient.

It's probably easiest to address the answer of *when* by identifying areas of conscious disobedience. We all have them. If you will just list on a sheet of paper the areas in which you feel there's a good likelihood that you're not being totally obedient, you can then begin to decide *when* you should submit yourself to a conscious process of accountability.

As you reflect on these areas of disobedience, ask yourself if you would be less likely to be disobedient if someone knew what you were doing in that particular area.

Not too long ago my wife, Pat, brought up an area for discussion. She has been a compulsive eater for years. I used to wonder how she exercised the discipline to not eat dinner, only to find out that she habitually ate junk food before or after dinner. The office where she works supplies free cookies and pastries, and in the course of trying to lose weight for her high school reunion she gained ten pounds. As we discussed her inability to get a handle on her eating habits, I suggested that she make a commitment to do two things. One: assess herself a fine every time she ate something she wasn't supposed to; and two: telephone me just before she took the first bite. The call to me wasn't for approval or disapproval, but just a step she would take as part of getting ready to be disobedient.

She agreed to try that plan. We're now several weeks into it, and she hasn't slipped one time. She has discovered that just knowing that she needs to notify me and assess herself a fine has helped her overcome — at least temporarily — a lifelong habit of disobedience. Incidentally, she still has the freedom to eat junk food on weekends. By the way, Pat is physically very attractive — she's never been fat, just disobedient.

When should you begin to hold *yourself* accountable? In some measure, that depends on how great you want the pain to become. Disobedience to God almost always produces pain; obedience usually brings freedom from pain; and accountability helps to produce obedience. That is a great motivation for accountability.

Where Should We Be Accountable?

What are some of the areas in which we should hold ourselves accountable to others? Actually the areas can be broken down into the same divisions that our priorities can be divided into: our relationship with God, our families, our jobs, and our efforts to serve others in God's name. Another way of looking at areas of accountability is: 1) our relationships, 2) our time, and 3) our money and material possessions. A third approach is to look at the natural and the spiritual.

All three of these approaches are all-inclusive. The key is not so much the system we use to obtain a balance as it is to do something to enable us to be more responsive to God than we're likely to be if we operate with no system.

We should realize that God holds us to a certain degree of accountability even when we make no effort to take the initiative. And far more than we realize, we are really held responsible for every single thing we do and say. There are natural and spiritual consequences to everything. If I draw a sharp knife across my finger, it will bleed. If I draw that same knife deeply enough across my wrist, I will bleed to death. These are natural consequences. If I lie and steal, I will bleed spiritually. If I worship other gods to the exclusion of

Jesus Christ, I will become spiritually destitute. God holds us accountable quite independently of our own efforts to hold ourselves accountable.

So what do we accomplish by holding ourselves accountable? We more closely find and follow God's plan for our lives. We find ways to reduce the cuts and bruises. We lessen or avoid the backsliding or stunting of growth that might otherwise occur.

Establishing a System of Accountability

There are three basic ways to proceed. One is to form a relationship with one person and submit your decision-making process to him or her. This approach requires a very high degree of commitment for you and the other person. It is also subject to the greatest danger. You run the risk of letting the relationship disintegrate into a controlling process, with the other person possibly assuming more responsibility than is healthy for either of you. But if the relationship retains a Christ-centered balance, it is probably most likely to produce real Christlike change in your life.

The second way to proceed is through participation in an accountability group that really does hold its members accountable for their actions, as opposed to the fellowship group we discussed earlier. This approach can be very effective if everyone understands how the process should work. There needs to be a willingness to assume responsibility for each other and to take the initiative in discovering each other's shortcomings.

The third approach is a combination of the other two. It is a one-on-one relationship with several different people. This runs less danger of abuse than a one-on-one with just one person and is less likely to suffer the dilution of intensity that a group approach often experiences. The biggest liability of this approach is that it requires a great deal of your time. You may spend much time in meetings; however, those meetings can produce great benefit.

If you have no accountability process in place, I encourage you to begin with either one individual in whom you have confidence or a small group. Work your way toward the balance that seems best for you and ask God to guide you. For the process to work, there must be mutual fulfillment. It's the process that's important, and God can supply the right people at the right time.

Accountability Can Reduce Stress

One of the primary benefits of designing a system of accountability which assures that someone else (or several others) is part of your decision-making process is that it can remove stress and accompanying anxiety from your life.

Suppose you lack confidence in your ability to make good decisions in a certain area of your life. If you enlist the help of one or more Christian friends, you could establish a system of accountability whereby you would spend one hour per week meeting with the group. Your concerns would be the focal point for that hour. After a couple of meetings to establish a comfort level, you would probably find that you could begin to share much detail about your life and problems. Your friends will not only help you make decisions, but will hold you accountable for your actions with regard to those decisions and will critique your performance after the fact. Before long you will have much greater confidence in your decision-making ability.

If you know there are areas of your life that are not pleasing to the Lord, you can gradually make the members of your group aware of your struggle in these areas. As you receive good advice and continuing prayer support, you should move toward overcoming these problem areas.

You will soon come to look at the challenges in your life through the eyes of your accountability group. You will anticipate what the group's reaction will be in advance, and you will start doing many things right on an almost automatic basis. As a result, your life will be more and more free of unproductive stress.

REMEMBER THE IMPORTANCE OF PLANNING

If you want to become responsible and reliable, you must have a regular time for personal planning and daily organization. Again, assuming you don't have any time set aside for that, you might want to begin with ten or fifteen minutes. Even that will sound like a long time until you learn to fill it wisely. Once you establish the habit of having that time available, you may very well find ways to use even more.

During this planning time, you need to do several things in order to improve your ability to be reliable. The first is to make a list of all the commitments you've made to others, including God. Remember your spouse, your children, your boss, your coworkers, your friends, your pastor, and everyone you talked to the day before. Ideally you might carry a 3 x 5" card and write down any commitments you make.

Next, you need to establish a date by which you will fulfill every commitment you've made. Some of them will be very short-term and should be done immediately. Others will take longer and may need to be broken down

NEW COMMITMENTS

During your planning time each day, you should list all commitments that you have made to anyone since your last planning session, and enter the date your effort will begin in the "Begin" column. Remember commitments made to pray for others, and commitments made to God, your spouse, your children, your boss, your coworkers, your friends, your pastor. Next, enter the date by which you plan to fulfill the commitment in the "End" column. This list should be reviewed daily, and used when you are formulating your Daily and Weekly To Do lists. When the commitment has been fulfilled, enter the date it was fulfilled in the "Completed" column. If you find that you are not fulfilling your commitment in timely fashion, contact the person you are committed to, and either establish a new "End" date, or ask to be forgiven and released from the commitment.

COMMITMENT/ACTIVITY	BEGIN	END	COMPLETED
Manage Deale campaign	12/15	3/1	
Fund-raising campaign	1/1	4/1	
Pra~ ~Dana	~12/1~		
~ganize coffee ministry at church	1/1	7/1	
Office Bible study	1/2	ongoing	
Teach at Singles Sunday School	2/14	2/14	

Figure 16—See Form 11 in back of book

into steps, each step with its own deadline. See Figure 16 here and Form 11 at the back of this book.

Finally, you need to report back to the person to whom you made the commitment. Even if you haven't done what you promised, at least report your progress or lack thereof. And if you need to undo a commitment, the sooner the better.

TO WHOM ARE YOU ACCOUNTABLE?

1) You Are Accountable to God

We each have many positions in life — spouse, sibling, parent, employee, friend, etc. — and in each of these positions we are liable to God for how we conduct ourselves. The Scriptures say that one day "each of us will give an account of himself to God" (Romans 14:12). And Jesus said, "I tell you that men will have to give account on the day of judgment for every careless word they have spoken" (Matthew 12:36). In everything we say and do, we are accountable to God.

But the fact of the matter is, it's not just hard to be responsible to God in all these areas — it's impossible, without His help. And He will hold us accountable whether or not we hold ourselves accountable. But if we take the initiative, we'll more likely be ahead of the game.

2) You Are Accountable to Your Spouse

Let's take a brief look at how accountability should work within marriage. If you're single, pick up some pointers; and if you're married, I hope you can use this discussion to improve your relationship with your spouse and with God.

The lines of authority that exist in a Christian home are unique. Just as there are often dual lines of authority in the Church (clergy and lay leadership), there are dual lines of authority in the family.

The Bible tells us that the husband is the head of the wife just as Christ is the head of the Church. The Bible also tells believers to be submitted one to another and instructs the husband to love his wife as his own body (Ephesians 5:21-33).

How does this work on a practical level? Using Pat and me as examples, we both acknowledge that if God has something to say to one of us, He can enable the other one to hear it also. Unless we agree on some matter, we are agreed in advance to not act. It may be that one or the other of us doesn't feel strongly and is willing to accede to the other's position just because that's the easiest thing to do. But if both of us do feel strongly, we know that we will not have achieved God's best in that situation until we are in agreement.

In the very rare times when we are not in agreement but circumstances dictate that a decision must be made or an action taken, Pat acknowledges my responsibility, as head of the home, to make the final decision. Since I know that one of God's most effective means for directing me is my wife's counsel, I'm perhaps even more likely to decide in accord with her position as not. Because she knows that, she seldom takes a very strong stand on something we disagree on. I know beyond question that if ever I make a decision that is contrary to Pat's position, I have missed God's best for us in that situation.

From Pat's perspective, she runs no risk if she lets me decide. She knows that God will protect her in the midst of my mistakes. Conversely, I'm happy to give her veto power over my decisions because then she assumes the responsibility, and God will protect me from the consequences. The overall result of our being submitted to each other is that we almost never disagree on anything of substance.

When children are involved, parents should demonstrate their commitment to mutual submission so the children can see it. And, fathers, that doesn't mean you can refer a child to his mother in every situation.

3) You Are Accountable to Your Brothers and Sisters in Christ

Galatians 6:2 tells us that Christians can fulfill the Law of Christ by bearing one another's burdens. That means that we are to have an attitude like that mentioned in the old hymn — "sorrow flows from eye to eye and joy from heart to heart." It also means we are to be accountable to one another. James 5:16 tells each of us to "confess your sins to each other and pray for each other so that you may be healed." When members of Christ's Church learn to be truly transparent with each other and fully accountable to each other, God's love and healing power will be in evidence among them.

James also says, in verse 19 of that fifth chapter, "My brothers, if one of you should wander from the truth and someone should bring him back, remember this: Whoever turns a sinner from the error of his way will save him from death and cover over a multitude of sins." In other words, I will be doing well if I not only make myself accountable to my brothers and sisters in Christ, but, as much as is within my power, also seek to hold them accountable for their actions.

If I am doing something that is not in keeping with my Christian walk, I expect my brothers and sisters in the Lord to point it out to me — although I hope they will do it gently and in a spirit of love. The reverse is true too, and if I see someone whose actions do not square with his profession of faith, I will be obligated to talk to him about it. I am accountable to my brothers and sisters, and I should not become angry about anyone speaking to me about a problem area in my life. Instead, I need to think seriously about what is being said and see what changes in my life are in order. I'm not talking about nit-picking one another to death, or going around looking for the faults in others, but I am talking about loving our brothers and sisters enough to hold them accountable when God wants us to and submitting to their counsel when God is speaking through them.

4) You Are Accountable to Your Boss and Coworkers

What is our responsibility on the job? Is it any different for a Christian than for anyone else? Yes and no.

Paul tells us that as servants we are to be submitted to our masters. The only exception to that is when your employer directs you to do something that is either illegal or contrary to God's Law. That part's pretty easy, or should be. If you have any inclination to compromise at that point, you definitely need to spend more time with God and in His Word. Not only do you need to know what God's Word says, but you need to have the strength of your convictions to help you withstand any temptation to compromise your faith or your beliefs. You're much better off to disobey your employer than to disobey God. And if you're put in the position more than once of having to make that choice, ask God whether you shouldn't find another employer.

But in most cases the choice isn't so clear-cut. It's not a matter of illegal or immoral action so much as it is a matter of attitude. Do you have the right attitude toward your employer and his interests? Are you loyal and faithful to him? Are you looking for ways to serve his interest that are outside your job description?

What about the problems associated with an intermediate boss — a supervisor? You have a good attitude toward your company or your company's owner, but you just can't stand the person directly over you. Do you know what the Bible says to do with him or her? Love him, do good to him, and lend to him without expecting anything in return. Pray for him and see him as the person in need rather than yourself (see Matthew 5:43-48).

How about a coworker you just can't stand? He has no authority over you nor you over him. Same solution. Love him; pray for him. God said if you'll do that, your reward will be great. Be merciful even as your Father is merciful.

Do you have authority over employees? Can you hire and fire? I believe that a Christian employer cannot hire and fire at will, and perhaps not even for incompetence. In fact, unless the employee has broken the law, I doubt seriously that God's will includes involuntary dismissal, and even then I think there may be exceptions. There is an excellent discussion of this subject in Larry Burkett's book *Business by the Book* (Thomas Nelson, 1990), which I highly recommend to anyone who has the ability to hire or discharge employees.

If you're unhappy in your job, should you quit? I doubt it. Chances are you need to become an excellent employee, serving your company as unto the Lord. Then you'll either get a promotion or a transfer — from within or from without the company. God is your ultimate authority on the job. Work for Him, and He'll give you peace within your present job. He may give you another and better job later on.

ACCOUNTABILITY WITHIN THE CLERGY

One of the most perilous occupations around is that of the ordained ministry. Not only is much expected of clergy, but all too often they are not adequately trained or prepared for the natural and spiritual pitfalls that lie in their paths.

Perhaps most serious, though, is the lack of institutional accountability. The problems are severalfold and vary with the background and tradition of the pastor's church or denomination.

Generally, though, what a pastor or priest does in his or her personal life is often neither scrutinized nor subject to any meaningful process of accountability. Very often the pastor's job security is dependent on his not exposing those very areas that most need to be shared.

The problem in part is that pastors are elevated in the minds of their flock. They are not supposed to have problems or display weaknesses. Unfortunately, many of them begin to believe that myth themselves. They either decide there is no need for accountability or they cannot appear to need it for fear of displaying weakness.

The answer is complicated. It includes an awareness on the part of individual members of the Body of Christ that we need to protect our pastors through prayer. It means designing systems that require a pastor to be accountable, even when he might otherwise resist it. And it includes the need for pastors to recognize the value of accountability and a willingness to submit themselves to personal oversight.

For you who are pastors, I would encourage you to seek out one or two men (or women if you are a woman) whom you consider spiritually mature and who most likely are not under your authority, then begin to build a personal *confidential* relationship. Run small risks with them until you have confidence in running larger risks. Don't let them see themselves as mutually accountable, but maintain the relationship so they see themselves as responsible for your well-being. Meet with them regularly, and work toward sharing as deeply as you can. Ask God to meet your needs through them.

ACCOUNTABILITY DOESN'T MEAN DICTATORSHIP

Before we move on, a word of warning.

In some circles there seems to be a tendency to feel that there should be someone in charge of everyone all the time — that anyone who is not following someone else's direction is "out on his own" or "not subject to authority."

Such an approach will almost certainly evolve into an unhealthy relationship. It's not that there isn't the need for clear lines of authority — there is. But whereas everyone needs to know whom to be accountable to and whom to report to when reporting is appropriate, we all need to have the freedom to make our own mistakes. It's an unfair burden to have someone feel he or she is responsible for all the mistakes someone else makes, and it's terribly constricting to have someone feel that he's not free to make his own mistakes.

And yet, God is a God of order. He says *He's* in charge. He also says that He appoints individual offices, governments and the Church to serve as His instruments. The key is to know whom God has designated to serve as His overseer or point of accountability in any given situation.

Let's take the situation where the Church's authority is invested in ordained clergy who are institutionally accountable to lay leadership in some fashion. Since there is no Biblical foundation for the ordained clergy in the New Testament Church, we don't have a solid Biblical basis for what follows. Nevertheless, for almost two thousand years the Body of Christ has recognized the ordained clergy as God's point of authority within the Church. To that end, each member of a local church is subject to the authority of his pastor. As long as a member feels God wants him to be a member of a particular church, he should accept the direction of the pastor of that church as God's direction for him.

While there should always be freedom to dissociate from a particular local church, there should also always be a commitment to be part of *some* local church and to be subject to the authority of that church. In my opinion, there is no room for lone rangers in the Body of Christ.

There is room, however, for long-range planning, and we'll discuss that in Chapter 15.

PRACTICE ACCOUNTABILITY

1) Name some problem areas in your life where you would particularly benefit from being accountable to others.

2) What are the benefits that can be derived from establishing a system of accountability?

3) What are the dangers that can arise from the lack of a system of accountability?

4) Make a list of the people to whom you should be accountable. Spend time thinking over your relationship with each person on your list, and see if improvement in the area of accountability is needed.

5) Make a list of the people who should be accountable to you. Do you need to strengthen your relationship with any of these people? If so, how can you go about doing that?

6) Should you be a part of an accountability group? Make a list of people to whom you would like to be accountable. Why have you chosen these people?

14

Looking Far into the Future

What are you going to do with the rest of your life?

Hopefully you're to the point now where you see the importance of planning ahead, and you know where you want to be four or five years from now. But how much time have you spent considering "the big picture"?

What do I mean by that? The big picture is the time between now and the day you graduate to Glory. Once you have an idea of what you believe God wants you to achieve by the end of your life on this side of eternity, you can gauge everything you do against that perspective. Back in Chapter 3, we discussed the importance of establishing objectives for your life. In this chapter we're going to take that a step further as we discuss devising a plan for the rest of your life.

Jesus told His disciples, "surely I will be with you always, to the very end of the age" (Matthew 28:20). He will always be with you, and as you trust your lifeplan to Him, you can have the peace of knowing that your life is unfolding as it should. You can trust Him for today, for tomorrow, and for the far distant future as well.

God says, "Fear not, for I have redeemed you; I have called you by name; you are mine. When you pass through the waters, I will be with you; and when you pass through the rivers, they will not sweep over you. When you walk through the fire, you will not be burned; the flames will not set you ablaze" (Isaiah 43:1, 2).

Isn't it wonderful to know that the plans God has made for us are good and that everything that happens in this universe is under His control?

PREPARING FOR THE NEXT TWENTY YEARS — AND BEYOND

I believe everything we do and become on this side of eternity has a very real effect on where we begin on the other side. In other words, who we become in this life will influence where we start in the next. The more obedient we are in this lifetime, the better equipped we'll be to "hit the road running" in the hereafter.

Because I believe that, I'm highly motivated to do my best now, and I am actively setting goals for fifteen to twenty years into the future. I have estimated that I have at least fifteen years to go in developing Christian Stewardship Ministries. At some point I'll try to turn it over to new leadership and plan to be around just long enough to be a constructive resource and not long enough to become an obstacle. Pat and I are actively planning and discussing our plans for life after CSM. We are visiting other geographical locations as part of our effort to set our twenty-year goals.

DRAWING A ROAD MAP TO THE FUTURE

Most of us tend to be rather near-sighted with regard to the future, but it is possible to draw up a long-range plan for your life. Here's how.

The first step to developing a long-range plan is to set aside sufficient quality time to be able to develop it without unnecessary interruption. My recommendation is that you set aside a full weekend in a setting that is conducive to contemplation and meditation. Go to the mountains, the beach, or a hotel. Make it a thoroughly pleasant setting — somewhere you're completely comfortable.

The next step is to start making a list of everything you'll need or want during this time of planning. Start with your clothes and accessories. If you're going to take food, think that through and make a detailed list.

After your creature comforts are taken care of, make a list of things you'll need to help you develop your long-range plan. You should have your Bible, writing implements, pads of paper, file folders, hole punch, loose-leaf binders, and so on. If you have an office or home calendar, take that, as well as your pocket calendar. If you don't have a calendar, get one. You may have a book that will help you think about the things that are important to you.

Next, begin to write down your thoughts as you get mentally prepared for your getaway. Have some 3 x 5" cards with you all the time. As you go through each day, you will have ideas you should capture for later development, so keep those cards within reach.

If you're married, you need to make a decision as to whether you will do this alone or with your spouse. If in doubt, I suggest you do it alone. You'll probably get more actual work and decision-making done. But if you both want to be together, by all means do so. The idea is to create as pleasant and positive an environment as possible, so let that criterion be your guide.

When you arrive at your destination, make yourself comfortable. Organize everything the way you want it. Decide where you'll do your writing, and establish a desk area that lends itself to comfort and efficiency. Try to have everything you'll need within easy reach.

BEGINNING THE PLANNING PROCESS

By this point you have already been thinking about what your long-range aspirations might be. You've made some notes and accumulated some thoughts. You're sure God has a plan for your life, and you're in the process of discovering more of what that plan is.

Now begin to concentrate on two or three things you're good at and that you like to do. Realize that God's best for you probably includes what I call your motivated abilities — certain talents and desires that God has placed within you. We discussed these in some detail back in Chapter 3.

You may not have identified all of them, but hopefully you're aware of some of them. I believe these motivated abilities — these things you like to do that you're good at — can help you discover God's long-range plan for your life, so make a list of them and then arrange the list in some kind of order. You'll see that some of the things on your list are related to others, and some will stand alone. Some you can do fairly quickly, and others seem totally impossible.

The next thing to do is develop a statement of what your long-term plan is. The more specific and measurable you can make it, the better. This statement should not be longer than two or three sentences, short enough to fit on a 3 x 5" card so you can carry it around and read it often. In fact, you might choose to memorize it.

For example, if you're single and your desire is to be married, your statement might read: "I plan to be married within five years. I will identify and change up to ten bad habits during these five years so that the man (or woman) of my dreams will wish to marry me." The timeframe of five years may be longer than you wish, but if you're not yet married and wish to be, you'll probably need to establish and pursue that plan before you can focus on longer-range plans. If you achieve it in less than five years, so much the better.

If your statement is career-related, it might read, "In fifteen years I will be the president of my company." Obviously there are many shorter-term goals and plans included in that statement. You'll need to think each of those through and make very specific plans for the ones that are closer timewise.

After you have identified your motivated abilities, you need to establish objectives and goals that are consistent with those motivated abilities. You may find it helpful to take aptitude tests which will shed more light on those areas. You might plan to see a professional who can guide you through career-related decisions. If you are multitalented, you may need to prioritize because there may not be enough time to develop all your strengths — at least not all at once.

Once you have decided on the long-range objective, you can begin to carve it into manageable bites which we call goals. Always remember that your long-range goals should be established with an attitude of obedience to God, wanting to discover and follow the plan He has established for your life.

If your objective is to become the president of your company in fifteen years, and you feel that objective is consistent with God's plan for you, you should establish some promotional timeframes. For example, you may need to plan on becoming senior manager within two years, department head within five years, senior vice president within ten years, and president within fifteen years. Then you need to develop a plan and goals within each of those timeframes.

It is important to remember that your plan does not have to become reality for you to be a success. Success is becoming the person God wants you to be, and that realization should always dominate your planning. God may use a good plan to get you to the point of developing another good plan. *It's not always the plan that's important — it's the process you go through to establish and pursue the plan that is often the most worthwhile.*

If you conduct yourself on a daily basis as God wants you to, you may or may not need to change the plan, but you'll always be making progress toward becoming who God wants you to become — and that is the ultimate objective.

FOLLOW-UP AND FOLLOW-THROUGH

Once you've drawn up your long-range plan, you need to decide what you're going to do between then and the time you will set aside to reevaluate your long-range plan. Get out your calendar and decide when you're going to have your next planning retreat. Will it be in three months, in six months, a year?

You also need to establish some action steps between now and your next long-range plan evaluation. You may need to take a course at a local college, get a second job, or develop a budget. You may need to get out of debt, save some money, or expand your vocabulary. What you definitely need to do is schedule specific things that need to be done in order to move toward implementation of your long-range plan. Some of those things may need to be scheduled only once or for a short period of time. Others may need to become lifelong habits.

Before you leave your planning retreat, go through your calendar and decide when you'll do what. Decide then, while everything is fresh in your mind, or you may never decide at all. Then you'll become discouraged, possibly lose momentum, and wonder why you aren't making progress.

ARE YOU DOING WHAT YOU SHOULD BE DOING?

We all have a perception of ourselves — of who we are. Some of us even have a perception of who we want to become. But if we look at ourselves objectively and determine who we are based on what we do, we often discover that we are not who we thought we were in various areas of our lives.

Once you have established a specific plan for the future, you need to take a look at your present use of time. Begin to compare who you are (which is a reflection of what you do with your time) with who you believe God wants you to become.

If you're typical, you'll be absolutely amazed at this point in the process. You'll begin to discover that much of what you do has little or nothing to do with what you have decided you want to be and become.

I counsel a number of businessmen on a regular basis. The actual people change over time, but the total number is usually between twelve and twenty. Most of those men have chosen to become accountable to me for a limited period of time in their lives because they can see the difference between who they are and who they believe God wants them to become, and they see the value of having someone help them oversee their activities and decisions.

It is often very helpful to have someone else involved in the process of evaluating the difference between who we want to become and who we actually are as evidenced by our use of time.

SHOULD YOU CHANGE CAREERS?

As you look at your long-range future, one of the most important considerations is your career. You don't want to be doing something you hate for thirty or forty years, and God doesn't want that either. He wants you to be content in all areas of life.

Are you getting ready to start a career, or thinking about changing your old job for something new? Again, it's important to remember that God's perfect plan for your life includes a career in which you will be able to utilize the talents He has given you and in which you will find fulfillment.

So again, the most important thing in considering a career change is to seek God's will in the matter. There are several other practical components that should be considered:

1) Look at Your Experience

The idea is to narrow the field of choices based on what you've already learned and done. That alone is not likely to show you what you will ultimately decide on as your career, but it's an invaluable resource.

It's also a good idea to seek the counsel of others who have already walked where you are going. Look not only at where you've been, but at where others have been.

2) Look at Your Present Situation

Now that we've looked at where you've been, the next step is to take a look at where you are right now.

If you are presently happy and fulfilled in your job, chances are good that you're on track for the future. But if you are unhappy or dissatisfied in your present job, you may or may not have a career change ahead of you. Basically there are two options. One is to learn to become happy and fulfilled where you are, and the other is to find your way to the job God has designed and prepared for you.

Now you may dislike your present job so much that you don't think you can stay in it for one more day. Chances are, the more you feel that way, the longer you'll have to stay where you are to discover the job God has for you. It's almost never a good idea to change jobs because you don't like being where you are. You must wait until you've identified the specific job God wants you to have.

As we discussed in the previous chapter, I believe you will be much better off to begin to look at your present job as the place God wants you right now. It may be that He has a plan for converting it into the job you're really looking for. Or it may be that He wants to use your present job to enable you to become the person He wants you to be so you can appreciate the job He has for you. It might also be that the job He wants you to move into may not even exist yet — He may be working on creating it. Whatever is going on, for you to be best positioned to receive what God has for you in the future, you've got to do your very best where you are right now. I have known people who were constantly moving from job to job, always dissatisfied for one reason or another, and never making much headway in their careers. They would have benefited by demonstrating some patience and perseverance — a willingness to "bloom where they were planted" until they were assured of God's timing regarding a change of jobs.

Is your problem your boss or supervisor? God can remove him or her in an instant. Is it the kind of work you have to do? God can change your job description just as quickly. Is it your salary? Money is certainly not a challenge for God. Is it your coworkers? Whatever it is, God can handle it.

3) Put God's Will Ahead of Your Own Interests

When I was practicing law after I became a Christian, I became increasingly uncomfortable with some of the things I had to do to represent my clients. I was always committed to high ethical standards, but I began to see conflicts between what I felt was in my client's best interests and what I felt God wanted me to do. For example, the whole field of family and divorce law was a problem. It became increasingly difficult to even participate in dissolving marriages when I knew God frowned on divorce. And when I represented Christians who were much more interested in the bottom line than in what God thought, I really didn't want to be involved at all. The other side of the coin was that my livelihood depended in part on those kinds of cases.

When I demonstrated to God that I took His principles more seriously than I did my own self-interest, He responded by giving me an entirely new vocation — one I didn't even realize He had prepared me for.

I started trying to convince my divorce clients, especially the Christians, to give their marriages another shot. I started trying to help business clients reconcile their differences. I began conducting myself as a counselor. For some that was very helpful. For others it was very unsatisfactory. For me it was the beginning of the end of my law practice. I could see much more potential in helping Christians who were interested in becoming more dependent on God discover how to do just that. God took my commitment to applying His principles in my job and converted my law practice into a ministry devoted to teaching those principles.

I can honestly tell you now that I am the happiest person I know, and I know a lot of happy people! I believe God will enable you to be perfectly happy and ultimately fulfilled in your job and otherwise as you commit yourself to a course of obedience.

4) Look for Areas of Disobedience

The final step is to ask God to show you any areas of disobedience in your life, and then to bring those areas under His Lordship. Once you've done that, you can at least relax in the knowledge that you've done your part. The next step is up to God.

Several years ago I met the wife of a man who I knew to be committed to understanding God's plan for his life. She wasn't all that interested in God's will and was putting all of her energies into her career. They had no children, and she didn't particularly want any.

She gradually began to open doors in her life for God to enter, but she was committed to retaining control of her career. She finally decided that she did want to have a child, but that she would return to work just as soon as she could after the baby was born. Well, it didn't work out quite that way. For one thing she had twins. Faced with the incredible demands that multiple children place on parents, she delayed her return to the work force.

Then God moved. She began to experience the joys of being a full-time wife and mother. Although the challenges are much greater than those in her former career, our new mother now wouldn't trade places with anyone. She has discovered the blessing of being where God wants her to be in her vocation.

How well have you been able to identify your God-given talents? To find the job or vocation or career that God has for you, take some time to understand the desires of your heart — those things you want to do that God wants you to do. Test those desires against Scripture. If they pass that test, and you continue to want to do them, develop a plan to achieve them, regardless of the challenges. You will have discovered God's plan for your career and a significant part of your long-range future.

PRACTICE LONG-RANGE PLANNING

1) Where do you want to be twenty years from now? Fifteen years? Ten years?

2) Are your present activities designed to move you toward that long-range destination?

3) If you are married, does your spouse know what your aspirations are? If not, why not?

4) Should you schedule a retreat for some long-range planning?

5) If yes, in what month should you plan to do this?

15

The Journey Begins!

Can you imagine what it would be like to wake up every day with a joyful, peaceful attitude because you know you're right in the center of God's will?

Can you imagine going for days without a single knot in your stomach because you know that God is directing your steps?

And what would it be like to get more accomplished than you've ever been able to do before and still have plenty of time for enjoyable activities with your family and friends? Can you imagine feeling that everything in your life is completely organized and under control?

Well, the absolute truth is that you can have all of these things simply by following the principles I've outlined in this book. This is no idle promise. I've seen it happen time and time again in the lives of many people — including myself.

Now that you've finished reading this book, you may be feeling either one of two ways:

1) Challenged.

2) Overwhelmed.

If you're feeling challenged, that's terrific. But let me urge you to act on that feeling now. The longer you wait to follow the principles we've discussed, the harder it will be. That's one of the reasons why it is so important that you decide exactly when you're going to do what with regard to getting your life in line with God's will.

Some people are always making plans and setting objectives, but they never get anywhere with them. Why not? Because they write them down but don't follow up. They don't do anything concrete toward reaching those goals.

It doesn't do a bit of good to buy a road map and plan your trip if you

never take it. This book can be your road map to a peaceful, ordered and —
most importantly — obedient life. But it won't do you a bit of good unless
you decide to make your plan and then actually take the trip.

Do not put this book in a drawer somewhere and then forget about it.
Keep it close at hand as a ready reference as you go through the process of
getting your life in order. Use it the way you would a textbook, realizing that
some of the concepts we've discussed may take some time and effort to incor-
porate into your life. It is not always easy to trade old habits for new ones.
Change or growth takes much in the way of effort and perseverance — but
any effort you put into following the principles I've given you will be well
worth it.

Now, instead of being challenged, what if you're feeling overwhelmed?

If you're thinking, "All of this sounds good, but I just don't know how
I could ever do all of these things," just remember that these concepts can be
built into your life one at a time. You cannot expect to read this book in one
sitting, absorb all of the knowledge and information, and immediately put it
into practice, especially if you've never heard many of these principles
before. But slowly, surely, bit by bit, chapter by chapter, they can be incorporated into your life. Then you'll see the benefit of spending a regular quiet
time with God, of taking the time to plan each day, of making schedules, of
establishing priorities for the use of your time, and all of the other things
we've discussed. You'll wonder how you ever got along before you did these
things.

Please, for your own sake, do not have the attitude that "I can't do this."
You *can* do it (Philippians 4:13), and your life will undergo a remarkable
transformation when you do.

On occasion when I am conducting a seminar I will see some of the people in the audience looking at me with a skeptical expression. Perhaps they're
not sure the principles I'm setting forth will work in their lives, or maybe they
don't think they will be worth the effort.

But I have received so many letters and phone calls and have run into so
many people who have told me, "You know, I wasn't too sure about what
you were saying. But I've tried it, and it's revolutionized my life!"

Please remember that my purpose in writing this book is to share with
you what God has taught me in the area of time management and personal
organization. My desire is not to sell books, but to see lives transformed. It
doesn't matter what sort of confusion your life might be in today — it *can*
be transformed.

You've bought the book. Wonderful!

You've read it. Terrific!

But unless you decide to put it into practice, we've both wasted a lot of time.

I've been trying to think about what would be the single most important thought I could leave with you, and I've finally decided it is this: "God loves you and has a plan for your life."

It sounds simple, but when a person gets to know, deep inside of himself or herself, that it is the gospel truth, life takes on an entirely new meaning.

In the first place, God loves *you* — so much that He was willing to send His only Son, Jesus Christ, to the cross to die in your behalf. Do you realize that He would have done that even if you were the only person on this planet who needed to be forgiven? Even if all of the other five billion people on this planet were perfectly righteous, and if you were the only one who had fallen into sin, Jesus Christ would have still gone to the cross for you.

How do I know that? Because Jesus described this kind of love when He told the Parable of the Good Shepherd who would not rest for a moment until he found and rescued the one small sheep that had been lost from his flock.

And I know that because I have come to know more and more as the years have gone by the incredible depth and breadth of God's love.

Because He loves you so much, you can know beyond any doubt that the plan He has established for you is perfect in every way. It will bring you contentment, fulfillment, joy, and all of the other ingredients of the "peace . . . which transcends all understanding" (Philippians 4:7).

Basically everything we've talked about in this book has been designed to help you uncover that plan. Now, knowing exactly what God wants for you and doing everything within your power to fulfill that plan, doesn't mean you won't have times when things go wrong. You may have a disaster at the office; you may have to cancel an important appointment because your car is out of commission or the kids have come down with the flu; you may miss an appointment because there was a massive traffic jam on the freeway.

But even when those sorts of things happen to you, you'll still find that the peace that passes all understanding rules in your heart. You've entrusted yourself to God, and you can know beyond a shadow of doubt that He is working everything together for your good — even on the bad days.

It took me quite a few years before I got to know God well enough to understand that the thing He wanted for me, more than anything else, was that I should be happy. And now I know that He wants the same thing for you. Why is it so important to Him that we obey Him? One of the reasons is that He knows the only way we can truly find happiness is by being obedient to Him, being intimate with Him on a daily basis, discovering and achieving His plan for our lives.

When you seek to discover and live out the plan God has established for you, you are living in obedience, and being obedient to God produces the fruit of His Spirit: love, joy, peace, etc. (Galatians 5:22, 23).

In the twenty-eighth chapter of Deuteronomy there is a list of the blessings that accrue to those who are obedient to God. It says:

"All these blessings will come upon you and accompany you if you obey the Lord your God:
"You will be blessed in the city and blessed in the country.
"The fruit of your womb will be blessed, and the crops of your land and the young of your livestock — the calves of your herds and the lambs of your flocks.
"Your basket and your kneading trough will be blessed.
"You will be blessed when you come in and blessed when you go out.
"The Lord will grant that the enemies who rise up against you will be defeated before you. They will come at you from one direction but flee from you in seven.
"The Lord will send a blessing on your barns and on everything you put your hand to. The Lord your God will bless you in the land he is giving you."

That's good enough, but there's more:

"The Lord will open the heavens, the storehouse of his bounty, to send rain on your land in season and to bless all the work of your hands. . . .
"The Lord will make you the head, not the tail. If you pay attention to the commands of the Lord your God that I give you this day and carefully follow them, you will always be at the top, never at the bottom."

Do you want those blessings for yourself?
This book has given you the keys. Now it's up to you to use them.

MY COMMITMENT

I pledge that I will generate and follow a schedule, as outlined in Chapter 5 of this book, and that I will, by God's grace, make the following changes in my life:

_____

_____

_____

_____

_____

_____

_____

_____(Signed)

_____(Date)

MORE HELP IS AVAILABLE

If you would like more information regarding seminars, tapes, and other materials available through Christian Stewardship Ministries, you may write to me at:

> Ken Smith
> Christian Stewardship Ministries
> 10523 Main Street
> Suite 200
> Fairfax, VA 22030
> Or call us at: (703) 591-5000.

We offer time and money management help in several ways:

1) Through Seminars

Christian Stewardship Ministries offers two basic seminars.

"God's Plan for Your Time" covers many of the same kinds of things as are discussed in this book. Its duration can range from one to three days, and it is taught as a course in seminaries and classrooms as well as through seminars.

"God's Plan for Your Finances" is taught as a one-day seminar. Larry Burkett's basic budgeting materials are used as the text for this seminar, and the object is to teach Biblically-based family financial management.

CSM's "Life Management Seminar" is a combination of the first two seminars and is taught in sessions of two or three days.

We are in the process of putting together a seminar that teaches Biblical principles of operating a business, with an emphasis on the practical application of those principles. This seminar is designed specifically for Christians who are the owners and operators of small businesses.

If you would like to have your church or organization sponsor a seminar, just have your senior pastor or the head of your organization write or call for more information.

2) Through Our Radio Program

"Time, Money, and Personal Organization" is a five-minute program available to Christian radio stations. Its emphasis is on teaching the practical applications that are contained within the pages of this book. It is reliant on local sponsorship, usually by Christian-owned businesses. Radio stations also sometimes agree to carry the program at a reduced rate or without charge as a service to the Christian community, when requested to do so by the listening public.

3) Through Audiocassettes

Tape recordings of radio broadcasts are available either as single releases or as albums.

Among the more popular albums are:

> The Life Management Series
> Techniques for Operating a Christian-owned Business
> Managing Your Money

Among the more popularly requested single programs are:

> How to Overcome Procrastination
> How to Become Punctual
> How to Overcome Overcommitment
> The Importance of Accountability

If you would like to order tapes, just call or write for a list of titles and an order form.

4) Through Business Consulting

Ken Smith does limited business consulting for companies owned and operated by committed Christians who are interested in knowing more about how to operate their businesses in accordance with Biblical principles. If you wish to know more about how to retain Ken, just indicate that on the following form.

5) *Glad Tithings*

Finally, if you wish to be placed on our mailing list, complete the form below, and mail it to us. You will receive our newsletter *Glad Tithings* with no obligation. In addition to articles by Ken Smith on time, money and personal organization, you will receive current information on upcoming seminars and future materials available through CSM.

We would also appreciate your comments on how this book has helped you and any suggestions you have for future materials you would like to have us make available to you.

Ken Smith
Christian Stewardship Ministries
10523 Main Street
Suite 200
Fairfax, VA 22030

Name:_____

Address: _____

_____

Telephone Number _____

❑ Please send me *Glad Tithings*.
❑ Please send me a list of materials available through your ministry.
❑ Please contact me with assistance in organizing and operating my business.
❑ Please let me know how I can help get your radio program on my local station.
❑ Please address the following topic(s) in your next book:

_____

_____

_____

❑ I have the following comments about this book (complimentary and critical). Use addition space if needed.

_____

_____

_____

_____

_____

_____

FORMS FOR PERSONAL USE

The following forms are meant for personal use as you schedule and organize your life according to the Biblical principles shared in this book. You are invited to reproduce these as needed, in whatever quantities you require. For the most part, samples of these forms have been given in the appropriate chapters to give you a better idea of how to use them.

I hope and pray that these forms will help in your own walk with God and your growing obedience to Him.

PERSONAL PROCRASTINATION WORKSHEET

Copy this form (or make your own). Make as many copies as you need. List everything you can think of that you have not done that you should have done, or that you want to do. Do not stop to do any of these things until you have completed the list to the best of your ability. You will find that as you continue to read this book, you will think of other things to add to the list. Just continue to build the list every time you think of something else until you have completed the book.

THE ACB TECHNIQUE

A — What is most important (Must do — high value)
C — What is least important (Can do — low value)
B — Everything that is not A or C (Should do — medium value)

AREAS OF PROCRASTINATION	PRIORITY	
	A-C-B	1-3-2
1.		
2.		
3.		
4.		
5.		
6.		
7.		
8.		
9.		
10.		
11.		
12.		
13.		
14.		
15.		
16.		
17.		
18.		
19.		
20.		

Form 1

THINGS TO DO TODAY

Referring to your Personal Procrastination Worksheet, as well as to your calendar and whatever else you use to remind you of what you have to do today, list those things that you would like to plan to do today. Prioritize the list as you have already learned to do, and then do the things in the order that your prioritizing dictates. Whatever you do not complete today will go on tomorrow's Things to Do Today list.

THINGS TO DO TODAY	PRIORITY	
	A-C-B	1-3-2
1.		
2.		
3.		
4.		
5.		
6.		
7.		
8.		
9.		
10.		
11.		
12.		
13.		
14.		
15.		
16.		
17.		
18.		
19.		
20.		

Form 2

THINGS TO DO THIS WEEK

Referring to the same sources as for the Things to Do Today list, list those things that you do not need to do today, but that should be done sometime this week. As you complete your Things to Do Today list, you can refer to this list for the next highest priority items. This list will soon become the source for the things that go on a future Things to Do Today list.

THINGS TO DO THIS WEEK	PRIORITY	
	A-C-B	1-3-2
1.		
2.		
3.		
4.		
5.		
6.		
7.		
8.		
9.		
10.		
11.		
12.		
13.		
14.		
15.		
16.		
17.		
18.		
19.		
20.		

Form 3

MAJOR ACTIVITIES

Indicate how much time is needed for specific daily activities.

ACTIVITY	HOURS PER DAY OR PER WEEK
Sleep	
Time with God	
Time for self	
Time for family	
Planning and organization	
Physical exercise	
Job	
Dealing with areas of procrastination	

Form 4

ANCHOR ACTIVITIES SCHEDULE

Indicate at what time you do or plan to do these specific activities.

ACTIVITY	WHEN/WHAT TIME
Getting up in the morning	
Going to bed at night	
Starting the workday	
Ending the workday	
Taking a midday break	

Form 5

DIVIDING THE DAY

SEGMENT OF THE DAY	SPECIFIC TIME	ACTIVITIES FOR THIS SEGMENT
Early morning	____ to ____	_____
		_____
		_____
		_____
Morning	____ to ____	_____
		_____
		_____
		_____
Midday	____ to ____	_____
		_____
		_____
		_____
Afternoon	____ to ____	_____
		_____
		_____
		_____
Dinner	____ to ____	_____
		_____
		_____
		_____
Evening	____ to ____	_____
		_____
		_____
		_____

Form 6

MAJOR ACTIVITIES SCHEDULE

ACTIVITY	SPECIFIC TIME
Time for sleep	____ to ____
Time with God	____ to ____
Time for planning and organization	____ to ____
Time for physical exercise	____ to ____
Time for spouse	____ to ____
Time(s) for child(ren)	____ to ____
Time for job (door to door)	____ to ____
Time for areas of procrastination	____ to ____

Form 7

CURRENT COMMITMENTS & ACTIVITIES INVENTORY

List randomly all of your present commitments and activities that involve the use of your time. Using the same system of prioritizing that you have already learned (A-C-B, 1-3-2), determine the relative importance of each commitment and activity. Now estimate how much time you presently spend per week on each item, and how much time you think you should spend (including 0).

COMMITMENT/ACTIVITY	PRIORITY		HOURS/WEEK	
	A-C-B	1-3-2	PRESENT	PLAN FOR

Form 8

PROPOSED COMMITMENTS & ACTIVITIES INVENTORY

List randomly all of those things that you ought to be doing that you are not presently doing, and all of those things that you want to be doing that you are not presently doing. Determine the relative importance of each of these things by using the same system in prioritizing (A-C-B, 1-3-2). Now estimate how much each time is needed for each of these things.

COMMITMENT/ACTIVITY	PRIORITY		HOURS/WEEK	
	A-C-B	1-3-2	PRESENT	PLAN FOR

Form 9

REVISED COMMITMENTS &
ACTIVITIES INVENTORY

After reviewing the two previous forms, decide which commitments and activities should be eliminated from your schedule and which new ones should be added. Any activity that you are able to eliminate immediately, just do so. Now list on this form all remaining present and proposed activities and commitments that you feel must be or that you wish to be part of your immediate future. Since it will probably take a while for you to extricate yourself from some of the things to be eliminated, use the Begin/End Date column on this form to indicate the date by which you plan to terminate any particular commitment. Likewise, you may not be able to immediately commence a new commitment, so indicate the date you plan to commence anything new.

COMMITMENT/ACTIVITY	PRIORITY		BEGIN/END
	A-C-B	1-3-2	DATE

Form 10

NEW COMMITMENTS

During your planning time each day, you should list all commitments that you have made to anyone since your last planning session, and enter the date your effort will begin in the "Begin" column. Remember commitments made to pray for others, and commitments made to God, your spouse, your children, your boss, your coworkers, your friends, your pastor. Next, enter the date by which you plan to fulfill the commitment in the "End" column. This list should be reviewed daily, and used when you are formulating your Daily and Weekly To Do lists. When the commitment has been fulfilled, enter the date it was fulfilled in the "Completed" column. If you find that you are not fulfilling your commitment in timely fashion, contact the person you are committed to, and either establish a new "End" date, or ask to be forgiven and released from the commitment.

COMMITMENT/ACTIVITY	BEGIN	END	COMPLETED

Form 11

DAILY SCHEDULE

	SUN	MON	TUE	WED	THU	FRI	SAT
4:00							
4:30							
5:00							
5:30							
6:00							
6:30							
7:00							
7:30							
8:00							
8:30							
9:00							
9:30							
10:00							
10:30							
11:00							
11:30							
12:00							
12:30							
1:00							
1:30							
2:00							
2:30							
3:00							
3:30							
4:00							
4:30							
5:00							
5:30							
6:00							
6:30							
7:00							
7:30							
8:00							
8:30							
9:00							
9:30							
10:00							
10:30							
11:00							
11:30							

Form 12

INDEX